the best of ASCD's *Update* newsletters

Transforming Classroom Practice

Edited by **John O'Neil** and **Scott Willis**

WITHDRAWN

Association for Supervision and Curriculum Development ✦ Alexandria, Virginia

Association for Supervision and Curriculum Development
1250 N. Pitt Street • Alexandria, Virginia 22314-1453 USA
Telephone: 1-800-933-2723 or 703-549-9110 • Fax: 703-299-8631
Web site: http://www.ascd.org • E-mail: member@ascd.org

On July 14, 1998, ASCD will move to new headquarters: 1703 N. Beauregard St.,
Alexandria, VA 22311-1714. Telephone: 703-578-9600.

Gene R. Carter, *Executive Director*
Michelle Terry, *Assistant Executive Director,*
  Program Development
Nancy Modrak, *Director, Publishing*
John O'Neil, *Acquisitions Editor*
Mark Goldberg, *Development Editor*
Julie Houtz, *Managing Editor of Books*
Charles D. Halverson, *Project Assistant*

Gary Bloom, *Director, Editorial, Design, and*
  Production Services
Eva Barsin, *Graphic Designer*
Tracey A. Smith, *Production Manager*
Dina Murray, *Production Coordinator*
John Franklin, *Production Coordinator*
Hilary Cumberton, M.L. Coughlin Editorial
  Services, *Indexer*
BMWW, *Typesetter*

Printed in the United States of America.   s6/98

ASCD Stock No. 198052   ASCD member price: $16.95   nonmember price: $20.95

Also available as part of a 2-volume set (ISBN 0-87120-312-X): stock no. 198198, ASCD member
price: $26.95   nonmember price: $32.95

Library of Congress Cataloging-in-Publication Data

Transforming classroom practice : the best of ASCD's update newsletters / edited by
  John O'Neil and Scott Willis.
     p.   cm.
    Articles in this book were originally published in Education update (formerly
called ASCD Update) and Curriculum update.
    Includes index.
    "ASCD stock no. 198052"—T.p. verso.
    ISBN 0-87120-310-3 (pbk.)
    1. School improvement programs—United States—Case studies.
  2. Educational change—United States—Case studies.   3. Education—
United States—Case studies.   I. O'Neil, John.   II. Willis, Scott.
III. Education update (Alexandria, Va.)   V. Curriculum update (Alexandria, Va.)
LB2822.82.T73   1998   98-3546
                                                                           CIP

03 02 01 00 99 98   10 9 8 7 6 5 4 3 2 1

TRANSFORMING CLASSROOM PRACTICE
THE BEST OF ASCD'S *UPDATE* NEWSLETTERS

Integrating the Curriculum

Multicultural Education

Multiple Intelligences

Preparing Students for the Workplace

Thinking Skills

Untracking

PREFACE

The pride of New City School in St. Louis, Mo., is its unique application of the theory of multiple intelligences (MI). For more than a decade, the New City faculty has been altering its curriculum, assessment, and ways of working with parents in light of what MI tells us about how people learn. La Salle Academy in Providence, R.I., has gained attention for its program supporting students' social and emotional growth. The program promotes community service and conflict resolution, and students helped to develop the school's "Goals of Community Behavior." Other schools are finding success through creative use of technology, peer coaching, integrated curriculums, or multi-age classrooms.

A consistent lesson from the literature on school change is that there is no single method, no sure-fire model—and certainly no panacea—for improving schools. Great ideas and great programs are as varied as the minds that conceive them and try them out.

In that spirit, this book brings together short articles on some of the most interesting and ambitious ideas and trends in education today.

All the articles in this book were originally published in *Education Update* (formerly called *Update*), the official member newsletter of the Association for Supervision and Curriculum Development, and *Curriculum Update*, a quarterly supplement focusing on trends and issues in curriculum. Both newsletters are sent to ASCD's entire membership, which includes principals, teachers, curriculum specialists, superintendents, and teacher educators, among others. Therefore, these articles were written to appeal to a broad audience of educators.

We've selected the articles included in this volume because we believe that they provide an interesting snapshot of the many changes being proposed and tried in elementary and secondary schools today. We think the articles identify some of the key issues and challenges in improving our schools, and these pages are punctuated with examples of real schools that are making a profound difference in the lives of their students. Our hope is that this book provides change-minded educators with some ideas and insights into a few of the many possibilities.

JOHN O'NEIL
SCOTT WILLIS

BILINGUAL EDUCATION AND ESL

◆

TEACHING LANGUAGE-MINORITY STUDENTS

SCOTT WILLIS

How schools can best serve students who are limited-English-proficient (LEP) has been hotly debated for decades. The main point of contention is whether LEP students should be taught in their native languages—and if so, to what extent.

Today, this debate is intensifying as the number of LEP students rapidly rises. Between 1985 and 1992, the number of LEP students enrolled in U.S. schools increased by nearly 70 percent, to a total of more than 2.5 million students, according to the group Teachers of English to Speakers of Other Languages (TESOL). During the same period, LEP students increased from 3.8 percent to slightly more than 6 percent of the total K–12 student population, and that proportion continues to expand. "The numbers are just phenomenal," says James Lyons, executive director of the National Association for Bilingual Education (NABE).

Much of the debate has focused on the relative merits of bilingual and English-as-a-Second-Language (ESL) programs: which type of program serves LEP students better? In simple terms, bilingual programs provide some amount of native-language content instruction for several years, while students also learn English skills during part of the day. The goal of these programs is to help students make a successful transition to mainstream classes. In ESL programs, by contrast, students receive content instruction in English (sometimes adapted to their level of profi-

This article was originally published in the June 1994 issue of ASCD's *Update* newsletter.

ciency) and are pulled out of the classroom for part of the day to learn English skills with other LEP students. Of the two approaches, ESL programs are more common, experts say.

Advocates of bilingual programs argue that LEP students need native-language content instruction to keep pace in the curriculum with their English-speaking peers while they learn English. If they are simply immersed in English instruction, LEP students miss too much academic content, these experts contend.

Young LEP children can pick up a fair amount of conversational English from their peers, but it's a mistake to think they can dive right into academic work, says Judith Lessow-Hurley of San Jose State University, author of ASCD's *Commonsense Guide to Bilingual Education*. Recent research has shown that LEP students need five to seven years of concentrated instruction in English to develop real academic proficiency in the language, she says. Therefore, it is unfair to expect them to compete in an English-language environment from the beginning. LEP students who receive no instruction in their native language often develop a negative self-concept, get held back, and ultimately may drop out of school, Lyons says.

Backers of bilingual programs also contend that if LEP students develop a strong base in their first language, they will learn English more readily—although this may seem counterintuitive. Students who understand how their native language works, they say, can transfer this understanding to English. In addition, advocates claim that bilingual programs reinforce LEP students' self-esteem and help them maintain their native language.

BILINGUAL DRAWBACKS?

Some in the field dispute these views vigorously, however. One outspoken critic of bilingual education is Rosalie Pedalino Porter of the Research in English Acquisition and Development (READ) Institute. Porter, author of *Forked Tongue: The Politics of Bilingual Education*, became disillusioned with bilingual education as a result of her experiences as a bilingual teacher. Although LEP students at her school were supposed to be mainstreamed after their third year in the bilingual program, "it didn't happen," she states flatly. In fact, she was dismayed to find 6th graders who still could not speak, read, or write English. This phenomenon—the failure of students in bilingual programs to acquire adequate English skills—has been documented across the United States, she asserts.

The problem with bilingual education lies in the program design, not in the way teachers implement it, Porter believes. Students in bilingual programs become reliant on native-language teaching, she says; the impetus to learn English is not strong enough. And in bilingual classes, LEP students are "segregated for years from their English-speaking classmates."

LEP students are better served if they are taught in English from the beginning, Porter believes. Young children are more capable of absorbing a second language than older ones, she says, and they are less self-conscious about making mistakes. Further, they have more time to devote to the task, simply by virtue of their young age. A skillful teacher can teach them content using "simple English and lots of illustrative materials," Porter says.

Like Porter, other educators dispute the claim that LEP students taught in English cannot keep pace with native speakers. ESL teacher Donna Clovis has found just the opposite to be true of her students. "Sometimes they're doing better than their peers" when they leave her program, she says.

Clovis teaches an ESL pull-out program at Riverside Elementary School in Princeton, N.J. Students remain in the program for one to three years. Clovis's students speak 19 different native languages, including Russian, Spanish, Hungarian, Japanese, and Hebrew. Offering all of these students a bilingual program would be well-nigh impossible, she notes.

Clovis focuses on helping her students develop academic English; her instruction emphasizes reading, writing, and grammar. "I know they'll learn speaking from their peers," she says. Her class is "a forum to make the mistakes" in usage and pronunciation that students might be unwilling to make in a regular classroom.

Nevertheless, Clovis believes LEP students should be part of a regular classroom from the beginning, because they must acquire the conversation skills they need to survive and learn to pick up teachers' cues. "We want everything to be as normal as possible" for them, she says. Although her students receive no native-language instruction, they do not have low self-esteem, Clovis says; in fact, they feel they have *more* to offer.

WHAT RESEARCH SAYS

What light does research shed on these issues? A major longitudinal study conducted for the U.S. Department of Education tracked elementary classes of Spanish-speaking LEP students from 1984–85 to 1987–88. Known as the Ramirez study, after its principal researcher, this study compared the long-term benefits of English immersion, early-exit, and late-exit bilingual programs.

In the immersion programs, all content instruction was in English, with Spanish used only for clarification. Children in these programs were to be mainstreamed within two to three years. In the early-exit programs, 20–30 percent of instruction (usually reading) was in Spanish, and children were to be mainstreamed after 2nd grade. In the late-exit programs, at least 40 percent of instruction was in Spanish, and students stayed in the program through 6th grade.

The Ramirez study found that all three programs helped LEP students improve their skills as fast as, or faster than, students in the general population. The late-exit program, however, showed the most promising results. Students in the immersion and early-exit programs had comparable skill levels in math and language arts (when tested in English) after four years, but their rates of growth slowed as their grade level increased. Late-exit students, by contrast, showed *acceleration* in their rate of growth and appeared to be gaining on students in the general population.

According to researcher Virginia Collier of George Mason University, nearly all the research looking at results over at least four years, including the Ramirez study, shows that the more native-language instructional support LEP students receive (if combined with balanced English support), the higher they are able to achieve in English in each succeeding academic year, relative to matched groups being schooled solely in English. Students who do not receive native-language instruction "appear to do well in the early grades, but their performance fails to match that of the norm group and gains go down as they reach upper elementary and especially secondary schooling," Collier has written.

Porter disagrees with these findings, and she too cites research to support her contention that teaching LEP students in English is best. A longitudinal study of programs in the El Paso schools commissioned by the

ESL Standards in Development

Spurred by concern that standard-setting efforts in the subject areas might harm language-minority students, the group Teachers of English to Speakers of Other Languages (TESOL) has begun to develop standards for English-as-a-Second-Language (ESL) instruction.

TESOL fears that ESL students will be considered failures if they don't meet standards set for all students, says Else Hamayan of the Illinois Resource Center, who chairs TESOL's task force on ESL standards. At the same time, however, TESOL doesn't want language-minority students to receive a watered-down curriculum. "We're having to deal with some very tough issues," Hamayan says.

The ESL standards will go beyond specifying what students should learn in ESL classes, says Fred Genesee, TESOL's president. They will also address the pedagogy ESL students need if they are to meet subject-area standards, he says, as well as ways to modify the curriculum for these students. In addition, the ESL standards will deal with issues such as teachers' professional development and the assessment of ESL students' achievement.

Assessment is a crucial issue, says Denise McKeon of the American Educational Research Association, a past chair of the ESL task force. McKeon believes educators should provide alternative ways for language-minority students to show what they know, so there won't be "a penalty for those who know content but can't express it in English." LEP students may understand concepts such as the evaporation cycle or mitosis and meiosis but not test well in English, Genesee says. "If use of [English] is the sine qua non of assessment procedures, then these kids will lose out."

Hamayan hopes the ESL standards will make all educators, including non-ESL teachers, more aware of the particular needs of language-minority students. She also hopes they will help ensure that ESL teaching is "up to par."

Appropriate pedagogy is essential if ESL students are to meet the content standards in the subject areas, Genesee emphasizes. "The easy part is saying what you want," he believes. "The hard part is figuring out how to do it."

READ Institute looked at the lasting academic effects of bilingual and English-immersion programs. The study showed that students in the immersion program outperformed their peers in the bilingual program in all subjects through 7th grade, when the latter group finally caught up.

Two key elements contributed to the success of the El Paso immersion program, says Russell Gersten, a professor of education at the University of Oregon, who was one of the study's researchers. First, the program started building academic language early on, using literature to ensure that English exposure went beyond the conversational. (Gersten notes that there is "overwhelming support" in the field for using literature and content as the vehicles for learning English, rather than a grammar-based approach.) Second, the program kept a modest native-language component for four years (decreasing each year), to provide "a safe anchor" for students.

Strikingly, the Ramirez study supports Porter's claim that bilingual programs launch too few students into mainstream classes. The study found that, despite program objectives, three-fourths of the immersion students and over four-fifths of the early-exit students had not been mainstreamed, even after four years.

TWO-WAY BILINGUAL PROGRAMS

Recently, another option for LEP (and English-speaking) students, "two-way" bilingual programs, has become increasingly popular, says Deborah Short of the Center for Applied Linguistics. In two-way programs, half the students are native speakers of English; the other half speak another language, usually Spanish. Instruction is delivered in English half the time, and in Spanish the other half. The goal is for all students to become fully bilingual and biliterate. There are about 170 such programs around the United States, Short says.

Key Elementary School in Arlington, Va., offers a two-way bilingual program in English and Spanish, says Principal Katharine Panfil. The school uses either one bilingual teacher or two monolingual teachers to deliver instruction; both approaches work, Panfil says. ("Children actually pick up language better from their peers than from the teacher," she notes.) Year to year, they alternate the language in which each subject is taught: math, for example, is taught in English one year, in Spanish the next.

The benefits of the program are many, Panfil says. "The children in the class become highly fluent in two languages," and they have positive feelings about themselves and speakers of other languages. The program has "a huge waiting list," she adds. "We can't possibly meet the demand."

River Glen Elementary School in San Jose, Calif., offers a variation on the two-way concept, explains resource teacher Linda Luporini-Hakmi. Although two-thirds of the children are English speakers, instruction is predominantly in Spanish; all students learn to speak, read, and write in Spanish. Spanish-speaking students also receive ESL instruction, while English speakers study English language arts.

In this setting, the native Spanish speakers' self-esteem "shoots up," Luporini-Hakmi says. They use their smattering of English to translate for their English-speaking peers. The mixed class gives speakers of Spanish a need to use English, while speakers of English have more opportunity to practice Spanish, she says. Another benefit of the two-way approach is that it mixes English- and Spanish-speaking students and allows them to become friends.

Whatever approach educators take to teaching LEP students, the United States needs to value bilingualism more highly, experts agree. The arrival of LEP students at the schoolhouse door should not be seen as a problem, Short says. If educators plan properly, "these kids can be a resource." Knowing other languages and cultures can only benefit students, she says. "If we start to value bilingualism, we will make the United States a stronger country."

KEEPING NATIVE LANGUAGES ALIVE

KATHY CHECKLEY

Maria Ramirez, daughter of immigrant parents who came to the United States from Mexico, insists that, had her school given students opportunities to maintain their native languages, it could have made a tremendous difference for her family. Even as she delights in the news that she has been named the bilingual teacher of the year by the National

---

This article was originally published in the March 1996 issue of ASCD's *Education Update* newsletter.

Association for Bilingual Education (NABE), Ramirez ponders what might have been for her six brothers.

"Our first language was Spanish, it's what we spoke at home," explains Ramirez. "At school, we were asked to always speak English. We were not encouraged to speak Spanish." While the lack of support kindled her competitive spirit, Ramirez says, it had the opposite effect on her brothers. As a result, only two of her six brothers finished high school; none of them pursued higher education of the sort Ramirez chose. Today she is a 2nd grade bilingual teacher at Alsup Elementary School in Commerce City, Colo.

Ramirez' experiences convinced her that if schools and teachers don't help students maintain their first language, they, in effect, tell these students that they aren't valued. "My language is part of who I am. If you take that away," says Ramirez, "you don't respect my whole person."

Ramirez' is a story shared by many students in the United States whose native languages are not English. The emphasis on English language development in U.S. public schools has precluded these students from maintaining fluency in their heritage languages, say experts.

"The attitude in the United States has historically been, 'lose the native language as soon as possible,'" says Marty Abbott, foreign language coordinator for Fairfax County Public Schools in Virginia.

"We're one of the few countries in the world that doesn't value bilingualism," agrees Deborah Short, TESOL/ESL Standards project director at the Center for Applied Linguistics. "We have quite a wealth of resources in immigrant students, but we try to trample their expertise, erase it."

There may now be a shift, however, in how educators cultivate the language resources that abound in our diverse student population. Recently released national standards for foreign language learning recognize the benefits of bilingualism and the need to help students recover their language if they've become English dominant. Soon-to-be-released standards for ESL instruction also support the belief that students should be given opportunities to maintain and develop their native language.

A BRIEF HISTORY

For several decades, public schools in the United States have been emphatically monolingual. As the student population grows more diverse, however, the question of how to assimilate non-English speakers into the U.S. educational system becomes more complicated. The debate can become heated.

Some educators continue to favor the so-called submersion approach—mainstreaming immigrant children into English-only classrooms. Advocates contend that this "sink or swim" method, used almost exclusively in U.S. schools for years, encourages students to master English quickly because they want to keep up with their English-speaking peers.

Critics challenge this approach, claiming instead that non-English speaking students who receive no assistance in the classroom often become so frustrated, the chances of their enjoying a successful academic experience are slim. These experts advocate transitional bilingual education programs in which students receive part of the curriculum in their native language, arguing that research shows that non-English speaking students schooled in their *first* language acquire the *new* language more readily.

Still, more and more experts are concluding that transitional bilingual education programs, while preferable to the submersion model, are short-sighted in this age of global competitiveness. What's needed, these experts say, is a comprehensive effort to develop fully what have been, to date, untapped foreign language resources. In this effort, foreign language teachers and ESL educators have a common purpose: to help students cultivate their native language.

THE LANGUAGE EDGE

"If you ask 'John Q. Public' if it's important for Americans to learn a foreign language his answer is 'yes,'" says Ronald Walton, deputy director of the National Foreign Language Center (NFLC). But, he adds, these same people don't see a need to help immigrant students develop their native language.

College-bound students, however, see the need. Enrollment patterns in higher education show that an increasing number of students with home languages other than English are signing up for courses in their native languages, eager to turn their linguistic advantages into economic assets.

Guadalupe Valdes, professor of Spanish and Portuguese and professor of education at Stanford University, identifies as "heritage language learners" those older students who have received all their schooling in English and are now ready to study their first language as an academic subject. "Many of these students say, 'I speak the language with my grandmother, but I never used it intellectually. I never learned to write it,'" Valdes explains. And, now, many of them want to use their native languages in entrepreneurial ventures.

Take, for example, the Korean-American business major who eventually wants to conduct business in Korea. Although she can use Korean informally, she needs to understand how to use the language in more formal contexts, such as in giving presentations or in writing sales reports; she needs to understand the discourse of the Korean business world.

Valdes, who represented heritage language learners on the task force that developed the new standards for foreign language learning, points out that most heritage language learners are secondary or post-secondary students trying to "recover" the language they lost as they became proficient in English, many through traditional bilingual education programs. In spite of the first few years in which these students received instruction in their native language, "after more than nine years of English-only education they become English dominant," Valdes explains. If they read and write in their native language, they "write like 3rd graders. They go into heritage language programs because they want to use two languages academically and professionally."

SHIFTING THE EMPHASIS

Although it's important to give all students at all education levels opportunities to develop their native languages, some educators, like Paquita Holland, wonder, why wait?

Holland is the principal at Oyster Elementary School in Washington, D.C., which has offered a two-way Spanish immersion program since 1971. In the Oyster model, two teachers are in the classroom every day, one to guide native English speakers as they learn Spanish and the other to assist native Spanish speakers as they master English. In the course of covering the curriculum, teachers and students use both languages equally, with half of the curriculum taught in Spanish and the other half taught in English.

"If you really want to make an impact, don't do transitional ESL," says Holland. Create, instead, "an educational setting in which the languages children bring to the school are celebrated and shared." The program at Oyster is based on balance, says Holland, a balance in which neither language dominates, and each language is considered valuable. "Never does the language minority child feel as though he or she has to give up something. The children here become as bilingual and biliteral as possible."

Holland says high test scores attest to the effectiveness of two-way immersion programs offered at the elementary level. As a result, Holland sees no need to delay foreign language instruction until high school.

Yet, as ideal as the Oyster model may be, there are some caveats. First, it's an expensive program. The per-pupil cost at Oyster is higher than at any other school in the District of Columbia. Second, the Oyster model can be successful only so long as the student population is relatively homogeneous. "We teach content in two languages, so the school population has to be mainly English-dominant and Spanish-dominant," explains Holland. In other schools and districts, where many different languages are represented among the student population, such a program would be very difficult, if not impossible, to administer.

It's these factors—expense and feasibility—that prompt some educators and policymakers to insist that families and communities bear the responsibility for helping students preserve their first language. Walton understands this argument. Indeed, he believes foreign language educators should call upon the linguistic abilities of community members to better serve students. "The Vietnamese community, for example, can help students retain their Vietnamese when that language is not offered at the school," he explains. The only obstacle Walton sees is a reluctance by schools to award credit for such nontraditional courses, taught by non-credentialed teachers. Walton brushes such concerns aside. Teachers, he says, can arrange for students to demonstrate their proficiency. "Why demand 'seat time' when it's possible for students to learn the language elsewhere?" Of primary importance, says Walton, who laments that too many languages and cultures are dying out, is that students have opportunities to learn or maintain their native language.

Other experts agree with Walton and conclude that those who understand the benefits of preserving language resources need to become more vocal advocates for the research that supports their position. "We have to become more savvy in talking to policymakers and community leaders," says Short, who maintains that most people don't know the benefits of bilingualism.

Those policymakers and community leaders should talk to Ramirez. Being bilingual, she says, will "open more doors" for English-speaking students. She cites her own experiences as evidence. Upon graduating from college, Ramirez says that, unlike her monolingual colleagues, she was offered a job "on the spot" because she is bilingual.

CHARACTER AND VALUES EDUCATION

THE CONTENT OF THEIR CHARACTER

PHILIP COHEN

Riding a wave of public response to the perceived moral decline of U.S. social and cultural life, character educators are renewing schools' emphasis on values and morality. After several false starts at values education in the 1970s and 1980s, character educators are uniting around a strategy of teaching core values developed through community consensus. To build public trust in schools' ability to teach character, schools and districts are enlisting parent and community participation in the design and implementation of character education programs.

The most successful approaches stress not only curriculum, but also changing the culture of schools to make them communities that reinforce positive values and character traits, advocates say. Using such strategies as literature-based curriculums in the early grades and service learning and ethical reasoning in high school, character educators hope to improve both the professional and economic prospects of their students, as well as the social and moral fiber of their communities.

Although enthusiasm among advocates is high, and early assessments of the new methods yield some promising results, the task of instilling good character is a daunting one. Many educators are unsure of the goals of character education, even as they search for effective strategies for their students.

This article was originally published in the Spring 1995 issue of ASCD's *Curriculum Update* newsletter.

Interest in character education has "really exploded around the country," says John Martin, executive director of the Character Education Partnership, of which ASCD is a member. The best estimate is that one school district in five has "some type of program in place," he adds.

PUBLIC DEMAND

"I've never seen such a broad-based public concern about values and character in our society, and such a strong statement of desire to do something about it in our schools," says Howard Kirschenbaum, author of *100 Ways to Enhance Values and Morality in Schools and Youth Settings*.

Thomas Lickona, author of *Educating for Character*, believes public acceptance of the idea is not universal, however. "There's some nervousness when the schools want to enter the values arena," he says. "But I think what's increasingly clear is that people are deeply disturbed about the state of our culture, about our moral condition. There's just this sense that our civilization is imploding, that there is a kind of moral collapse from within, and that we can't take for granted any longer that we'll have a moral society. So there is a real sense of crisis, a sense of urgency."

Public trust in U.S. schools is not at an all-time high. But a recent survey of Michigan parents showed that one reason parents support voucher programs is that public schools don't do enough to teach values and character. Advocates conclude that character education is one way to win back community support. Repeated surveys have shown that more than 90 percent of adults think schools should teach such noncontroversial values as honesty and democracy.

Schools influence student character whether they try to or not, says Henry Huffman, author of *Developing a Character Education Program* and director of the Character Education Institute at California University of Pennsylvania. The question is not if schools should teach character, he contends. "The question is *how* will they do it?"

SCHOOLS STEP IN

The demand for character education dovetails with a rising concern about youth problems. In the past six years, hundreds of communities have established curfews. Several states have increased their prosecution of young people as adults when they are charged with violent crimes. Also, character educators argue that many children live in an environment that is unhealthy to moral development. One survey found that 39 percent of 6- and 7-year-olds in the District of Columbia had seen a dead body, and 31 percent had seen someone shot. A large survey in Connecticut revealed that many children had their first alcoholic drinks in 3rd grade. All these problems—and more—are reflected in the mass media and popular culture. It's more than some parents can handle—and parents are more often single. In schools, some analysts trace growing discipline and safety problems to fractures in family and social life.

"Schools must step in where parents fail and supplement them when they succeed," says Amitai Etzioni, University Professor at George Washington University and founder of the Communitarian Network. "There are a large number of parents these days, who—either through no fault of their own, or because they are drug addicts or alcoholics, or because they run away on their families—leave children characterologically underdeveloped." However, Etzioni also believes that some "successful" parents are failing their children as well. "They can also fail because both of them are commodities traders or lawyers who are more interested in making a million before they are 30 than in having any real time for their children," he concludes. "So the schools must reinforce, supplement, and augment what the families do when they are at their best."

Not everyone wants this sort of help. House Majority Leader Rep. Dick Armey is among those who oppose any values education in schools. "I for one, would not tolerate anybody having the presumption to dare to think they should define who my children are, what their values are, what their ethics are," he has said.

Character educators do not want to take over the role of parents, says David Miller, vice president of Quest International. "But from what we can see coming into schools, they need some help," he says. Huffman agrees. "We're not about to solve all the problems in the world" with character education, he says. But together with other institutions, such as the family, religious institutions, and government, schools can make a difference. "Everyone has a sphere of influence"—and a responsibility to act within it. Or, as Dayton, Ohio, school board member Charles Scott puts

Reading for Values

In Jody Colby's 1st grade class at Foster Elementary School in Pittsburgh, Pa., story time means more than just a well-told tale. The stories Colby uses emphasize seven characteristics: courage, loyalty, justice, respect, hope, honesty, and love. "We define them with the children, and then we read stories that apply them," she says. "When those words come up again, at home, or at play, the children have a more specific understanding of what they are" after reading the stories. Colby's program is from the Heartwood Institute, which develops materials for literature-based character education.

Because Foster is a "very homogeneous" school, Colby is also glad that Heartwood stories help "develop a respect for other cultures," by drawing from diverse cultures for myths, legends, and folktales.

In one story focusing on courage, an Aleut child goes on her first excursion into caves under the frozen surface of the sea at low tide to collect shellfish. The children, Colby says, are riveted. They pay especially close attention because they know "it's not just a story. It's more unusual, and there's going to be a follow-up activity."

Before the story, "We've already talked about what the term is, and when they listen to the story, they listen for when it comes up," Colby says. Afterwards, she gives them the beginning of a sentence: "I showed courage when. . . . " Students complete the sentence with words or pictures and share their work with the whole class.

In a story teaching honesty, the emperor of China is looking for a successor, and he announces a flower-growing contest for all the boys in China. Each gets a set of seeds, which are all sterile. Every boy but one cheats, substituting healthy seeds, and brings in a beautiful flower pot. Only one is honest enough to bring in a barren pot, and he is chosen. After the story, the children form cooperative learning groups to compose a sentence about honesty in school.

Colby, who spent four years on committees to help her district get its character education program off the ground, is optimistic about the effects of the literature, although she knows that any long-term results will not be seen in her classroom. She also knows that "whether students change depends on a lot of things that we can't control," including their home lives, personalities, and other experiences. But she does hope to see an improvement in school behavior, especially as the school starts using the values more broadly through its discipline policies.

Heartwood stresses that the stories alone are not character education. Students preview the ideas before reading the story, then use critical thinking, problem solving, or conflict resolution strategies through hands-on or cooperative learning activities. In a wrap-up activity, teacher and students are encouraged to make connections to other aspects of the curriculum and their lives.

The Heartwood Institute is in Wexford, Pa., and may be reached at (412) 934-1777.

it, "From kindergarten to senior year of high school, we have the children 15,000 hours. If we can't modify their behavior in all that time, then we're doing something wrong."

Still, the current character education movement is young, diverse, and relatively untested, these experts say. "These periodic expressions of concern have in the past sometimes been superficial or short-lived," Kirschenbaum notes. "This feels a little bit more serious and deep, but it also requires a real commitment of time and resources to implement. So we'll see how far it really goes."

No nationally agreed-upon standard or curriculum for character education exists; approaches and curriculums abound. But Martin considers that healthy: "The fact that there are a variety of strategies adds synergy to the movement." That diversity is fueled by the commitment to crafting character education programs at the local level and according to local community values.

The program at Bel-Air Elementary School in Albuquerque, N.M., is less than two years old, but school counselor Mary Jane Aguilar says that already "it's creating a school climate where there is a common humanity working together." With that beginning, proponents say, character education has begun to pay off.

WHAT VALUES?

The identification of "core" or "consensus" values lies at the heart of most new character education programs. These are usually lists of values or character traits developed to address the needs of the local district and community. One of the most common starting points is the Aspen Declaration, the product of a 1992 character education conference. This statement lists six values: respect, responsibility, trustworthiness, caring, justice and fairness, and civic virtue and citizenship. Educators can make such a core list available to their communities, or they can start from scratch.

By focusing on such basic and noncontroversial values, educators hope to head off political controversies that could stop character education in its tracks. They also avoid the pitfalls of the much-maligned "values clarification" model of the 1970s, which left values choices to the student.

Controversy erupts whenever schools approach the gray areas where the easy application of right and wrong fails to provide answers. But Etzioni sees no reason to debate the specific controversial questions that have bogged down character education before some basic values are established. "My first thing to say to the student, the parents, the community," he says, "is that a child who does not have self-discipline, and does not have empathy, could not abide by *any* values. Whatever the values—you name them—not telling a lie, being compassionate, being just, being tolerant, respect for others and self—they all presume these two capacities."

Kirschenbaum agrees with the emphasis on basics, at least to begin with. "Things are more moral, or more right, among other reasons because they're more consistent with values of respect, fairness, and justice," he says. "We have to help students understand that we can go back to commonly agreed-upon understandings of these basic values and moral principles, which they can use when making individual value decisions. It's not that one choice is just as good as another choice. Some choices are better. You can think about universal ethical principles—such as universality and reciprocity and other principles—by which we judge whether something is right or good."

Both Lickona and Etzioni believe some basic values have an objective basis that is not subject to individual interpretation. For them, these are at the heart of successful character education. "In American thinking today," says Lickona, "there is still a predominantly subjective notion of conscience—you've got to follow your conscience. But there is very little attention to the other side of that—that you have to form your conscience in accordance with moral norms that have objective validity."

Etzioni agrees. "For me," he says, "these values are independent moral clauses, which speak to us in unmistakable terms in their own force—directly to our hearts in a very compelling voice—if you just listen to them." If a student asks where they come from, he says, "I don't care. God or nature. To me it's important they are there."

Once this ethical groundwork is established, these experts agree, then students (and communities, for that matter) are better prepared to discuss and debate the thorny social issues of the day—especially those surrounding such topics as teen sexuality, abortion, and homosexuality. Kirschenbaum says schools should "educate people to the principles of respect and civility that enable them to explore those differences in a way that doesn't tear the fabric of society apart, but allows them to grow and learn, and if not agree with one another, at least work out a way to live peacefully together."

MAKE VALUES STICK

In the Dayton (Ohio) school district, character education revolves around a word of the week. From *punctuality* in the first week of school, to *patriotism, perseverance, politeness,* and *cooperation,* each week the district promotes the virtues of a new value. Local television stations air spots promoting the word, fliers go out to parents, place mats bearing the word adorn cafeteria tables—even religious groups are encouraged to plan sermons and lessons around the word of the week. Dayton is a model of a program that stresses repetitive inculcation, especially in the younger grades, as a way of making a lasting impression on children.

"Language leads to attitudes, and attitudes lead to behavior," says David Brooks, president of the Jefferson Center for Character Education. "We're in the advertising business." Advertisers successfully promote desired behavior by encouraging conformity through repeated messages, Brooks says, and schools can, too.

This approach has its critics, however. Alan Lockwood, chair of Curriculum and Instruction at the University of Wisconsin–Madison, says much of character education is guided by an "unexamined assumption" that needs to be challenged. "The presumption is," he says, "that the bad behavior of young people is a consequence of their not holding the right values. The notion that behavior flows directly from values in some unmediated way—that is, that if you're behaving badly it means you've got bad values, if you've got good values you won't behave badly—that is simply not true." People who engage in destructive behaviors often believe their actions are wrong, Lockwood says. And many people who hold good values can be led into bad actions by force of circumstances.

While Lockwood concedes that a direct link between values and behaviors "has a certain commonsense appeal," he says, "I just think that it's a mistake to the extent that character education advocates are giving the public the impression that if only kids had the right values that these problems would either go away or be attenuated. That's just not persuasive to anyone who looks at the research." Research dating to the 1920s, he believes, "simply makes clear that there is not a simple equation from values to behavior."

This research does not mean that such pressing problems as youth violence, drug abuse, pregnancy, and other troublesome behaviors should be left alone, Lockwood adds. "I strongly support efforts to address these kinds of issues," he stresses. "But the efforts at promoting civic decency have got to be thought through a lot more carefully."

Kirschenbaum says that successful character education requires a combination of inculcation, modeling, and facilitating of values. The appropriate method is often suggested by the question at hand, he says. "There are some areas of values that involve more personal choices," he says, "such as career choice or marriage partners, or perhaps choices about religious practices, which don't necessarily involve moral issues. Whereas there are other issues—regarding stealing and getting along with others in society, and participating in groups, and doing good work that you're responsible for—that do involve questions of right and wrong, moral issues." Finally, "there are lots of areas of life—like sexual choices and behavior—that involve both personal choices and moral decisions. So depending on what the issue is," he concludes, "inculcating may be more appropriate or important, or giving people skills and facilitating their own best thinking may be more appropriate or important."

Character education has an important cognitive element, Lickona says. "It's crucial, even in the elementary grades, to get kids to be thoughtful about why one is kind or honest or brave. Kids have to be moral thinkers from the beginning." But cognition cannot be the whole approach, he believes. "You have to have the feeling, the commitment, and finally the behavior."

Simple formulas are easy to learn, says Lockwood, but they are just as easily undermined by real-life events. Children will quickly find that "general values conflict in concrete situations," he explains. When a relative asks a child if the dry turkey tastes good, for example, honesty and politeness clash. "To reason your way through, you've got some overarching moral principles that you apply in situations to help you sort out the dilemma of which value to endorse," Lockwood says. "Just endorsing a single general value doesn't give you as much guidance as you think it might."

In the civil rights movement, demonstrators broke the law to overcome racial segregation—undermining the edicts to "play by the rules," "obey laws," and "respect authority" now put forward by the Character Counts Coalition, for example. Good citizens need the skills and the morals to confront such choices when they arise. "In some cases, you do sacrifice one principle for the sake of the other," says Bel-Air's Aguilar. Conflicts such as the civil rights movement can be turned into valuable lessons, she believes, by stressing the high morals and peaceful means advanced by Martin Luther King Jr. Similarly, in the school, Aguilar says children are expected to follow rules, but the rules in turn are expected to be fair. "If the rule is not fair, then we want that brought to our attention," she says.

BUILDING RELATIONSHIPS

"The mere exhortation or the urging of good behavior on the part of children can be effective under some circumstances," explains James Leming, professor of curriculum and instruction at Southern Illinois University at Carbondale. "And those circumstances are that the person doing the exhortation is a person that is significant to you, and the person's opinions matter to you—and those sorts of influences are more powerful than other forces acting on you in the environment. But by and large," he concludes, "that's not what happens." Building such influential relationships in a school environment is central to the challenge of character education.

To create an environment that nourishes character-building relationships, advocates say changing the culture at the school level is essential. "Character education must be led by the principals," says Dayton

Finding Out What Works

There are almost as many character education programs as there are schools and districts attempting to teach character. Some use literature classes to impart values; others employ service learning. A program may be school- or districtwide, combined with other reforms such as dress codes, or confined to a few classrooms and hours of the day. For a movement trying to gain credibility by proving its effectiveness, the different approaches pose a problem. How do we know what works?

"We're dealing with some of the most difficult aspects of human development and trying to influence those in certain directions," says James Leming, professor of curriculum and instruction at Southern Illinois University at Carbondale. "We ought to be realistic in what we can achieve."

Partly because of its decentralized nature, Leming says, character education in its latest incarnation has produced little systematic evaluation of its results. "Evaluation is the last thing people think about," he says. "It just isn't a glitzy, pretty thing to engage in, and it's also very expensive to do it well."

Leming fears such a weakness may have harsh consequences. "As the field starts to come under attack, people start to ask hard questions: 'What evidence do we have that these programs work?' The answer is, 'Well, we really don't have a lot.' That's a lot of ammunition for the critics. So I think it's really important that the field itself acquire some discipline and do some tough-minded inquiry into the effect the programs are having—and produce some credible answers," he asserts.

Discipline

Some schools and districts recorded rapid improvements in discipline after they began character education programs. An independent survey of 25 K–8 Los Angeles area schools using curriculum from the Jefferson Center for Character Education found substantial declines in the median number of discipline problems reported by school administrators in the first year. The Allen Elementary School in Dayton, Ohio, reported similar results.

"I think those early positive results are encouraging signs," says Howard Kirschenbaum, author of *100 Ways to Enhance Values and Morality in Schools and Youth Settings*. "But it's not initially clear what those results mean," he cautions. "For example, just the fact that a group of teachers is enthusiastic about doing the program, and have come up with activities that are interesting, could be enough to get some initial positive results, which is a great start. The question is, will the results last and spread and deepen, so they'll lead to permanent changes in values, attitudes, and behavior? We need to stick with these programs, keep improving them," he concludes, "and eventually start measuring the results in a more rigorous way."

Early discipline gains mean that "if we as teachers pay attention to these matters, students pay attention to them and change their behavior," Leming says. "But whether or not the curriculum that's associated with these changes is responsible" is not clear from these studies, "because maybe another curriculum would have had the same effect," he notes. So these results do not offer much guidance to educators trying to compare the effectiveness of different programs.

Another worry is that the effects may not last. Discipline results "are mostly short term and situationally specific," Leming says. "They don't seem to generalize to subsequent years unless the program is continued. That is, if the child has an intense 3rd grade curriculum, we'll notice some very nice things happening. But then if that child changes school districts, or goes into a 4th grade where the environment is different and those values aren't reinforced and aren't developed and elaborated on, the research seems to indicate that these gains that we've made tend to wash out in the following year."

Comprehensive Results

The Child Development Project (CDP) has undertaken an in-depth research effort, producing the most comprehensive results of character education research yet, experts say. The program includes classroom, schoolwide, and family components. Stressing intrinsic motivation in the classroom, the program uses literature and cooperative learning activities to promote the values of concern and respect for others, fairness, and personal responsibility. And CDP coordinates at-home activities with curriculum and school events.

CDP has conducted longitudinal studies at two school districts in California, using classroom observations and extensive interviews. Classroom practices such as supportiveness, cooperation, student thinking and discussion, and the emphasis on prosocial values, led to improved interpersonal and academic behavior. That, in turn, affected such student outcomes as learning motivation, concern for others and conflict resolution skills, according to CDP. CDP also followed a group of students from both "program" and "control" schools from elementary grades into middle school and found that these positive effects lasted beyond the life of the program itself. The "program" students continued to show improved behaviors.

John Martin, executive director of the Character Education Partnership, says making the link between character education and improved academic performance will be a watershed for the movement. "I think at that point everybody in America is going to be clamoring to get involved," he says. For now, although most programs rely on anecdotal evidence, he says, "we're generally pleased with the assessment data. But that clearly is one of our biggest needs."

Superintendent James Williams, "with the teachers buying in." In Dayton, which uses site-based management, the district supports school efforts, but each school sets its own tone, he says.

Allen Elementary is an inner-city school in Dayton, with 60 percent of its students living in single-parent families, and more than 70 percent on Aid to Families with Dependent Children, according to Principal Rudolph Bernardo. He says the school began to emphasize character education because order and discipline in the building had broken down.

"The teachers could no longer teach in the classroom because of the constant interruption," he recalls. After a needs assessment, including a parent survey and focus groups, Allen staff decided to embark on a program that would "immerse the student in a totally new way of learning," Bernardo says.

The efforts at Allen go beyond the word of the week, which is the core of the school's character education program. Teachers improved their own relationships through staff development workshops on building trust, working by consensus, and working in teams. Bernardo arranged for summer orientation sessions for parents to help them understand the new attitude of discipline and mutual responsibility that would govern the school. Those parents who did not attend orientations were invited to one-on-one sessions with the principal. Those who failed to respond to invitations for such conferences were eventually required to attend. Parents and students alike signed memorandums of understanding for participating in the school, and uniforms were required. Parents who did not participate were warned their children would not be permitted to stay at the school. "Unless parents understand that you mean business," Bernardo says, "they won't listen."

Each week, in a typical Allen classroom, the word of the week is defined on Monday and illustrated with simple examples. The next three days feature short homeroom discussions related to the word. Teachers are encouraged to connect classroom activities to the word's theme. Then at the school assembly on Friday, one class offers a performance—story, drama, pantomime—extolling the virtue of the character trait.

In the first two years of the program, suspensions dropped drastically, teacher absenteeism declined, and PTA fund-raising increased. Now children are sent to the principal's office for compliments when they behave well, Bernardo says.

"We believe that all experiences at the school should be aligned so that they support the values we care about, rather than undermine them," Etzioni says. "So what we need to do is kind of take stock of everything we do in schools: on what grounds we dish out the grades, how people behave in the corridors, what happens in sports, and see that all these experiences support our educational purposes rather than undermine them."

For many people interested in character education, discipline and safety problems are an immediate concern. Character education gives these educators a way to pursue a disciplined school environment without simply increasing punishments or focusing exclusively on negative reinforcement.

"You can teach what these values mean, you can teach that they are important," Lickona says. "But then you have to hold students accountable in some way so that when they violate the value, there is some kind of a correction, that they're held responsible for their behavior, and there's accountability in the system."

Charles MacQuigg, a shop teacher at Hoover Middle School in Albuquerque, N.M., who trains other teachers in character education, says discipline has slipped to the point where "I can no longer tell a kid that cheaters never win, because very often they do." A lack of discipline undermines the whole program, he says, because teachers who advocate playing by the rules appear hypocritical or out of touch. "There have to be meaningful consequences for people who behave unethically," he believes. "If a kid cuts in line in the cafeteria, and the only consequence is he ends up where he would have been anyway—at the end of the line—then there's no downside" to his unethical behavior, MacQuigg argues.

CURRICULUM INTEGRATION

Few schools use stand-alone character education programs. Instead, most integrate the ideas into existing curriculums. Many use character education units that can be incorporated into English or social studies courses. At Hoover Middle School, MacQuigg says teachers are planning to work character education into existing courses. "The curriculum is so packed right now that there isn't room to add much more," he says. Still, he thinks teachers will find that the time dedicated to the program is well invested because it stands to improve discipline and student participation in other areas.

Most character education programs are in elementary schools, but districts and curriculum developers are now training their sights on middle and high schools. There is "no question" that character education is "a bigger challenge at the secondary level," Martin says. Teachers have less time with students, and the integrated approach favored by character educators is less compatible with most high school curriculums.

Aguilar hopes Albuquerque can take its program to the higher grade levels, but she concedes such an undertaking will be more difficult. The sheer size of the high schools presents a challenge, as does the greater fragmentation of the high school faculty. Also, high school students must take a more active role in the program if it is to be successful, she believes. "The students will have to be leaders to change the culture," she says. But with the increase in school-related violence in high schools, she also thinks students and faculty may rise to the challenge. "Desperate times force people to take risks they wouldn't usually take," she concludes. In character education, incidents of violence and acts of good character become the moments of teaching opportunity.

"High school is a tough nut to crack," Lockwood says. "And adolescents are very different from young children. So we should not generalize from a program that might be effective with 3rd graders and assume that its principles, if translated to the high school, will have equal effectiveness." Huffman believes that a single required course in 9th grade may be necessary to establish a program, before character content can be successfully implemented throughout the upper-level curriculum.

Middle and high school students will also need to spend more time engaging in critical thinking and moral reasoning, Huffman adds—and that time must include helping students make their own decisions about those controversial issues on which the school will not take an official position. Young children can usually concentrate on learning to choose between clear-cut right and wrong decisions, which are not true ethical dilemmas, Huffman says. Older students face values issues of increasing complexity.

Advocates say peer- and service-oriented programs can provide the combination of cognitive and behavioral factors needed to be effective with older students. Research in pregnancy and drug prevention programs has shown the effectiveness of peer- and community-based approaches, Leming says.

In programs such as Quest International's Skills for Action, according to David Miller, high school students combine critical thinking, problem solving, multicultural understanding, accountability, and communication skills in a community service program. To "seal in" the learning, the program includes an extensive classroom component that includes discussion, reflection, and writing, Miller adds.

"Character is formed in the crucible of experience," Lickona says. "Morality is not a spectator sport. If you want kids to have good character, they have to have countless real-life moral experiences that teach them, through their human relationships, through their everyday interactions, what it means to care, what it means to be fair, what it means to be trustworthy."

Educators must "teach our young people the skills to solve problems, to think for themselves, and to make their own responsible decisions," writes Kirschenbaum. "Anything less would not be worthy of an educational system in a democracy and in a changing world."

Community Involvement in Character Education

Philip Cohen

Successful character education programs rely on community support and involvement for several reasons, advocates say. First, the presence of controversial issues in the classroom increases the chance that strong organized opposition will threaten the entire program. Second, if children are to receive a consistent message regarding character education, com-

---

This article was originally published as "The Community Approach" in the Spring 1995 issue of ASCD's *Curriculum Update* newsletter.

munity members—including families—must bolster the message received in school, and vice versa.

Experience suggests many communities are prepared to work together for character education. "I'm very optimistic," says Howard Kirschenbaum, author of *100 Ways to Enhance Values and Morality in Schools and Youth Settings.* "Because in community after community, when adults, parents, community members, and teachers have sat down with one another and asked, 'What are the values that we want to teach?' they've found that they have a lot more in common than that which was dividing them. They really can agree on the vast majority of moral questions when it comes to basic standards of right and wrong."

Supporting good character is a community responsibility, says Thomas Lickona, author of *Educating for Character*, and that idea is being rediscovered. "There is a growing sense that we have to do more than just keep our own families happy and healthy," he says. Character education does not have to spark widespread controversy, says James Leming, professor of curriculum and instruction at Southern Illinois University at Carbondale. "Most of the ideological spin comes from the extremes; it doesn't come from the center. I think astute school boards, and astute superintendents and principals around this country are people who know how to develop a curriculum that represents the center of the political debate. The center of the political debate accepts the basic principles that character education is trying to develop."

MAKING A LIST

Popular lists of values overlap, but they also differ in their emphasis. The "six pillars of character" distributed by the Josephson Institute and Character Counts Coalition are trustworthiness, respect, responsibility, fairness, caring, and citizenship. On the other hand, the Heartwood Institute advocates a literature-based program that has seven traits: courage, loyalty, justice, respect, hope, honesty, and love. Only "respect" appears on both lists. A Baltimore County task force sifted through the U.S. Constitution to produce a list of 24 values, which includes equality of opportunity, order, tolerance, and truth.

Henry Huffman, author of *Developing a Character Education Program*, recommends a concerted effort to reach community consensus on a short list of one-word core values. These values can be "stated at such a high level of abstraction" that everyone can agree with them. "What can be more challenging," he concedes, "is bringing them down to lower levels of abstraction." For example, at the Mt. Lebanon school district in suburban Pittsburgh, where Huffman spearheaded the character education program, the community could agree that students should "demonstrate active responsibility for the welfare of others." But one sub-statement of that value was "caring for one's country," which "could take the form of civil disobedience to bad policy," he writes. This vagueness masked a potential controversy.

The trend toward simplicity in a list of character traits has some advocates worried. "I am concerned about this for two reasons," says Amitai Etzioni, University Professor at George Washington University and founder of the Communitarian Network. "First of all, a list of virtues does not give you the psychological equipment to abide by any of them. Second, I understand why people are driven to those lists, because all education is controversial, and they hide behind those lists because they believe they are safe. So who can quarrel with *respect*? But the lists are either simplistic and not compelling, or if you try to enrich them, you're back to controversial material."

Lickona is less worried about this trend "at this stage of the movement, because it will help us make some progress in the short run," he says. "Making it all kind of simple—so everyone can get on board—that's probably the American way. We're pragmatists, and we want to fix a problem fast. Partly it's that the problems in this case are so serious that we want to move quickly. And partly the challenge of pluralism makes us want to get the maximum amount of agreement. Let's get on with stopping food fights in the cafeteria and sexual harassment in the corridors."

ENTER THE COMMUNITY

Mary Jane Aguilar, school counselor at Bel-Air Elementary School in Albuquerque, N.M., says of the "six pillars," "These words are pretty basic and fundamental." But she finds they are too often ignored. We have to "weave this back into the American culture and the community culture," she feels, and schools can only do part of that themselves. "Schools reflect communities, and communities reflect schools."

Etzioni believes that unrealistic expectations from character education are a real danger. "The first thing we have to say to the community is that we are all partners here," he says. "And the notion that somehow the parents will go on and neglect their children, and the neighborhoods will be unsafe, and unemployment will be rampant, and drug use will be common, and violence prevalent, and then we're going to come to the schools and say, 'Fix it,' is preposterous. If we all participate to the maximum, we still have our hands full."

In *Developing a Character Education Program*, Huffman lists several lessons learned from working with his community.

• **Prepare an adequate communications plan.** The district needs a comprehensive approach to communicating with school staff, parents, and community members. Everyone should have access to information and a means to be heard.

• **Follow up on initial communication.** Early enthusiasm, especially among staff, may not be maintained unless program planners continue to seek out and include stakeholder input.

• **Communicate the priority of character education.** Instead of sticking character education in a reform corner, make sure that all aspects of school operations are considered under the program. Employee recruitment, evaluation, and staff development can all be used to convey the importance of district values.

• **Do not dismiss critics quickly.** Writing off critics as extremists will only increase public fears. In responding to critics, schools should model the respect for others that is central to all character education.

WHAT'S WRONG WITH CHARACTER EDUCATION

SCOTT WILLIS

Character education, as it has been defined by leaders in the field, has deep flaws, contended Alfie Kohn at ASCD's 1996 Annual Conference, during his session on "How Not to Teach Values." Although he "heartily endorses" educators' efforts to help students become good peo-

This article was originally published in the May 1996 issue of ASCD's *Education Update* newsletter.

ple, Kohn has many reservations about the character education programs schools are using. "The dominant, mainstream approach [to character education] in the country right now" manipulates students' behavior to produce "unreflective" actions, he charged. "This is what I see in classrooms—with some sterling exceptions."

Kohn discussed five concerns about character education programs as they are currently conceived.

• They take a "fix-the-kid" approach. Programs attempt to solve problems at the level of the child, Kohn said. They imply that problems rest solely within individuals; teachers should fix the child so that he "has character."

This approach ignores what we know from social psychology—that structural characteristics help to drive individual behavior, Kohn said. Besides focusing on individuals, we also need to look at the structure of the school and classroom. If students' cheating is a problem, for example, we need to scrutinize the competitive system that fosters cheating.

• They take a dark view of human nature. "Character education theorists are refreshingly explicit about their views" of human nature, which are quite cynical, Kohn said. They see people as self-centered, willful, and aggressive, with their desires fighting their reason. According to this view, human beings' natural impulse is to be antisocial, and we must overcome selfish desires by force.

Kohn objected to this view. "I'm not Carl Rogers; I'm not Mr. Rogers," he said, "but I believe it's *as* natural to be prosocial, cooperative, and distressed by others' distress." Educators must question programs whose practices grow out of a dark view of human nature, he said.

• They aim to maintain the status quo. The ultimate goal of character education programs is conservative, Kohn said; they respond to concerns for social stability. He suggested other possible goals: to promote social justice, to meet children's needs, to develop active participants in democracy, and to make students part of a caring community. We shouldn't "throw out" tradition, he said, but "it's a matter of emphasis."

• They beg the "Which values?" question. It's a cliche, Kohn said, to wave away this question with bland assurances, such as, "Don't worry about it. There's broad consensus on basic, underlying values."

"Not so fast," Kohn said. Character education programs, in the values they emphasize and the values they eclipse, are promoting "an extremely right-wing agenda," he alleged. These programs define the values they emphasize—such as obedience, patriotism, respect, responsibility, and citizenship—in ways that foster "uncritical deference to authority," he warned.

• They ascribe to a "transmittal" theory of learning. The basic theory on which character education is based is one of instilling values in children, or indoctrination, Kohn said. As a result, programs rely on exhortation (using banners and posters, for example), and reward or punish students until they do what adults want.

If teachers know that children construct their own meanings, why would they use a character education program that transmits knowledge as if to empty vessels? Kohn asked rhetorically. "Kids are not clay to be molded, computers to be programmed, or pets to be trained," he said, and they won't become committed to values when the transmittal method is used to teach them.

Instead, teachers should help students "become thinkers about how we want ourselves and others to be," Kohn urged. Students and teachers should decide together what they want their community to be like, so students will understand values "from the inside out." Adults have a key role in this process, as models and facilitators, Kohn emphasized. Teachers must frame the discussion. "A constructivist teacher poses challenges and dilemmas," he said. "This critique is not an argument for relativism."

Kohn noted that some character education theorists claim that it's "a waste of time to get kids to reinvent basic values." His own view is the opposite: "Folks, there are no shortcuts."

"In most schools where I visit," Kohn said, "students are expected to follow the rules, regardless of whether they're reasonable, and to respect the adults, whether or not they've earned respect." Most schools also endorse competition as natural and desirable, making students' peers potential obstacles to their own success. "Are these the values we want to promote?" he asked. He cited Central Park East High School, with its values of "empathy and skepticism" as an alternative.

TEACHING STUDENTS TO BE MORAL

SCOTT WILLIS

Too many of today's students seem to have no moral compass. Increased youth violence, teen pregnancy, substance abuse, and cheating are cause for alarm among educators and parents alike. More and more communities are calling for their public schools to play a more active role in shaping students' sense of morality.

Reflecting this trend, several speakers at ASCD's 1994 Annual Conference discussed the need for schools to help students become moral adults. Whereas in years past, public school efforts to teach values have bogged down in controversy over *whose* values would be taught, today there is widespread agreement that schools should teach "core" values. These include the civic values inherent in democracy—such as equality, tolerance, and justice—and the moral values that essentially all Americans share, such as honesty, respect for others, and fairness.

How can teachers instill these core values in their students? Drawing on his 30 years' experience in the field of character education, Howard Kirschenbaum of the State University of New York at Brockport attempted to answer this question, describing dozens of practical ways to teach students to be moral.

The most direct method to transmit values is inculcation, Kirschenbaum told his overflow audience—a method educators are "rediscovering" today. Teachers can inculcate values in many ways:

• Use literature and nonfiction selections. "World literature provides many valuable reading experiences" that impart good values, Kirschenbaum said. Even simplistic Horatio Alger works, in which virtue is always rewarded, can reach students, he has found. Rather than responding cynically, his students have been "moved by the simple morality of the tales."

This article was originally published in the May 1994 issue of ASCD's *Update* newsletter.

- Use quotations, such as "Ask not what your country can do for you, but what you can do for your country." Post them on the walls so students can see them daily, he advised. Students will internalize them "almost by osmosis."

- Use praise and appreciation to reinforce moral behavior. This technique is most effective when teachers describe precisely what behavior they appreciated, and its moral implications.

- Establish rules. A system of rules (and punishments for breaking them) provides a moral structure and allows students to feel safe. Malcolm X Elementary School in Washington, D.C., for example, highlights one overarching rule: "No aggressive, violent behavior."

- Use American history as a vehicle. "If taught right, our history can be an effective way to inculcate respect, tolerance, courage, fair play, and faith in the future," Kirschenbaum said. Over the course of American history, respect has been extended to more and more people, including women, minorities, and the disabled. "It's a great story," he said—one that students will find inspiring. Our history also conveys the message that even when we fail to live up to our ideals, we can strive to do better.

- Use codes, pledges, and guidelines. According to survey data, slightly more than half of all students who say they would cheat in school also say they would *not* cheat if they had signed a pledge not to, Kirschenbaum said.

- Clarify moral questions. Teachers can help students think about the consequences of their actions, to others and to society. They can ask questions such as, "If you were on the other side, how would you feel?" and "What does your conscience say?" Through such discussions, students absorb the idea that these issues are important to think about.

ROLE MODELING

Teachers can also instill values by modeling them, Kirschenbaum said. "Students are hungry for adult models," he asserted.

Besides practicing what they preach, teachers can share their moral convictions with students—telling them, for example, "I believe it's wrong to steal, and that's very important to me." Teachers can also talk about community service they perform, as well as events that have shaped their values. Kirschenbaum tells his own students about his experiences registering voters in Mississippi during the civil rights movement. "When my students hear this, I believe it makes a difference," he said—not because his story is so dramatic but because he, the students' own teacher, is telling it. Teachers can also discuss exemplary people in history, such as Abraham Lincoln or Harriet Tubman, he added.

But besides telling and showing students what good values are, teachers must also encourage young people to internalize values and make their own decisions, Kirschenbaum said. Teachers must give students opportunities to respond to moral issues themselves—or their other efforts to teach values will be "like teaching map-and-compass but never sending students out into the world to do it." Teachers need to help students build their *own* commitment to act in a moral way, he emphasized.

One simple way teachers can do this is by giving students lots of opportunities to make choices. Even when students merely rank their ice cream preferences, they learn how to take turns and how to listen, and they see that "we're different but we can get along."

Teachers can instill *civic* values by holding discussions of controversial issues and by conducting class meetings to discuss problems such as pilfering, cliques, or too many interruptions. Teachers can introduce students to "democratic problem solving," encouraging them to consider minority viewpoints and to reflect on whether proposed solutions are fair.

A fourth way teachers can help students become moral is by teaching them *skills* for acting morally, Kirschenbaum said. These include how to listen, communicate clearly, and stand up for their own beliefs; how to resolve problems in a nonviolent way; and how to resist peer pressure and maintain their self-respect (by withstanding pressure to have sex, for example). "Teach them how; don't just moralize to them" about what they should do, he advised.

In conclusion, Kirschenbaum cautioned that educators need to teach values in conjunction with parents and the larger community. "We can't just plunge ahead ourselves," he said.

LEARNING THROUGH SERVICE

SCOTT WILLIS

Students at North Carroll Middle School in Hampstead, Md., are no strangers to community service. Through a program offered by their school, many of them volunteer at a nearby nursing home, says social studies teacher Craig Giles. After receiving six hours of training, students pay visits to the nursing home on their own time, to assist and socialize with the residents. Then, once a month, the students meet for a "reflection session" to discuss their experiences and share suggestions. Last year, forty 8th graders participated in the program. "They love it," Giles reports. "They enjoy doing what they perceive as an adult job."

As a high school student, Bob Giannino also volunteered at a nursing home. Today, he's a program consultant at the Thomas Jefferson Forum at Tufts University, which coordinates student service projects. From the senior citizens he helped, Giannino learned much more about the Depression and the two World Wars than he could have learned from reading textbooks, he says.

Giannino also participated in other service activities while in high school: tutoring, environmental clean-ups, and political service (as a student member of the school board). While he found much of his classroom learning—"reading Hawthorne and learning about the Civil War," for example—hard to relate to his own experiences, service activities provided him "an opportunity to bring some reality to everyday school life."

As these examples reflect, many students are eager to help others in their community, and when they do, they benefit from the experience. Students who serve others actually help *themselves* most, advocates of service learning believe.

More and more schools are using service activities to support learning, experts say. In fact, two dozen school districts around the country and

This article was originally published in the August 1993 issue of ASCD's *Update* newsletter.

the state of Maryland now *require* students to perform community service. Mandatory service learning remains controversial, however.

WHAT STUDENTS DO

In well-designed service learning programs, students do more than ladle out soup to the homeless or pick up trash in public parks, experts say. They apply what they've learned in the classroom, develop leadership and communication skills, become more caring and responsible citizens—and help meet community needs in the process.

Service learning activities are extremely diverse. Students work at hospitals, soup kitchens, homeless shelters, and day-care centers. They promote recycling efforts, monitor air and water quality, and clean up pollution. They plant bulbs in parks and supervise recreational play. They tutor other students, check people's blood pressure, and raise money for charities. They advocate civic action and lobby their elected officials.

Tutoring is a common service activity. Middletown High School in Middletown, Md., for example, offers a course for students who want to be peer tutors, says Joey Hoffman, who teaches the course. Hoffman gives her students "a pretty comprehensive training" in tutoring strategies and topics such as learning disabilities. Then, four days a week, students tutor elementary, middle, and high school students. On the fifth day, the class convenes to discuss their experiences.

Students at Middletown also do projects that combine research and a service activity, Hoffman says. One student developed lessons on saving the Chesapeake Bay and taught them to elementary students. Another student renovated an apartment in a homeless shelter. Other students have developed educational pamphlets on drinking and driving, child abuse, and teen pregnancy.

At Washington Elementary School in Mount Vernon, Wash., every student engages in at least one service project each year, says Kathy Fisk, who teaches 2nd grade. For example, the 2nd graders do composting, while the 3rd graders use the rich, composted soil for beautification projects. The school's 4th graders do cross-age tutoring, and the 5th graders maintain a bird sanctuary (and study birds and migration).

One of the key principles of service learning is providing time for students to reflect on their experiences, experts emphasize. Through discussions, journals, and essays, students should explore the larger dimensions of their service.

"Working in a soup kitchen can be very menial if there's no reflection or discussion," says Samuel Halperin, who directs the American Youth Policy Forum in Washington, D.C. But when students explore related questions—such as why there is hunger and how our society might combat it—"even the menial can become significant."

"Reflection is the key," affirms Alice Halsted of the National Center for Service Learning in Early Adolescence. During the period of service, "there are so many teachable moments, if you can capture them," she says—especially with early adolescents, who are developing abstract thought. Halsted also emphasizes students' need for preparation and training *before* they do their service.

SUPPORTING LEARNING

How do service activities support learning? Service learning is *active* learning, advocates emphasize. In fact, the growing interest in service learning stems, in part, from research showing that many students learn especially well through hands-on, experiential activities, Halperin says.

When students have a real purpose for what they do, they are more motivated to learn, says Maggie O'Neill, deputy director of the Maryland Student Service Alliance. In writing a persuasive letter, for example, service learning provides real consequences. In a traditional class, if a student's letter advocating recycling is mediocre, it may get a "C." In a service learning context, the student won't persuade others to back recycling efforts.

Students want to have authentic experiences, O'Neill adds. They are "tired of the vicarious experiences the classroom provides—filmstrips, somebody else's stories—they want to have their own experiences."

Because service learning provides a way for students to apply knowledge and skills, it should not be seen as an add-on, experts say. Instead, it should be closely coordinated with the curriculum.

If students serve by monitoring the water quality of a river, for example, they should study related issues in the classroom, Halperin says. How did the stream get polluted? Who pays for pollution? How can we develop good public policy on pollution? "You make the questions real by engaging in the service," he says. "It makes the curriculum alive."

Educators can integrate service activities into the curriculum in a variety of ways, experts say. In science classes, students can take on environmental projects, for example. In art classes, students can consider how their art could make life better for people. (They might decide to donate it to a homeless shelter.) In home economics classes, students can use their newly acquired skills in cooking and child care to help those in need.

In teaching a novel or autobiography, an English teacher can help students examine social problems, Hoffman says. The novels of Dickens, for example, explore poverty and the oppression of children. Having students lobby or write letters to the editor about such issues is "a wonderful way of applying what you're learning to today," she says.

Teams of teachers in Boston schools have used service activities to support interdisciplinary learning, says Pat Barnicle of the Thomas Jefferson Forum. If students serve in a soup kitchen, for example, teachers might organize instruction around the theme of hunger: biology classes could study nutrition; social studies classes could examine hunger throughout history and its causes; English classes could read literature that deals with hunger.

Service learning is truly *learning*, advocates emphasize. When students serve, they develop both new skills and positive attitudes. Students who serve learn communication, problem-solving, and leadership skills, says O'Neill. They also learn practical knowledge, such as how to tutor, how to weatherize a window, or how to find their way around community agencies. According to Halperin, service activities teach "the kinds of things employers are looking for: responsibility, teamwork, problem solving, and learning to learn."

Service activities "reconnect" students to the community, Halsted says. In contrast to our former agrarian society, "we have postponed work for the adolescent," she points out. "The young are now alone, disconnected from institutions." Service learning provides "a way to reconnect them, to show them they are people of value."

The list of benefits to students is long, Hoffman says. They gain a sense of self-esteem; they feel and become more responsible; they stop thinking only of themselves; and they begin to think about solutions, asking: "What can *I* do to make a difference?"

REQUIRED OR VOLUNTARY?

In light of these benefits, some advocates contend that schools should *require* students to participate in service learning activities. ASCD supported required service programs in a resolution passed last March. But experts are divided on this issue.

"Pedagogically, it's a real question," says Halperin, "because kids resist what they're forced to do." But schools make many things mandatory because they're important, he points out. And students often need a nudge before they become interested in any pursuit, be it geometry, swimming, or community service. The real issue, he believes, is not whether service learning is required but the *quality* of the experience.

Requiring service learning is "a wonderful idea," says Giles. "Why should we deny any student the joy of serving?" he asks. "We wouldn't deny them the joy of reading." Maryland's requirement is not burdensome, he says, because it allows both in-school and out-of-school service. "Students get to choose from all sorts of activities."

"The whole mandatory/voluntary argument is a red herring," says Halsted. The students who benefit most from service activities are the ones who would never volunteer, she asserts: "Those who think they're going to hate it end up loving it." Students who are troublemakers often show great maturity and infinite patience in situations where they are needed, she says. While Halsted concedes that some students may develop a negative attitude about service, she endorses a requirement because the experience is "so good for so many"—and life-changing for some.

Others vehemently disagree. The idea of required service is "a joke—an oxymoron," says Cynthia Parsons, coordinator of SerVermont in Chester, Vt. "It's very hard to teach anyone what it means to volunteer, in a mandatory program," she asserts. "I have yet to find a kid who doesn't think compulsory service has a negative effect."

"Overwhelmingly, the students vote against it," says Debra Mead of Good Shepherd Services, who runs a community service program at Sarah

J. Hale High School in Brooklyn, N.Y. Students say a requirement would devalue the fact that they volunteered, she reports.

Mead also has practical concerns about required service. When unwilling students "mess up," not only is that one more failure for them—they are also letting someone else down, or even hurting them. "It's not like failing geometry," she points out. "This affects others."

Giannino has mixed feelings about a service requirement. He finds "very valid" the argument that requiring service undermines the spirit of it. Having a requirement also "tarnishes" the young people who are really altruistic, he believes, by lumping them with all the others. "An agency won't know *why* you're coming to it," he says—by choice or by compulsion.

If a school system or state does require service, then it should put the onus on schools to integrate it into the curriculum, as in Maryland, Giannino says. It should not be an add-on, where students are told they must serve a certain number of hours and then left to find opportunities through service agencies. (This latter scenario happens all too often, experts admit.)

Requiring service is a good idea, but only if schools are given time to develop high-quality programs, says Bernadette Chi, a CalServe regional coordinator for the California Department of Education. Before a program is launched, teachers must be prepared to integrate service into the curriculum, and students must be oriented. Schools need about four years of preparation to gear up for a mandate, she believes.

"I'm concerned about the slapdash approach" when administrators and school boards get excited about the idea and just do it, Chi says. "If the infrastructure and preparation aren't there, it's going to create a backlash." Young people might be turned off from service, and service agencies might never want to work with the schools again, she warns.

Schools should start slowly, plan carefully, and consider service agencies' needs and teachers' feelings, Chi advises. They should also seriously explore how students can participate in the decision-making process.

TAPPING IDEALISM

Whether or not service learning is required, advocates are emphatic about its value.

"Young people grow both academically and personally through service learning," says Barbara Gomez, director of the Service Learning Project of the Council of Chief State School Officers. "It's a win-win situation. You can't go wrong if it's done well."

After hearing students discuss their service experiences, "you come away convinced," Halsted says. "They take on a maturity that is so unexpected, because we don't usually ask it of them. They do incredible things."

Service learning "taps into kids' idealism," says O'Neill. They want to take on big problems—end bias or hunger, for example. "Students really do have a lot to offer," she says. "It's up to us to provide them opportunities by changing how we teach."

CONFLICT RESOLUTION

HELPING STUDENTS RESOLVE CONFLICT

SCOTT WILLIS

Schools are hardly immune to the violence that plagues American society. At some high schools, students are as likely to be carrying weapons as textbooks, and violence can erupt over incidents as trivial as the way one student looks at another.

Although the problem at most schools is not so acute, more and more educators are coming to believe they must show their students constructive ways to resolve conflict. By teaching students how to negotiate and mediate disputes, and by developing a climate that fosters collaborative problem solving, many schools are hoping to reverse the trend toward violence they see in society at large.

More than 5,000 schools nationwide offer some kind of conflict resolution program, estimates Annette Townley, executive director of the National Association for Mediation in Education (NAME). Interest in these programs is rapidly rising, she adds.

The most popular kind of conflict resolution program is peer mediation, experts say. In peer mediation programs, a cadre of students are trained to help their schoolmates resolve disputes. Peer mediators do not impose solutions; rather, they help the "disputants" work out their *own* solution to the conflict. Mediators work alone or, often, in pairs.

Though the details of the process may vary, most peer mediations follow the same basic steps. First, the mediator and disputants come together. This can happen in several ways: The mediator may intervene

This article was originally published in the December 1993 issue of ASCD's *Update* newsletter.

in an ongoing dispute (in the cafeteria or on the playground, for example), an adult may refer a dispute to mediation, or the disputants themselves may seek it.

After the disputants have agreed to participate in the process, the mediator lays some ground rules: no interrupting or put-downs, for example. Then each disputant tells his or her side of the story, speaking only to the mediator. The mediator paraphrases and summarizes what she hears and asks clarifying questions.

After both disputants have told their stories and expressed their feelings, the mediator tries to help them see the conflict not as a competitive situation, but as a shared problem they must solve together. Then the disputants brainstorm ways to resolve the conflict. Once they have agreed on the best solution, they pledge to abide by it. Sometimes the solution is put in writing and signed by both parties. The mediator may check with the disputants later to make sure their agreement is "sticking."

Around 80–90 percent of peer-mediated agreements hold—a higher rate "than if the principal just lays down the law," says Virgil Petersen of the University of West Virginia. "The disputants own the solution," he says, because they have hammered it out themselves.

What kinds of conflicts do peer mediators help resolve? Conflicts run the gamut from playground fistfights to arguments over whose turn it is to use the classroom computer, experts say. Many disputes stem from rumors and gossip, name calling and harassment, and boyfriend/girlfriend troubles.

Of course, not all student conflicts lend themselves to mediation. Experts agree that conflicts involving violence, weapons, illegal activity, or blatant injustice need to be settled by adults. Peer mediators should not get involved in disputes over drugs, for example, says Jim Halligan of the Community Board Program, which provides conflict resolution resources. "We're not going to mediate for a kid who thought he got shorted on the amount of cocaine he bought for $300," he says wryly.

A fundamental rule of peer mediation is that if the disputants agree to a solution, adults must respect it—even if they do not consider it the best solution possible. (This assumes there has been no intimidation.) Some adults fear that students will devise solutions that are objectionable—that accommodate prejudice, for example, says Halligan. "That's not going to happen," he asserts. "Kids have more sense than that."

Peer mediations often take place during lunch or recess and sometimes during class time. David Sponheim, who teaches at Highlands Elementary School in Edina, Minn., does not want his students to miss instruction while they mediate disputes. "This is where the ideals of the program meet the realities of the classroom," he says. If a conflict arises while he's teaching, he either postpones the mediation or settles the problem himself then and there. But overall he has found peer mediation "a very positive part of our school and my classroom, both in management and in teaching kids some very important life skills."

MEDIATION SKILLS

Peer mediators need many skills if they are to succeed in their role, experts say. First, they must be good communicators: They must be able to listen carefully, restate and clarify what they are told, and ask neutral questions. They must be able to detect the underlying cause of a conflict—the disputants' differing perceptions or assumptions, for example. Equally important, they must know how to defuse anger and develop empathy between disputants. And, finally, they need the self-control to keep the mediation process confidential (unless they have heard allegations of abuse or threats of serious violence). To develop these skills, peer mediators need 15–20 hours of advance training, with follow-up sessions every two weeks, Petersen recommends.

Surprisingly, experts agree that popular and successful students are not the only candidates for peer mediators. "The mediator doesn't have to be a kid who's looked up to by everybody," says Terry Amsler, executive director of the Community Board Program. "Negative leaders"—bullies and troublemakers—often make good peer mediators. When given responsibility within the system, these students often rise to the occasion.

To select peer mediators, most schools survey students, asking them, "Whom would you trust? Whom would you like to talk to?" But schools should also hold some slots for appointments, advises Terry Kelly, who ran a peer mediation program at a junior high school in Booth, W. Va., for three years. This allows the school to balance the pool of mediators in terms of gender and race, she says.

One sensitive issue in peer mediation is the degree to which mediators should address causes of conflict such as racism and sexism. Does eliciting issues of bias help restore harmony among students or merely widen estrangements?

Mediators *do* need to deal with these issues, believes David Johnson, a professor of educational psychology at the University of Minnesota and co-author of *Teaching Students to Be Peacemakers*. But he concedes that it's "tricky" to do so. "There's a lot to be learned if it's [done] in a constructive context," he says—but care must be taken to ensure that the discussion doesn't "escalate in a negative way."

Issues of bias should be dealt with "as much as appropriate to resolve the problem," says consultant Marcia Peterzell, who ran a conflict management program at a San Francisco high school for over six years. "It's good for disputants to be challenged" on their prejudices, she believes, as long as the focus remains conciliation, not therapy.

"You don't go deeper than what the disputants are presenting," advises Ellen Raider of the International Center for Cooperation and Conflict Resolution. But if a larger pattern emerges—if a school has recurrent conflicts with racial overtones—then educators should recognize the need for training in multiculturalism and understanding bias.

Terry Kelly adds a practical footnote: If a dispute involves issues of gender or race, "always make sure you have a balanced team of mediators" to work with the disputants.

Research on peer mediation programs is too scanty to determine how successful they are, says Daniel Kmitta, a doctoral student at the University of Cincinnati, who is studying this question. But there is a wealth of anecdotal evidence in favor of such programs, he notes. Students report that they are fighting less often, and teachers say their school climates have improved.

TEACHING ALL STUDENTS

Some experts believe peer mediation programs, while worthy, do not go far enough. Schools should teach *all* students negotiation and mediation skills, they believe, rather than just a cadre of peer mediators.

David Johnson advocates this approach. "You need every kid trained in the same system," he says, "so that when a conflict arises, everybody knows what to do." In teaching these skills at an elementary school, Johnson gave 25-minute lessons daily for three or four weeks, then one or two lessons per week to explore topics in more depth.

"This stuff needs to be way overlearned," Johnson emphasizes, because the process of negotiation is contrary to our instinctive desire to strike back during a conflict. To override such instincts requires "hundreds of repetitions" of the process. "You just don't get this at a conflict awareness weekend or day of training," he says.

Besides learning to negotiate and mediate, all students can benefit from learning good communication skills, anger management, and perspective taking, says Larry Dieringer, executive director of Educators for Social Responsibility, whose Resolving Conflict Creatively Program is being used "in a lot of tough areas in New York City and New Orleans," among other cities. Students should also learn about prejudice and discrimination, as well as how to be assertive without attacking others, he believes.

Where in the curriculum can these skills and concepts be taught? According to Dieringer, they can be infused into the traditional subject areas. In studying literature, for example, students could identify and analyze conflict themes. In math and science, they could study the conflicts raging over acid rain and the destruction of the rain forest. Although teaching this content takes up instructional time, in the long run teachers *save* time because they don't have to spend so much time resolving disputes, he says.

CHANGING THE SCHOOL CULTURE

Some experts urge that efforts to address conflict resolution should involve everyone at a school—not just students. "Most schools initially gravitate to peer mediation programs, because they think if they fix the kids everything will be okay," says Townley of NAME. Although peer mediation programs are "wonderful," they are limited to a small group of people—and therefore provide only a limited impetus for changing behavior and attitudes.

At best, schools should take a systemic approach, Townley recommends. They should begin with staff development for adults so they can serve as role models. "Kids see the way adults resolve conflict all the time," she notes. If everyone in the school tries to "live" the skills and philosophy, the program becomes part of the fabric of the school, not just an add-on.

To change the school culture, staff members must learn and practice the skills of negotiation and mediation, Raider agrees, because adults can't say to students, "Do what I say, not what I do." Adults need to learn these skills "at their own level," or they will have false expectations for students. Through role playing, adults need to learn how hard it is to change behavior, she says. "They have to feel it viscerally."

Can conflict resolution programs prevent serious violence in schools? Experts are quick to point out that these programs are not a panacea. "We don't believe these programs in and of themselves solve violence," says Amsler. However, they are an important "tool toward that end." Serious violence won't be reduced until educators "work at the organizational level" by involving the whole school community, Raider believes.

Raider is "very hopeful" regarding the future of conflict resolution programs in schools. "A critical mass is building, of folks who understand this stuff," she says. But she adds that the movement is "still in its infancy."

"More and more, people are thinking it's a really good idea" for schools to address conflict resolution, Halligan says. "We look at it as a basic skill for kids today."

CONSTRUCTIVISM

WANTED: DEEP UNDERSTANDING

JOHN O'NEIL

Until recently, Sheila Frost's method for teaching ceramics skills to students at Shoreham-Wading River Middle School, located in Long Island, N.Y., was consistent. For the first week of a 10-week unit, she demonstrated some skills for working with clay, and how various tools could be used to produce clay pieces. "I wouldn't let the kids touch the clay" until they had sat through the explanation and demonstration, Frost says.

Her approach now is quite different. With a group of 6th graders recently, Frost had clay in students' hands from the start. She showed them an example of a "slab"—a flat piece of clay about a quarter-inch thick that can be etched with impressions or used as part of a clay product calling for a flat surface—and then had students break into groups to discuss how they might turn lumps of clay into slab form. They shared their groups' findings and proceeded to experiment with water and various tools, with Frost and some of the students themselves facilitating and coaching.

Frost and others in the Shoreham-Wading River School District are part of a group of educators and researchers hoping to transform educational practice that has been driven, for decades, by behaviorism, a theory about how humans learn. Critics of the behaviorist approach claim that it has resulted in students who can parrot a theory or set of ideas given by the teacher without truly understanding important underlying concepts.

This article was originally published in the March 1992 issue of ASCD's *Update* newsletter.

To educators in Shoreham-Wading River and elsewhere, the new banner is "constructivism," another theory about learning, which emphasizes the importance of the learner's active construction of knowledge and the interplay between new knowledge and the learner's prior knowledge. Its supporters, leading cognitive researchers and curriculum theorists, believe that constructivism holds the promise of deeper understanding and retention. Constructivist views strongly influence the "whole language" movement in English, the curriculum standards developed by the National Council of Teachers of Mathematics, and new recommendations on effective science practices issued by the National Center for Improving Science Education (NCISE).

Learning about constructivism "has changed my teaching dramatically," says Frost, who has attended several staff development activities on the topic sponsored by her district. As students in her class work with clay, she walks from one table to the next, asking students: "How else could you do that?" or "What other technique might work?" Students learn some strategies from peers and some on their own—and rely less on Frost to tell them the answer. "They're much less dependent on me," she says with pride. "They don't think I'm an integral part of their work."

BEHAVIORIST TIDE TURNING

Constructivist literature on learning, experts note, calls for a marked departure from the vestiges of behaviorist theory still driving much educational practice. Popularized by B.F. Skinner and others, the behaviorist view of learning, when translated by schools, was characterized by lengthy lists of measurable behavioral objectives and tightly sequenced curriculums. Knowledge and skills were broken down into smaller and smaller bits, under the assumption that mastering simpler steps would add up, in the end, to complex thinking. These "bits" tended not to be placed in the context of an authentic problem situation, and students had difficulty applying what they had learned in new contexts. Little attention was given, moreover, to the conceptions and misconceptions that learners held about the skills or knowledge being introduced; so misconceptions frequently resurfaced after the learning task concluded.

Such practices are now under siege. "Thinking is more than just the sum of its parts," says Lauren Resnick, a leading cognitive researcher and director of the Learning Research and Development Center at the University of Pittsburgh. "You can know every bit of arithmetic and not know how to solve a problem." According to traditional learning theory, curriculum is a "conceptual analysis of the subject matter but ignores what is already in the learner's head," adds Senta Raizen, director of the NCISE. "The result of this is that children can play back memorized canonical knowledge and conceptions but return to their own ideas when confronted with unfamiliar questions or nonroutine problems."

The key tenet of constructivist theory, experts say, is that people learn by actively constructing knowledge, weighing new information against their previous understanding, thinking about and working through discrepancies (on their own and with others), and coming to a new understanding. In a classroom faithful to constructivist views, students are afforded numerous opportunities to explore phenomena or ideas, conjecture, share hypotheses with others, and revise their original thinking. Such a classroom differs sharply from one in which the teacher lectures exclusively, explains the "right way" to solve a problem without allowing students to make some sense of their own, or denies the importance of students' own experiences or prior knowledge.

In other words, "frontal teaching" is minimized. "All people ever have is their own understanding: you can tell them all sorts of things, but you can't make them believe it unless they also construct it for themselves," says Eleanor Duckworth, a professor at the Harvard Graduate School of Education. "Giving students the ideas" impairs "the robustness of what students learn, their depth and breadth of understanding, and their self-confidence," adds Martin Simon, a researcher and teacher educator at Pennsylvania State University.

EXPLORATION FIRST

In Lucio Costanzo's mathematics class at Shoreham-Wading River High School, students are working on a set of unfamiliar problems. "We've never done these before," Costanzo says, "but I want to see what you can do."

New York District Champions Constructivist Approach

A small group of kindergartners in Pat Remek's class at Briarcliff School, which is housed in a remodeled mansion built around the turn of the century, are helping to write a poem about snow. "What do snowflakes do?" Remek asks the group. "Snowflakes fall," says one student, and Remek writes that as the poem's first line on a piece of construction paper in elementary-sized print. "S—that's how my name starts," notes Steven.

"Snowflakes come down from the sky," says another pupil, and the poem's second line provokes other observations. "That's the same word," says Cheryl, pointing to the word *snowflake* in each line. *Snowflake* is similar to the word *snow*, she adds. "How do you know?" asks Remek. "It starts the same," Cheryl points out. At another activity station, students paint pictures of a snow scene. At a third, children are constructing Lego pieces into forms of various shapes and sizes and immersing them in water to discover which ones float and why.

Down the hall, in Carolyn Reynolds' classroom, kindergartners are using Dixie cups, with plastic wrap and a bit of water placed on top, to construct primitive microscopes. After observing objects through the "microscope," students begin to list other things that magnify—binoculars, telescopes, and magnifying glasses—and a discussion follows on who uses these tools. Beginning with the knowledge students already have, and ensuring that skills are placed in authentic contexts, is a marked departure for many teachers, Reynolds notes. "When you watch kids, you'd be amazed by what they know and bring to the situation," she says. Until a few years ago, she says, Briarcliff teachers focused on a "letter of the week," but that practice has given way to lessons drawn from students' need to use language for useful purposes.

Although many schools use approaches that resonate with constructivist views on learning, the Shoreham-Wading River School District, where Briarcliff is located, is unusual in the explicit attention it gives to constructivist theory and its implications for curriculum, student assessment, and teaching strategies.

At least two-thirds of the district's teachers have received some staff training in constructivism and its implications for practice, says Assistant Superintendent Martin Brooks. Each of the district's five schools has one or more faculty "constructivism coordinators," who receive extra pay to help plan activities based on staff input. The district discourages the use of basal readers in favor of classroom sets of trade books. Teachers are encouraged to use an experiential approach to science. And the district has dropped its standardized testing program (although students must still take state tests), because leaders considered multiple-choice exams an obstacle to lessons congruent with constructivist views. "We've built a program with constructivism at its very core," says Brooks.

The attention to constructivism began more than 10 years ago with a local study group of teachers and administrators, and the grassroots emphasis has continued. Some of the district's teachers have used peer coaching, observing, and videotaping one another, to focus on the extent to which learning activities reflect constructivist thought. That has proven to be a powerful force for change, says Reynolds. "Because it's from a colleague, and not an administrator, teachers can take a lot more constructive criticism."

Local faculties recently went through the process of examining school mission and philosophy, and "a constructivist philosophy came through loud and clear," says Superintendent David Jackson. But the key question is whether educators are changing their behaviors, as well as beliefs, Brooks notes.

Learning about constructivism "certainly made me reflect on everything I was doing," says Jane Wittlock, a teacher at Shoreham-Wading River Middle School. "I now give kids more time to think for themselves, to talk in groups. I think more about what the children already know. And it's really helped me key into how children think. I expect more from them because I see how much more they can do."

Given a set of equations, such as $(x-2)(x+7)=0$ or $x(x-11)=0$, Costanzo has the class break into small groups to try to find the solution sets by solving for all possible values of x. "Ultimately, I'd like you to find the rule that works here," he says. "Anything multiplied by zero must equal zero," so one of the factors must be zero, one student says a few minutes later, explaining how he arrived at his answer. "This is referred to as the zero law," Costanzo tells the class.

Those attempting to imbue their schools with a constructivist perspective extol the virtues of having students explore and discover. "The way human beings learn best is by 'discovering' first, because that's the only way to create the cognitive disequilibrium necessary for learning to take place," says Martin Brooks, deputy superintendent for the Shoreham-Wading River schools. "It's through reinventing the wheel that students move along."

Proponents of constructivist theory are careful to point out, however, that the discovery and exploration that takes place as students "construct" meaning is not random; teachers must have overall curriculum goals and key principles and concepts they'd like students to understand. "You could go into a classroom where kids are doing a lot of wonderful things, but where's the direction?" says Maureen Powers, a Shoreham-Wading River reading specialist. "The discovery is on the part of the child, but the teacher's ability to mediate the learning environment is essential."

It is also wrong to assume that, in classrooms influenced by constructivist theory, all student "constructions" are considered equally valid. In visiting science classrooms, "I've seen some really funny things—like kids voting" on the explanation for a scientific phenomenon, says Raizen. Teachers have to guide students toward "current, best understandings." Adds Resnick: "There isn't just one truth, but there isn't no truth either." Many teachers, Raizen admits, "are extremely uncomfortable" handling discrepant observations and theories, however.

Not all types of learning, moreover, are conducive to constructive practice. "There's nothing about the theory that says that everybody ought to discover everything," says Simon. Memorizing basic facts is often essential, and separate practice on discrete skills is sometimes called for. But the more likely it is that students have misconceptions, and the more important deep understanding of a concept is, the more educators must "minimize the amount of direct telling to students and maximize [pupils'] direct construction," Simon says.

MODEST INROADS

Despite the accumulating body of support for a constructivist view of learning, schools that organize curriculum and instruction to take advantage of the research findings are relatively rare, experts acknowledge. Several large-scale studies of schools have shown that teachers more frequently lecture or directly show students how to solve problems.

One barrier to broader acceptance of constructivist practice is the considerable time needed to settle on central organizing concepts and to plan strategies so that students will have opportunities to "construct" their own meaning, experts say. Teachers frequently feel pressure to cover a considerable amount of content. Standardized tests, moreover, rarely measure the deep understanding teachers seek. Constructivist teachers "have to juggle what's important for learning and what's necessary for bureaucracy," says Duckworth.

Broader application of constructivist principles also is hindered by a lack of understanding of the instructional issues raised by the theory, others say. Because Socratic dialogue, hands-on science, process writing, and other practices share some common tenets with constructivist thought, some educators mistakenly believe that they're already "doing" constructivism. "Constructivism has become the new catchword," says Simon. "There are people who are using the term who don't know what it means." Applying constructivist research is more complex than most educators realize, he says.

Some of the teachers who have read the literature on constructivism and attempted to put it into practice say the effort is worth it, however. "It's not easy to do well," Costanzo admits. "It was much easier not knowing what the kid was thinking while you're lecturing in the front of the room." But students in his classes are more comfortable taking responsibility for their own learning, he says. "I'm giving kids questions that have multiple answers that I never would have dreamed of giving before."

PROBLEM-BASED LEARNING

KATHY CHECKLEY

When U.S. journalist R.W. Johnson noted that "any solution to a problem changes the problem," he probably wasn't thinking about K–12 education reform. Still, Johnson's observation that every answer ultimately leads to more questions could guide educators as they consider how students today should be taught. So say experts who hold that it's the job of educators to prepare students to live and work in a world where they will encounter perplexing puzzles and bewildering questions.

This article was originally published in the Summer 1997 issue of ASCD's *Curriculum Update* newsletter.

The Basics of Problem-Based Learning

PBL is an instructional method that uses a real-world problem as the context for an in-depth investigation of core content.

The problems that students tackle are ill-structured; they include just enough information to suggest how students should proceed with an investigation, but never enough information to enable students to solve the problem without further inquiry. These problems cannot be solved by using formulas—students must use the inquiry process and reasoning—and there may be more than one way to solve the problem.

Teachers who use a problem-based learning approach become tutors or coaches, helping students understand their own thinking and guiding them as they search for new information.

Through problem-based learning, students become better problem solvers because they hone skills such as reasoning, collaboration, and persistence in their self-directed search for solutions.

And, say these experts, those best equipped to cope with complicated real-world issues once they leave school are those who struggle with similar issues while still *in* school, through an approach to teaching and learning called problem-based learning.

ILL-STRUCTURED PROBLEMS

Only in school can students expect to be given all the information they need to solve a particular problem; only in school can students use a formula to arrive at a single solution to that problem; and only in school can students be absolutely certain that the solution they propose is the right one, says Howard Barrows, chair of the medical education department at Southern Illinois University School of Medicine, in Carbondale, Ill. Only in school, he contends, are students given well-structured problems that do little to inspire student-initiated inquiry.

What students should be given instead, Barrows asserts, are *ill-structured* problems—problems that give students just enough information to guide an investigation. Such problems cannot be solved using algorithms or formulas, they may change as more information is gathered, and they have more than one solution. With ill-structured problems, he says, student-directed inquiry becomes the heart of the problem-solving process. "Students must be able to inquire, to investigate," Barrows explains. "When students grapple with open-ended problems, they discover what it is they need to know in order to propose a solution." Students can then determine *how* they'll find the information they need.

And in their quest for knowledge, students acquire more than just a collection of facts. "We want students to become effective problem solvers, to become self-directed learners, and to be able to work collaboratively with others," he says. Searching for solutions to ill-structured problems "gives students experience in those areas."

MAKING THE GRADE IN MEDICAL EDUCATION

The ill-structured problem is the centerpiece of an approach to teaching and learning called problem-based learning (PBL). Medical schools have been using PBL since the early 1970s, thanks to Barrows and others, who helped create the first problem-based curriculum for the medical school at McMaster University in Ontario, Canada. Barrows then developed the Problem Based Learning Curriculum (PBLC) at Southern Illinois University School of Medicine—the first such alternative curriculum option available to medical students in the United States. More than 60 U.S. medical schools have since converted all or part of their curriculum to a PBL approach.

"To be frank, I was skeptical at first," admits Sarah Meredith, first-year coordinator of curriculum and admissions for the PBLC at Southern Illinois University in Carbondale, Ill. "Although I saw that there would be real advantages to the PBL approach, especially the value of early clinical experiences, I was uncertain that students would be able to take the responsibility to learn what they needed to," she explains.

Meredith's concern is not uncommon, yet Barrows points out that students *do* take responsibility for their learning because "the problems are so real, the learning really turns the students on." Turning students on was, in fact, one of the reasons McMaster University decided to try problem-based learning. Research showed that most students hated medical school. "What a contrast that was to first-year residents who loved what they were doing despite long hours and challenges," he says. "We wanted to return that love of medicine to medical education."

To do so, Barrows and his colleagues created a series of simulations that allowed students to act as practicing physicians when confronted with a medical question. For example, instead of asking students to attend a lecture on the brain stem and to copy and memorize a multicolor diagram of that organ, "we gave students an actual patient case—complete with symptoms that would indicate that something was wrong with the brain stem."

Before students were able to provide a diagnosis, they had to generate multiple hypotheses, determine what they did and didn't know about the brain stem, and then search for more information, Barrows notes. Through that process, students covered the material they were required to learn. "PBL is not devoid of content," Barrows emphasizes, "the content is just organized around the kinds of problems students will encounter in real life."

"PBL gives students a way to learn that is more engaging to them than a lecture," agrees Meredith. "Many students say they can learn that way [through a lecture], but they just don't want to—they're tired of passive learning."

Meredith is now a firm supporter of the PBL approach. She's seen PBL-trained medical students perform as well on national exams as their traditionally-trained peers. And she's seen that those medical students are better prepared to interact with patients. Students see up to 70 patients a year in PBLC, Meredith explains, "so they have a two-year advantage of reading signs and symptoms and linking them to the diseases they represent. These students also have practice talking with patients, and they become more comfortable with difficult things, such as taking a sexual history or breaking the news to someone that he has cancer." Early on, she says, students in PBLC learn how to present distressing news to their patients and their patients' families.

"There's just no question about what PBL has accomplished in medicine," Barrows observes. And what's more, he adds, "medical students are now enjoying their education."

A PRESCRIPTION FOR K–12 EDUCATION

The success of problem-based learning in medical education has proved irresistible to some K–12 educators who wanted to fuel students' enthusiasm for learning.

Problem-based learning can restore "romance" to the pursuit of knowledge, says Shelah Gallagher, professor of education at the University of North Carolina at Charlotte. "If you read the biographies of very creative innovators, they all talk about problems that ignited their interest," she states. Gallagher makes this point when explaining to teachers how PBL can spark the same passion in their students. When students are given ill-structured problems to solve, "they are placed in the role of real-world professionals—as architects, historians, archaeologists, and so on," she says. And Gallagher's research shows that students love "to think how the experts think."

Thinking like an expert requires that students first analyze a problem to determine what pieces of the puzzle are missing—called the *learning issues* in PBL parlance. Most students read a problem and jump to a solution, Gallagher observes. "Students have to be taught to find the *real* problem first," she says.

To find the real problem, students follow a process of first identifying what they already know about the problem and making hypotheses based on that knowledge. Students then identify the learning issues and decide what new information they need to test and refine their original theories. Only after students have taken the problem through this process do they finally propose a solution.

"With this kind of process, students develop new understandings of the learning issues in the problem while simultaneously having an experience in real-world problem solving," says Bill Stepien, director of the Consortium for Problem-Based Learning, which is housed at Northern Illinois University in Dekalb, Ill.

Stepien has worked to bring a problem-based focus to K–12 education for more than 10 years. He has found that although many teachers embrace PBL in theory, they may shy away from actually using the approach in the classroom because crafting ill-structured problems can be a time-consuming challenge. Another reason for resistance, Stepien notes, is that PBL asks teachers to assume a new role in the classroom—teachers must be willing to let students take the lead and must be ready to guide students along the way.

STARTING SMALL

To address the concern that creating ill-structured problems is too difficult a task for teachers, Stepien always recommends that teachers start small. "It isn't realistic for a teacher to convert an entire course. So we try to help teachers have a good experience with one problem," he explains. "When we work with regular schools, there's a pretty well-defined curriculum, so I help teachers find ways to teach that curriculum in a problem-based fashion." Stepien advises teachers to look through textbooks and curriculum guides "to find problems, dilemmas, issues to resolve."

Stepien reminds teachers that not all problems have negative connotations. When a watercolor artist makes decisions about how to paint a still life, she's problem solving, he explains. The artist has to decide what colors to use, and she conducts experiments to determine which blend of colors will result in just the right shade. She also has to think about how to use perspective and how to add positive and negative space. "In essence, she's behaving like a scientist. The real rigor in the arts is in the problem solving," he observes.

Other problems can be structured around current events to link real life with learning objectives, he notes. Consider this scenario: *A large oil company wants to dispose of an abandoned oil rig by dropping it into the North Sea. Activists, who are concerned about the effects of such a move on the environment, have taken over the rig and are now living there.* Teachers can ask students to be mediators and determine how to resolve the conflict peacefully, says Stepien. "In solving this problem, students will learn about how toxic substances are typically disposed of." Then, he adds, teachers can extend the lesson and help students use what they learned in this exercise when considering similar problems, such as how to dispose of spent nuclear fuel rods or used medical supplies.

When teachers become comfortable in delivering curriculum through a problem-based approach, it's then much easier for them to begin to create ill-structured problems that are interdisciplinary in nature, says Stepien. "It's really nice for students to see how different subject areas connect," he says, noting that it's also important that students tackle problems in all of their classes, from biology to algebra, social studies to fine arts. "Students need to see that problem-solving is required in all of these disciplines," he asserts.

Gallagher agrees, adding that for problem-based learning to be truly meaningful, students have to grapple with more than just one problem. "Students don't get the powerful benefits of PBL if it's only done once a year. The metacognitive gains come in repetition," she argues.

FINDING A PLACE FOR PBL

To offer more problem-based units, teachers will have to introduce fewer topics to students each year, and administrators must support that decision, experts argue.

"A lot has been made about less is more, and that leaves a bad taste in my mouth," says Stepien. "I'd like to turn that phrase into 'doing more with less.' Instead of trying to cover an increasingly filled-up curriculum, why don't we concentrate on doing more with fewer topics?"

"We encourage teachers to do more than one problem a year, but teachers need to hear a clear commitment to PBL from their administrators," Gallagher adds.

That clear commitment is essential if PBL is to be more than an "add on," she contends, warning that PBL is at risk of becoming the "flavor of the month" in reform. If PBL is to be seen as "a permanent component of the new educational system," teachers, administrators, parents, and community members need to understand how this approach enhances learning. "We need to link the problems to standards and high-quality content" so that teachers and administrators will see how PBL can meet learning objectives, Gallagher maintains. Students' enthusiasm will do much to convince parents and community members, she adds, recalling that at one school in South Carolina, teachers were encouraged to design more PBL units because students and parents demanded them. "Students can be great advocates for PBL," she says. "The grassroots push has got to be there."

For More Information

ASCD's Problem-Based Learning Network (PBL Net) offers opportunities for K–12 educators to share information, methods, and materials, and enhance their understanding of problem-based learning from the perspectives of learner, coach, and problem designer.

"As with any change initiative, you have one or two people in one place working on PBL," explains Linda Torp, the network's facilitator. "To sustain change, you need to expand your professional community and be able to ask questions and engage in professional dialogue with other practitioners."

PBL Net encourages its members and interested educators, parents, students, and community members to post questions and share ideas about problem-based learning through a listserv and an electronic interactive forum on ASCD's Web site <http://www.ascd.org>. Other PBL Net services include a newsletter and a meeting at ASCD's Annual Conference.

For more information about PBL Net, contact Linda Torp, Strategic Coordinator for PBL Initiatives, Illinois Mathematics and Science Academy, 1500 W. Sullivan Road, Aurora, IL 60506 USA. Telephone: 630-907-5956. E-mail: <ltorp@imsa.edu>.

Other PBL resources available from ASCD

✦ *Problem-Based Learning,* a video-based staff development program, will be available in October. The program includes two videotapes and a comprehensive Facilitator's Guide. The first tape in the series introduces viewers to problem-based learning theory. The second tape in the series is designed to help viewers craft ill-structured problems.

✦ *Problem-Based Learning,* a Professional Development Inquiry Kit, will be available in September. This kit is designed to help school study groups improve their understanding of PBL. Each folder in the kit contains resources such as journal articles, book chapters, case studies, and video clips. Activities and suggestions for group study of the resources are included.

For more information, call the ASCD Service Center at 800-933-2723, or 703-549-9110, and then press 2.

Students' enthusiasm can also convince teachers who resist making changes in their instructional styles.

"Many teachers feel threatened by PBL," says Barrows, who has been working with teachers in elementary and secondary schools since the early 1980s. "The interesting thing is, once teachers take that step and witness the students' excitement, it's amazing how quickly they change."

"A teacher does have to develop a certain mind-set, to understand that it's okay to say, 'I don't know the answer to that question, let's find out.' Teachers who aren't inclined to be coaches need to take a leap of faith and trust that students will admire them more for taking that role," Gallagher adds.

NEXT STEPS

Advocates of problem-based learning say they are heartened by the growing interest in this instructional approach. "It's exploding in special education, gifted education, in every discipline, at every grade level," says Stepien, who would like to use that interest to introduce PBL to the primary grades. "The sooner we start, the better," he states.

Are students in the primary grades ready to undertake this kind of learning experience? Yes, Gallagher asserts. "PBL is inherently, developmentally appropriate. Students generate the questions, so the learning issues are at their level of understanding," she explains.

Gallagher says the reaction of 2nd graders to a science unit she created with colleagues from The College of William and Mary proves her point. "We gave the students a problem about Carl Lewis, asking them to help him train for the Olympics," she says. "The students were so excited." They studied books about health and nutrition, they talked with a nutritionist who visited the class to learn which foods provide the best fuel for an athlete. "These 2nd grade students were eager to learn because they were responsible for getting Carl Lewis ready for the Olympics," Gallagher recalls. "It was tremendous."

Barrows agrees that it's important to give students an opportunity to direct their own learning early in their educational life. Indeed, the Southern Illinois University School of Medicine is now helping educators apply PBL to all areas of elementary and secondary education, in all subject areas, and for students of all ability levels.

Still, Barrows worries that the prevailing practice of interspersing PBL units throughout the curriculum is too piecemeal an approach to reform. PBL should be a complete curriculum replacement, he argues. Otherwise, "it will be a nightmare to try to have problem-based learning in each of the isolated hours carved out for math, science, social studies, and so on. It will be too much for students to keep track of." What's more, he points out, by segregating the subject areas, educators rob PBL of much of its power. "By its very nature, problem-based learning is integrated," Barrows maintains.

Schools need to be reorganized so that subjects can be fully integrated, he states, and so that students will have the authority to decide what information they need—not teachers who believe they have a certain "body of knowledge" they must provide.

Stepien concedes that there is a need for systemic change so that students who learn through a problem-based approach one year can continue to hone their problem-solving and decision-making skills the next year—and beyond. "We're involved in training teachers from K–12 so students can build on what they learn in prior grade levels," he says.

But Stepien doesn't think it's realistic to completely replace existing curriculums with PBL—the system simply won't allow it, he says. He chooses, instead, to work around what he calls the "inertness" of the system. "I like to create a little chaos. If PBL is any good, the bigger, larger educational system will begin to feel the pressure" and change. "PBL will have staying power," says Stepien, "because it gives students and teachers a chance to get more out of what is already in the curriculum."

USING REAL-LIFE PROBLEMS TO MAKE REAL-WORLD CONNECTIONS

KAREN RASMUSSEN

As soon as the 8th grade students in Harriet Carlson's science class enter their classroom at Indian Trail Junior High School in Addison, Ill.,

This article was originally published in the Summer 1997 issue of ASCD's *Curriculum Update* newsletter.

they realize it won't be a typical school day. A video showing a prom night automobile accident plays at the front of the room and on each student's desk is a folder containing accident reports and a name card identifying them as "Inspector." As the students take their seats, Carlson steps to the front of the room and addresses them as investigators for the state attorney's office. A drunk driving accident occurred the previous night, and the students are in charge of the investigation. They have five days to review existing evidence and investigate further. Then they must recommend an indictment to the state attorney's office and notify the press of their conclusions.

This lesson is part of the Inspector Red Ribbon Unit, a problem-based learning (PBL) project that involves all of the 8th graders at the school and 15 teachers from various content areas, including English, math, physical education, science and social studies. Teachers at the school are enthusiastic about the PBL unit because it allows students to develop and exercise problem-solving skills as they identify the actions that should be taken during the mock investigation. The teacher's role throughout the unit is to guide students as they search for solutions to this real-world problem. During the next five days, students will work individually and in groups to interview witnesses, visit and assess the scene of the accident, review medical reports, and make their recommendations in a press conference.

Carlson and two of her colleagues, a math and a social studies teacher, created the unit after receiving PBL training from the Center for Problem-Based Learning at the Illinois Mathematics and Science Academy in Aurora, Ill. Developing the Inspector Red Ribbon Unit has proven to be "the most exciting and exhausting project" she's ever been involved in, says Carlson, a teacher for 27 years. "This was a shot in the arm for a lot of teachers. For experienced teachers, the project was something new and different. For beginning teachers, this gave them an approach to add to their teaching methods," states Carlson.

Ninety percent of the material covered in each subject over the course of the project is part of the 8th grade curriculum, according to Carlson. During the unit, students work on the case in each class. They analyze accident reports, learn how to differentiate between fact and opinion, and write a report to meet language arts requirements. In science, students perform lab experiments to determine blood alcohol levels and impaired reaction time, while in physical education they administer field sobriety tests to each other.

For math class, students visit the school athletic field where teachers, working with the Addison police department, have spray painted an intersection and positioned two cars as if they had been in an accident. Aluminum foil affixed to the teachers' cars indicates the point of impact. In teams, students examine the evidence and measure skid marks. Later they develop computer spreadsheets and calculate the speed of the cars based on what they observed at the scene.

During the mock press conference, each student reports what charges they recommend be brought against the driver who caused the accident based on the evidence he has gathered during the past five days. Students receive a memo from a fictional police captain stating whether their findings were appropriate for the police to act on or if more information is needed. Other assessments occur in each class. Carlson's students, for example, conduct three labs on which they are graded.

The best measure of the unit's success can be found in the students' excitement. Although student conversations in the hall and cafeteria usually focus on what occurs outside of the classroom, Carlson reports that with this project "you hear, 'This witness said she had six drinks, but another said she had less.'"

BEYOND THE BASICS

The activities included in the Inspector Red Ribbon Unit at Indian Trail Junior High School are examples of the kind of learning experiences students receive through problem-based learning. PBL activities allow students to assume roles of real-world professionals, experts say. The problems also help students see the connections between various content areas.

PBL allows students to study interdisciplinary material that is organized around a common goal, says Brad Martin, a 5th grade teacher at LaEntrada School in Menlo Park, Calif. What's more, he contends, "the benefit of PBL is that it meets curriculum requirements and allows students to go beyond required learning." Martin adds that for PBL to be successful, "the teacher needs to accept that he or she has less control and must act as a coach or mentor." Martin has been using PBL in his class for four years but says he's been working toward a PBL-approach throughout his 30-year career.

To study anatomy, local history, cultures, and religion, Martin took his class to a nearby building site where they "discovered" a plastic skeleton. Artifacts such as a woven basket, stones, and shells were found near the remains. After discussion, the students decided they should call the police. Martin had made arrangements with the police department, so the dispatcher was prepared for the students' phone call. A doctor volunteered to act as a coroner and prepared a mock report for the class.

The class was charged with deciding how to bury the skeleton, and they determined that they needed to learn about religious and cultural burial customs before making that decision. The students invited a rabbi and priest to speak to them and searched the Internet in teams for information about cultures and religions.

Teachers using PBL must discover how to set parameters for a project without dampening the students' enthusiasm. "My biggest challenge is how to turn the kids *off* to the problem. At some point, you must shut it down, but they want to keep going and engage further. I have students who are now in the 8th grade coming to me to discuss problems we worked on three years ago," says Martin.

COMMUNITY CONNECTIONS

At its best, PBL helps students understand how they can use what they learn in school outside the classroom. Teachers at Urbana East Elementary School in Urbana, Ohio, for example, channel their students' enthusiasm into improving the community while also helping them learn how to communicate with various audiences.

When students and teachers noticed that graffiti and gang activity were becoming prevalent in their town, Kathy Norviel, a 5th/6th grade teacher, and Joanne Petty, a 4th/5th grade teacher, decided to take advantage of PBL training they had received through Ohio SchoolNet. They asked their classes, How can we improve the image of Urbana?

Planned originally for a four- to six-week period, their project has grown into a yearlong activity. "We thought we could get in and out of the problem, but it has grown as the Urbana business community has become more involved," says Norviel.

The teachers introduced the project by asking students to define "community." After a brainstorming session, students wrote acrostic poems using the letters of Urbana. "By writing the poem, the students were able to identify and present their perceptions of their hometown," explains Norviel.

As a large group, the students created a list of interview questions for each student to ask three people: two who lived in Urbana and one who did not. Questions included, What do you really like about the community? What do you dislike about the community? What could improve the city park?

After completing the interviews, the students developed graphs and presented their findings in groups as either a multimedia presentation, a poster, or a brochure, or a video. Members of the Urbana business community evaluated the presentations using a rubric developed by the students and teachers. At the request of the business leaders, students are creating a community Internet Web site and are offering to link local businesses' home pages to the site.

"The kids at our school are used to working in cooperative groups, doing projects, and using rubrics, so PBL is a natural progression for everyone involved," explains Norviel. The project includes aspects of the curriculum—such as making graphs and spreadsheets and learning about civics—that Norviel and Petty would have covered in class using other teaching methods, but PBL "has made what the students learn more meaningful for them," Norviel maintains. "Students are showing interest in the community and giving something back to it by highlighting the positive aspects of Urbana."

LEARNING OUTSIDE THE CLASSROOM

Rick McKelvey agrees that PBL can help students make connections between school subjects and the world outside of school. For that reason, he's based his 12th grade geoscience class entirely on ill-structured problems, teaching six PBL units during the school year. Each unit lasts six weeks. "We want to tie together the students' high school experiences in each subject and teach the kids that science happens outside of the classroom" says McKelvey, who teaches at Cary Grove High School in Cary, Ill.

For one unit, students receive a letter stating that a volcano in Yellowstone Park is showing signs of activity. If it erupts, the middle third of the United States could be wiped out. In response, students work in groups to study volcanoes, determine the probability that such an event would occur, and describe the effect a major natural disaster would have on jobs and politics in the region. Rather than invite speakers to the class, McKelvey encourages his students to locate information on the Internet.

Students prepare a final paper for this unit, but may present oral reports for the other units. Their suggestions range from drilling into the volcano to relieve the pressure and developing evacuation plans to not informing the public because, as students reason, the volcano is unlikely to erupt, there is no way to predict or prevent an eruption, and widespread panic would lower property values and scare industry away from the area. None of the suggestions are right or wrong, says McKelvey, but each suggestion must be supported by student research.

TYING IT ALL TOGETHER

Experts point out that virtually any lesson objective can be taught through a PBL approach. For example, Gerri Appleberry, a 10th grade geometry teacher at Dumas High School in Dumas, Ark., asked students to take on the roles of marketing representatives and tie designers for a problem based on neckties. "PBL doesn't replace what you normally teach," says Appleberry, the material is just taught in a different way. The tie project meets state standards in basic math, geometry, and statistics.

Appleberry distributes PBL guidelines to her students and shows them ties discarded from her husband's closet. "They laugh at the ties because they are too short or too narrow by today's fashion standards," says Appleberry. Students work in groups organized around the learning issues—the missing pieces—of the problem, such as What are the most popular colors? What are the most popular patterns? Who is the target audience?

PBL stimulates students to creatively seek answers, Appleberry has found. "PBL trains students to find places other than the encyclopedia to find information. One student called Dillard's, the local department store, to ask a salesperson what kinds of ties were selling," she explains.

For the final project, students create a tie and an accompanying advertisement, which are judged during a tie fair in the school's auditorium. Judges, who don't know anything about PBL, receive guidelines so that it's not the prettiest tie that wins, but the one that shows a student's understanding of geometric and spatial properties. The advertising copy that students write is expected to show an analysis of marketing statistics and must convince the judges that the tie will improve corporate profits through increased sales.

Students receive the equivalent of a test grade for the project, which concerns some students, Appleberry observes. "A lot of top-notch students feel threatened by PBL because they know they are good at taking tests but aren't sure they'll get a good grade this way. Students that some consider low achievers get into PBL; they get excited, have a game plan, and think," she says.

For students and teachers alike, PBL can be an adventure, Appleberry adds. "PBL allows students to learn by discovery, not by listening to the teacher in the front of the class saying 'this is what symmetry is.' It teaches students life skills."

EARLY CHILDHOOD EDUCATION

TEACHING YOUNG CHILDREN

SCOTT WILLIS

A kindergarten student, having observed the classroom aquarium carefully over several days, notices that the water level is slightly lower each day. He says to his teacher: "We have to put more water in the tank because the fish are drinking it."

How should the teacher respond to best support the child's learning? Should she leave him to continue his observations unaided? Should she try to teach him about evaporation and molecules, simplifying the concepts as far as possible? Or should she do something else?

How best to teach young children—pupils in preschool, kindergarten, and the early grades—has long been a subject of lively debate. Over the past decade, however, a consensus has arisen among experts in early childhood education, most of whom endorse the idea of "developmentally appropriate practice." The National Association for the Education of Young Children (NAEYC), in particular, has championed this idea through its position statements and publications.

What do experts mean by this unwieldy phrase?

Simply put, developmentally appropriate practice "takes into account those aspects of teaching and learning that change with the age and experience of the learner," says Lilian Katz, director of the ERIC Clearinghouse on Elementary and Early Childhood Education at the University of Illinois, Urbana-Champaign. Today "we have better research

---

This article was originally published in the November 1993 issue of ASCD's *Curriculum Update* newsletter.

Assess Your Curriculum

The National Association for the Education of Young Children (NAEYC) recommends that educators reviewing a curriculum for young children consider these questions, among others:

Does the curriculum

✦ promote interactive learning and encourage the child's construction of knowledge?

✦ encourage active learning and allow children to make meaningful choices?

✦ foster children's exploration and inquiry, rather than focusing on "right" answers or "right" ways to complete a task?

✦ lead to conceptual understanding by helping children construct their own understanding in meaningful contexts?

✦ embody expectations that are realistic and attainable at this time, or could the children more easily and efficiently acquire the knowledge or skills later on?

✦ encourage development of positive feelings and dispositions toward learning while leading to acquisition of knowledge and skills?

✦ help achieve social, emotional, physical, and cognitive goals and promote democratic values?

✦ promote and encourage social interaction among children and adults?

Condensed from NAEYC's Reaching Potentials: Appropriate Curriculum and Assessment for Young Children, Vol. I.

than ever on how children learn at different ages," she notes—and that knowledge has many implications for schooling.

We know, for example, that children aged 4–6 learn better through direct, interactive experiences than through traditional teaching, where the learner is passive and receptive. (The latter might be "okay" for children aged 8 or older, Katz says.) Further, the younger children are, the more their learning needs to be meaningful on the day they learn it, not just in the context of some future learning.

Developmentally appropriate practice has two dimensions, says Sue Bredekamp, director of professional development for the NAEYC. First, it is age-appropriate: it reflects what we know about how children develop and learn. Second, it is appropriate to the individual child: it takes into account each child's own development, interests, and cultural background. Teachers need to consider both dimensions, she says.

In choosing a learning experience for a child, knowing what's age-appropriate "gets you in the ballpark," Bredekamp says, but the teacher must also consider the individual. She offers an analogy to choosing a toy for a 3-year-old. Knowing the child's age gives one a general idea of what kind of toy would be suitable, but without knowing the individual child— her interests, whether she's "young" or advanced for her age—one can't choose with confidence.

Given the diversity seen in any group of young children, attention to individual appropriateness is crucial—yet too often neglected, Bredekamp says. "There's a wide range of individual variation that everyone recognizes, but it's rarely paid the attention it deserves," she asserts. This neglect occurs because the curriculum imposes a norm, and because teachers find it easier to plan to some predicted norm. But teachers whose instruction is developmentally appropriate "don't expect all the children to learn the same things in the same way on the same day," she emphasizes.

Teachers must also consider all aspects of the child, experts advise. Developmentally appropriate practices "challenge individual children to learn and reach their potential in all areas of development," says consultant David Burchfield, who teaches at Brownsville Elementary School in Albemarle County, Va. Teachers must attend not only to the cognitive domain but to children's social, emotional, and physical needs as well. "Typically in schools, we pay too much attention to the cognitive," he says. "We shouldn't ignore the complexity of children."

Developmentally appropriate practice is not a recipe but a *philosophy* for teaching young children, experts explain. "It's not a curriculum or an exact prescription," says Burchfield. "It offers guidelines." Some teachers may find this unsettling. "Teachers are so used to being told, 'Do it this way,'" he notes. By contrast, the developmentally appropriate philosophy says, "'Keep these things in mind' when considering your kids, the classroom environment, what you teach and how."

Developmentally appropriate practice is "a set of principles, not a methodology," agrees Barbara Bowman, vice president of programs at Loyola University of Chicago's Erikson Institute. Beyond advising teachers to honor the sequence of child development and their pupils' individual differences, "you can't make hard and fast rules," she says. Instead, teachers must exercise their professional judgment, based on training and reflection. "That's the piece that's gotten lost" in the past, she believes.

PUSHED-DOWN CURRICULUM

In large measure, early childhood experts are promoting developmentally appropriate practice in response to a phenomenon dubbed the "escalated" or "pushed-down" curriculum. Over the past few decades, observers say, preschool classes and kindergartens have begun to look more like traditional 1st grade classes: young children are expected to sit quietly while they listen to whole-class instruction or fill in worksheets. Concurrently, teachers have been expecting their pupils to know more and more when they first enter their classrooms.

Experts cite many reasons for this trend. The urge to catch up with the Russians after the launching of Sputnik led to "young children doing oodles of sit-still, pencil-and-paper work"—a type of schoolwork inappropriate for 5- to 7-year-olds, says Jim Uphoff, a professor of education at Wright State University in Dayton, Ohio. (Today, the urge to compete with Japan yields the same result, experts say.) Another cause of the pushed-down curriculum is the widespread—yet incorrect—notion that one can teach children anything, at any age, if the content is presented in the right way, says David Elkind, a professor of child study at Tufts University.

In addition, more children today attend preschool, and preschools market themselves as academic, says Marilyn Hughes, an education consultant and veteran elementary teacher from Aspen, Colo. Some parents, too, favor the pushed-down curriculum in their zeal to give their children a head start in life. And, in general, Americans believe that faster is better. "We worship speed," Uphoff says. "That's an integral part of our beliefs."

Jacqueline Feare, principal of Todd Hall School in Lincolnwood, Ill., says that a pushed-down curriculum used to prevail in her district. Under pressure from parents and the central office, kindergartners were expected to use workbooks—despite their teachers' concerns. "Now we're saying, 'Less is more'; then, it was just the opposite," she recalls. "We were saying, 'Let's see how much we can cram into their heads.'"

While the intentions of those pushing down the curriculum may be good, the effects on children are bad, experts say.

For one thing, giving children material far beyond what they can do is simply inefficient, says Elkind. While 4-year-olds need "eons" of time to learn subtraction, 6-year-olds can grasp the concept in a few hours, he says. Similarly, 4th graders typically need months to learn decimal fractions, whereas 6th graders can master them with far less effort. Although educators *can* push down the curriculum, "what's the point?" Elkind asks. "Certainly there should be challenge, but it should be intelligent challenge."

Requiring young children to do overly advanced work has another harmful effect: it causes them to miss something else they *should* be doing, says Hughes. If children are only responding to teacher cues, "they are missing natural learning experiences"—direct, sensory experiences of their world—which form the foundation for later, more abstract learning.

Yet another drawback of the pushed-down curriculum is its effect on children's attitude toward learning. When young children are introduced to formal instruction too early, in a form that is too abstract, they *may* learn the knowledge and skills presented, but at the expense of the disposition to use them, Katz says. Obviously, destroying students' enthusiasm for learning in exchange for some short-term gains is a poor bargain. Further, when young children are repeatedly coerced into behaving as though they understand something—such as the calendar or arithmetic—when they really do not, their confidence in their own abilities is undermined, Katz says. "If you can't relate to what's going on, you believe you're stupid," she says. And over time, children bring their behavior into line with this belief.

ACTIVE LEARNING

If traditional, lecture-driven teaching is not appropriate for young children, then how *should* they be taught?

According to Katz, what children learn generally proceeds from "behavioral" knowledge to "representational" knowledge—from the concrete and tangible to the abstract. Therefore, the younger the learners, the more opportunities they need to interact with real objects and real environments.

In a developmentally appropriate classroom, Bredekamp says, the teacher provides lots of organized activity. Children are actively involved in learning: writing, reading, building with blocks, doing project work, making choices. Young children need hands-on experiences and social interaction around content, she says. In math, for example, students grasp concepts better when they grapple with real-life problems and work with manipulatives.

Teachers must respect how young children learn best: through social interaction, Bredekamp says. "It shouldn't be chaos," but children should be discussing their pursuits with peers. Research shows that children learn problem solving better when they work in groups, she says. So while some whole-group instruction may be useful, teacher lecture should *not* be the rule of the day.

For the most part, teachers should avoid whole-group instruction, Katz agrees. When a teacher tries to teach something to the entire class at the same time, "chances are, one-third of the kids already know it; one-third will get it; and the remaining third won't. So two-thirds of the children are wasting their time." To learn a particular concept, "some children need days; some, ten minutes," says Hughes—but the typical lockstep school schedule ignores this fundamental fact.

Because children learn idiosyncratically, teachers need to provide a range of learning opportunities, says Judy Zimmerman, principal of Indian Fields Elementary School in Dayton, N.J. If a teacher wants to teach that every sentence begins with a capital letter, for example, she could introduce that idea to the whole group, perhaps by pointing it out in a "big book." Some children will immediately grasp the concept; others might recognize an individual capital letter; still others might miss the point entirely, Zimmerman says. Therefore, the teacher must continue to provide opportunities for pupils to learn the concept. "The teacher should constantly expose them to this [idea], and push them along."

Teachers can help individualize instruction through small-group work and opportunities for children to do their own investigating, Katz

A Look Inside a K–2 Literacy Portfolio

What kinds of student work and other information should be collected in a literacy portfolio? In the South Brunswick (N.J.) School District, a pupil's K–2 literacy portfolio contains the following:

✦ Self-portraits drawn by the child at both the beginning and end of the school year.

✦ Notes from an interview, conducted in September, during which the child is asked about his or her favorite pastimes and reading activities at home.

✦ A questionnaire sent to parents at the beginning of the school year that solicits their input and helps build a working relationship between parents and the teacher.

✦ A test of the child's understanding of the conventions of books and print that is administered at both the beginning and end of kindergarten.

✦ A "word awareness" writing activity, administered at the end of kindergarten and at the beginning and end of 1st grade.

✦ Unedited samples of the child's free writing, which may include translations by the teacher if invented spelling or sketchy syntax make them difficult to read.

✦ A "remodeling" sample, collected three times a year, that allows teachers to appraise the strategies each child is using to deal with print. Two techniques are used: a running record for emergent readers and a miscue analysis for independent readers.

✦ A record of the child's ability to retell a story, recorded three times over the course of the school year.

✦ A class record that profiles the accumulated knowledge about the class on a one-page matrix.

Adapted from The Education and Care of Young Children: Report of the ASCD Early Childhood Consortium.

says. "Children are born with a powerful natural impulse to investigate their environment. *That's* what we should be capitalizing on in the curriculum," she asserts. For young children, investigation is a natural way of learning; they make hypotheses all the time. To capitalize on this inclination, educators should consider how to provide contexts for worthwhile investigations.

How, for example, could the teacher* in the anecdote at the beginning of this article best help her pupil investigate whether the fish in the aquarium were actually drinking the water? According to NAEYC's *Reaching Potentials: Appropriate Curriculum and Assessment for Young Children* (the source of this example), the teacher should enable the child to test his hypothesis. She could say, "Oh, do you think that if we had another tank of water with no fish in it, the water level would stay the same? Let's try it and find out." By responding in this way, the teacher engages the child's participation and challenges his thinking, the NAEYC document says.

One excellent way to encourage student investigations is through the project approach, Katz says. Children should study real phenomena in their environment through in-depth projects that combine all the disciplines, she advises.

Children in a small Vermont town, for example, investigated the question: "Who measures what in our town?" They studied the daily measurements of length, time, cost, distance, and so on, made by people throughout their community. The project lasted for weeks, and parents and businesses were involved. The children collected measurement devices and created an exhibit. "The kids got into it," Katz reports.

Long-term projects help teachers nurture students' interest—which is not to be confused with excitement, Katz says. One mistake teachers make, she believes, is to confuse getting kids excited—"a short-term turn-on"—with engaging their interest: inducing them to "wrap their minds around" a topic for an extended period. Projects help children develop this ability, she says.

---

*Diane Trister Dodge of Teaching Strategies, Inc., in Washington, D.C.

Using Themes

The traditional curriculum is fragmented, many experts complain. In too many classrooms, children study South America in the morning and Colonial America in the afternoon, making school studies a "giant Trivial Pursuit," says Teresa Rosegrant, an associate professor of early childhood education at George Mason University and a former kindergarten teacher. The pieces don't fit together, especially for young children.

Teachers can avoid this pitfall by using a thematic approach, Rosegrant says. For example, a 1st grade class could study the five senses in language arts, science, math, and art. A thematic approach makes learning more coherent, Rosegrant says; it also makes the curriculum accessible to parents, who can reinforce learning at home. A young child is incapable of summarizing "what happened at school today" if learning is a confusing array of unrelated facts, she notes. But with a thematic approach, a young child could say, "We learned about the tongue, and we tasted salt, sugar, and spices."

Kindergarten teacher Lynn Michelotti uses a thematic approach in her classroom at Todd Hall School. "We do a lot with pumpkins and apples in the fall," she says, citing one example. Her pupils take a field trip to a pumpkin farm; then they observe pumpkins in science, weigh and measure pumpkins in math, read about how pumpkins grow, and learn to cook pumpkin pie.

Without a thematic approach, the curriculum may ask teachers to do some illogical things, Rosegrant says. As a kindergarten teacher, she was expected to teach about the moon, although teaching about the sun was reserved for 1st grade! (The district has since moved to a thematic approach, she says.)

Learning Centers

Many teachers of young children use learning centers to individualize instruction and to allow pupils some choice and control over their learning, experts say. "Learning centers are designed to give an experiential approach and to provide for student differences," says early childhood expert Barbara Day of the University of North Carolina–Chapel Hill, who is a Past President of ASCD.

In his rural Virginia classroom, Burchfield provides many learning centers, including areas devoted to art, math and science, a library, a computer, blocks, and a stage. Allowing his students some choice yields several benefits. "I see them being able to persist in their work much longer," he says. His pupils also strive for quality, feel a sense of ownership, and have a tremendous sense of pride. "They see value and meaning in their school experience," Burchfield says.

Learning centers "allow for the broadest range of interactions," says Hughes. Her own classroom featured 20 hands-on learning centers, which were run on student contracts. Some of the centers were set up for independent work; others, for pairs or small groups. Students could respond to the centers in a variety of ways: linguistic, visual, kinesthetic. Hughes taught her pupils how to move independently through the centers, giving them a chance to pace themselves. The centers placed "hundreds of materials within the reach of the children," she says.

THE ROLE OF ACADEMICS

A common myth about developmentally appropriate practice, experts say, is that it is not academically rigorous—that it allows pupils to "do whatever they want." Advocates are quick to refute this charge.

Developmentally appropriate practice is not unacademic, Elkind says; it's simply academic in a more appropriate way than traditional instruction. It encourages curiosity, not rote learning, and it creates a sounder base of knowledge that is more retainable.

The belief that developmentally appropriate practice lacks rigor is a misunderstanding, says Bredekamp. "The opposite is true. It can be *more* rigorous than a basic skills approach" because it is not limited to skills alone. Skills are infused and taught in context—through project work, for example.

Others, however, would prefer more emphasis on the direct teaching of skills.

Donna Siegel, an associate professor of education at the University of Science and Arts of Oklahoma, is a stout supporter of teaching basic skills to young children, especially the disadvantaged. Children who aren't exposed to literacy at home need to be taught basic decoding, she believes. (Children from middle-class backgrounds fare better with less direct teaching because their parents teach them basics such as the alphabet, she says.) Siegel is concerned that an emphasis on allowing children to explore and discover may leave them unprepared academically. "It's hard to *discover* how to do math or how to read," she says. "Some things you have to sit down and learn."

Young children learn basic skills much faster through direct instruction or modeling than through exploration, Siegel says. Further, adults can teach academics to young children without harming their disposition to learn, she believes. The teacher should explain in a step-by-step fashion, help pupils along, and keep them trying. "I'm not talking about drill all the time," she emphasizes. "You don't want to stress children out."

If a child can read on entering 1st grade, he or she is more likely to have success all through school, Siegel says. "Reading is so critical to later school success; a little head start can only be beneficial."

Bredekamp believes formal reading instruction, such as phonics drill, is not appropriate until 1st grade, and then only when needed. She too is concerned about disadvantaged children, but she diagnoses their needs differently. "The key is to have a program in which kids are getting numerous experiences with print, starting at age 3 probably," she says. In particular, they should be read to constantly.

Too often, children who have not been exposed to literacy at home get only the alphabet and phonics at school, Bredekamp says. They are "drilled and killed on basic skills in isolation," despite their lack of experiences on which to "hang" this learning. (Children who are exposed to literacy in many ways outside of school can better weather a decontextualized skills approach, she says.)

"In the past we taught language as though it was a jigsaw puzzle: hopefully, by magic, sometime the pieces would fit together," Uphoff says. By taking this fractured approach, "we've taught a lot of kids to read but to not *want* to read."

CHALLENGE TO THE TEACHER

Experts in early childhood education agree that teaching in a developmentally appropriate way is more demanding than traditional, lecture-driven teaching. It "requires more input, time, and energy," says Elkind, because it demands more individualized instruction "geared to where kids are."

"It's more challenging," agrees Bredekamp, because it requires teachers to use their judgment. The traditional notion that "the curriculum rules" is being overturned. "There's no such thing as a teacher-proof developmentally appropriate curriculum," she points out—a fact some teachers find hard to accept.

Rather than following a skills-based, lockstep approach, teachers must guide and support children through a broad range of strategies, so each child has "more than one pathway," says Rosegrant. Teachers must be experimenters, willing to try different means to reach a child, sensitive to the fact that children respond differently to materials and strategies. "You can't think that there's *a* way" to teach a concept, but "many, many alternative ways," she says.

Teaching in a developmentally appropriate way is "much more difficult," says Feare. "Ego is part of it." The teacher used to be the center of attention, the know-it-all, she says; now the teacher must act as a facilitator. Making this shift is difficult for some veteran teachers who are used to being the focal point. "You must have the disposition not to need to be the center of your own universe," adds Hughes.

Elkind, however, cautions that we must allow a wide range of teaching styles, because some teachers are more at home with direct instruction. Often, this preference is a matter of temperament, he believes—not a reflection of training and habit. Some younger teachers prefer teaching in the traditional way, he notes.

"I don't think we've taken sufficient account of these personality factors," Elkind says. "Some teachers just feel more comfortable with a traditional, structured classroom organization," as opposed to giving children more choice. And some children need more structure. "It's wrong to say the traditional approach is wrong for everybody," he asserts.

Given the challenging nature of developmentally appropriate teaching, it's not surprising that experts underscore the need for better teacher training.

"Generally, teachers are not well-prepared to do this," Bredekamp says. "A lot of states don't even have an early childhood certificate." Training is especially important, she says, in light of the fact that more knowledge is being generated all the time—about how children learn in small-group settings, for example.

Teachers "absolutely need training" in developmental appropriateness, says Hughes. "It just isn't happening at the college level." Schools of education should spotlight the finest teachers of young children as master models, she proposes.

Child development needs to be seen as an integral part of education courses, says Shirle Moone Childs, director of curriculum and instruction for the Windham Public Schools in Willimantic, Conn., who heads ASCD's Early Childhood Education Network. "It's important that we make the connection" between child development courses and education courses, she says, noting that when she was in college, child development courses were considered part of Home Economics.

BETTER ASSESSMENT

Like curriculum and instruction, assessment practices should be developmentally appropriate, experts agree. Most recommend a move to "authentic" forms of assessment.

Compared to paper-and-pencil tests, portfolios and performance assessments give teachers "a much better read on what children really know," says Feare. "You can see how the child is progressing—and not progressing." These forms of assessment are "far more diagnostic."

For many reasons, paper-and-pencil assessments of young children tend to be inaccurate, Elkind says. Children are not very good with symbols; they tend not to understand—or follow—instructions well; and their mood can greatly affect their performance. Fortunately, there are many observational ways to assess children, Elkind says. Their use of language is very revealing, for example. If they use the words "shorter" and "longer," they have mastered the unit concept. Similarly, if they play games with rules, they have grasped syllogistic reasoning.

Teachers need to be close observers of young children, experts agree. With less direct instruction, "keeping track of what kids know becomes terribly important," Bowman says. "The teacher must spend a good part of the day *not* talking," but "watching and listening a lot," adds Rosegrant.

Kindergarten teacher Michelotti says she devotes much of her time to observing and evaluating her pupils. "The teacher's a facilitator; the process is more important than the product," she explains. "I'm trying to spend more time really watching kids and making more anecdotal records."

Good ways to assess young pupils include observation, portfolios, and interviews, says Bredekamp. "We do far too much testing," she says, to the degree that our teaching looks like testing: children sitting quietly, filling in blanks. Instead, she believes, the influence ought to flow in the opposite direction: assessment should resemble good instruction.

Portfolios and journals are more appropriate for young children, Uphoff says, because they "allow children to do more at their own rate of development." Moreover, "the child is part of his own assessment; he can see his own progress." Thus, the child gains the ability to self-evaluate: "It's not just 'the great expert' evaluating you."

Literacy portfolios are central to the program offered at Indian Fields Elementary School, says Principal Judy Zimmerman. Over the course of each child's K–2 school career, pieces of student work and other indicators are collected in the portfolio. Teachers do not collect exactly the same information on every child (more is collected on children who appear to be having difficulties), but what *is* the same is standardized through a six-point scale.

The portfolios provide "a failsafe method for explaining to parents what we're doing," Zimmerman says. The school's program is validated when parents see the progress their children are making in writing and spelling. As a public relations tool, the portfolios have been "a savior for us."

But use of portfolios alone to assess what children know is not adequate, cautions Rosegrant. "You need more than the work itself," she says. "You need the critical adult," probing what understandings the

Staff Development Key to Success

As assistant superintendent for curriculum and instruction in Lincolnwood, Ill., Mark Friedman was asked to plan an early childhood program for the district. Staff development was a major focus, says Friedman, who is now superintendent of the Libertyville, Ill., public schools.

When changes in instruction were proposed, some teachers felt an "invalidation" of what they had been doing in the classroom, Friedman says. To counter this inevitable feeling, he tried to convey the message that "we've learned that there are other ways to do things."

Teachers were given training in a variety of instructional strategies. Consultants showed them how to teach reading without reading groups, for example, and how to integrate reading with other disciplines, Friedman says. Teachers were also trained in the "Math Their Way" program, which makes extensive use of manipulatives. In addition, the district provided a lot of "awareness training" about developmental appropriateness, using video-tapes and "fireside chats" (informal discussions with teachers about their concerns). They also put together "article banks"—phonebook-sized volumes of articles on the topic.

A "big issue" for teachers, Friedman says, was the definition of developmentally appropriate practice: teachers wanted to know just what was expected of them. Some teachers wanted almost a checklist, he recalls—but this was precisely what the central office did not want to give them. They did not want teachers merely to adopt the "surface aspects" but to grasp the underlying philosophy.

Classroom visits were an especially powerful staff development tool, Friedman says. Through networking with other districts, teams of teachers (of the same grade level) were able to visit classrooms in other districts—including private schools and the laboratory school at the University of Chicago—to "get a flavor of good teaching practices at various sites." The teacher teams "culled some good stuff out of every visit," he says.

child's work represents. "The issue here is to get closer to the process," she asserts.

Teachers must avoid the "trap" of providing developmentally appropriate instruction yet asking children to show their learning on a written test, Hughes says. Instead, teachers must allow children to demonstrate their learning in a variety of modes. For example, after a science exploration on weather, children could show what they learned through writing, creating charts, or building a model. "It's the children's responsibility to choose a way to show the *most* they know," she says—with the proviso that children also need to expand their repertoires.

"Assessment is the key to a developmentally appropriate program," Hughes says. "It tells you how sophisticated [students'] connections are." And, she adds, given the power of testing to drive other aspects of schooling, "if your assessment is not developmentally appropriate, nothing else you do will be."

RELATIONS WITH PARENTS

Developmentally appropriate teaching can sometimes be a hard sell with parents, many of whom find the break with tradition disturbing. "Most parents want workbooks and papers to put on the fridge; they understand these things," says Uphoff of Wright State University. "Parents are anxious to help students at home," Zimmerman adds, and they feel "insecure and frightened if they don't have worksheets to help them with."

To give parents confidence in a developmentally appropriate program, educators need to spend time with them, helping them understand what they see in their children's work, Zimmerman says. "We have to help our parents put on a new set of eyes. It's very hard to do." Teachers at her school communicate with parents frequently, Zimmerman says, explaining what children are learning about and describing what they'll bring home. They use Voicemail and leave messages almost daily. For example, they tell parents, "Ask your child how we measured the perimeter of the classroom" or "Ask how they dug their garden and what they planted." Individual conferencing with parents also helps allay concerns, as does inviting parents to observe or volunteer in the classroom.

"The communication is absolutely key," Zimmerman emphasizes. Teachers need to be "clear, consistent, frequent communicators—and partners—with parents," she says. And they must show parents, all along, that their children are learning more than they would in a more traditional program.

Teachers do a disservice by not communicating with parents at least weekly, Feare says. (Teachers at her school send home a newsletter.) If parents are kept informed, and their children are happy in school, parents are satisfied, she says.

"We've been highly successful in changing our model," Feare says. "We've made changes in my school that people said couldn't be done"—including the elimination of workbooks, worksheets, and the spelling book. They won public support for the changes because "parents could see that kids were learning."

LOOMING OBSTACLES

Despite the consensus among early childhood educators that developmentally appropriate practice is best for young children, obstacles loom between theory and practice.

To spread developmentally appropriate practice will be "an uphill fight," says Bowman, primarily because it is expensive. "The cost factor has not been faced up to," she says. "To get wonderful results, you have to invest in the program," including improving teacher-to-pupil ratios and providing training for teachers.

Bredekamp also sees "a real challenge in terms of school financing" to provide smaller class sizes, more materials, and richer experiences—in a time of tighter budgets. "The challenge is to use budgets more wisely," she believes. For example, rather than buying 30 desks, a school might purchase several tables and some hands-on materials.

For Rosegrant, the main obstacle lies in the lockstep curriculums from publishers, which meet the needs of so few children, yet are so expensive. Developmentally appropriate practice will never become widespread "as long as the curriculum comes in boxes," she asserts. When teachers must meet the requirements of the curriculum, "there's so much to juggle, they drop concerns for individuals to plow through stuff." To overcome this obstacle, teachers need time, far in advance of the school year, to plan, she believes.

Yet another obstacle, says Feare, is the tyranny of the expectations of the teacher at the next level, who might complain that incoming children were not well prepared. "The bashing has just got to stop," she declares. At her school, 1st grade teachers have a new faith that the kindergarten teachers are "giving it their best shot," she says. "Our philosophy is that we're not getting kids ready for the next grade; we're getting them ready for life."

"It takes nerve and money" to move to developmentally appropriate practice, Feare adds. "You need to acquire all kinds of hands-on things." But, she notes, these purchases are actually cost-effective in the long run: manipulatives last a long time, whereas workbooks are consumables.

Burchfield sees an obstacle in the mismatch between instruction and assessment. Teachers are being asked to change their instruction (to literature-based reading, for example) while assessment remains unchanged (most often, standardized tests). The lack of congruence has spawned a great fear among teachers that he finds justified. "We're running into some dangerous territory."

People in power positions—administrators, school boards, superintendents—are still appealing to "the numbers" for accountability purposes, Burchfield says. *Qualitative* evidence of children's learning needs to be made understandable, he believes—although he wonders, "How do you take a portfolio and make it understandable to a school board, when you can't present it in an aggregate way?"

LOOKING TO THE FUTURE

What do experts foresee for the movement toward developmentally appropriate practice?

Most are cautiously optimistic that the trend will continue, primarily because of the great number of complementary trends, such as the new process orientation in mathematics and the widespread interest in integrated curriculum. Bredekamp is heartened by the congruence she sees among these trends, but she also fears that the impetus toward national standards could mow down any progress if it perverts the curriculum to a reductive skills-based approach.

"I am optimistic," says Burchfield of the prospects for developmentally appropriate practice. But he emphasizes that those in leadership positions, including principals and central office staff, need to be involved in training and discussions about the concept. Like teachers, "they must be given a lens to see what good practice can look like."

BUILDING A FOUNDATION FOR SOCIAL, EMOTIONAL, AND INTELLECTUAL GROWTH

KAREN RASMUSSEN

• Individually or in small groups, the children in the Child Care Education Program at the University of North Carolina at Greensboro pursue art projects, sit in bean bag chairs looking at books, play listening games on a computer, and try on secondhand adult clothing. The 17 children in the class, ranging in age from $2^1/_2$ to 5 years, have been allowed to choose which activities they would like to pursue. Later the children will eat lunch and choose books to take to their cots for a few hours of quiet reading and rest.

• After a teacher finds a mouse in her office at the Child Development Laboratory at Pennsylvania State University (University Park, Pa.), she tells her class of 3- to 6-year-olds about her experience. The class decides to learn about how mice live, to identify the differences between a white rat and a field mouse, and to build mouse houses. To find answers, they visit the library and talk to experts.

• At the First Presbyterian Weekday School in Watkinsville, Ga., 10 of the class's 2-year-old children are taking turns painting with orange paint under the watchful eye of a teaching aide. Just outside the door, at a table in the hall, two of their classmates are engaged in a color-matching activity with their teacher.

Although the children's ages and their activities vary, the children in these three classrooms are learning new vocabulary words, interacting with their peers, and exploring their environments. Many of the children at the first two child care centers remain there from the time their parents drop them off in the morning until they are picked up in the evening. At

This article was originally published in the Winter 1998 issue of ASCD's *Curriculum Update* newsletter.

the weekday school, programs last from 9:00 a.m. to noon, several days a week.

Despite the variations in these classrooms, preschool and child care programs share the same goals, say experts: to provide high-quality experiences that address all aspects of child development, including social, emotional, and intellectual growth.

DEFINING EARLY CHILDHOOD EDUCATION

The National Association for the Education of Young Children (NAEYC) defines the age of young children as birth through 8 years. The age range is "a developmental definition, not one based on the structure of schools and organizations, but on how children develop," explains Sue Bredekamp, director of professional development at NAEYC. As a result, educators of young children provide a level of care different from that of their colleagues who teach older children.

Children under the age of 8 have certain things in common: they are in the midst of the foundation years, on which later experiences will be built, and they are still connected strongly with their families, Bredekamp explains. Because of their strong dependence on adults, young children need to be in high-quality child care settings, regardless of their age, experts say.

Programs that last more than a few hours per day must meet children's requirements for rest and nutrition, but all early childhood programs should strive to meet children's emotional, social, and intellectual needs, contend early childhood education professionals. In fact, most teachers of young children view early childhood education and child care as interchangeable. "Caring and learning go hand in hand," says Jennifer Kuhlman, a lead teacher at the Child Care Education Program at the University of North Carolina at Greensboro. "Where it happens doesn't make a difference."

A BRAVE NEW WORLD

Although a variety of types of early childhood education programs exist, experts say that the need for them is growing. According to the U.S. Department of Education's *Building Knowledge for a Nation of Learners: A*

Framework for Education Research—1997, the percentage of children aged 3–4 who have enrolled in nursery schools during the past three decades has increased from 11 percent to 48 percent. As recently as 1993, the U.S. Bureau of the Census reported that 9.9 million children younger than 5 years needed care while their parents worked. As the number of children born to working parents and single parents increases, and as new welfare laws requiring that recipients find work are implemented, more high-quality education programs will be required than ever before, say those who study the issue.

To illustrate how quickly the need for child care has grown, Linda Duerr, coordinator of the Child Development Laboratory at Penn State, cites an activity that took place at a recent conference on child care: Participants over the age of 40 were asked to raise their hand if they remembered their own child care experiences outside the home. Few raised their hands. As the age decreased and the same question was posed, however, more and more people revealed that they had spent time in group child care programs.

THE IMPACT OF BRAIN RESEARCH

As advocates for young children seek to educate the public on the need to improve care for young children, educators continue to explore the best ways to provide high-quality educational and care experiences.

To support the importance of the early years of children's lives, there has been a focus on brain research, originating with the Carnegie Corporation's 1994 report *Starting Points: Meeting the Needs of Young Children*, says Bredekamp. The report, which emphasizes the impact that experiences during the first three years of life have on a child's development, cites the importance of a healthy and nurturing environment for brain development.

However, the report and educators stress that such research simply documents what early childhood educators have known for years—that the early years of a child's life profoundly affect later ones. Pictures of children's brains that show the difference between children who have been neglected and children of the same age who have been nurtured, she continues, have made brain research compelling to a wide audience.

Although reports about how the brain works and develops in young children have been highly publicized, early childhood educators warn that such research should not be overstated. While compelling, pictures of the brain do not reveal to educators the best ways to stimulate brain development, suggests David Elkind, professor of child study at Tufts University (Medford, Mass.). "Just because you have the capacity to learn a foreign language, you may not have the motivation to do it," he says. "You need to hear the language, be able to practice it, and have support from those around you."

Lilian Katz, who directs the ERIC Clearinghouse on Elementary and Early Childhood Education at the University of Illinois at Urbana-Champaign, joins Elkind in cautioning educators to be careful about how much importance they place on results of brain research. She worries that "people will say, 'Well, kid, you're 4 years old now, it's too late for you.'"

PLAY LEADS TO LEARNING

Rather than rely on brain research to report benefits of good early childhood experiences, educators need to focus on how to best teach and nurture children, experts say. Fortunately, kids come to preschool with a willingness to learn, says Katz. "Educators need to ask, What curriculum will support this? We must find ways to strengthen children's dispositions to learn, hypothesize, and look for cause and effect. This intellectual element is missing from most programs."

Education of young children needs to be redefined because they learn in different ways than older children, says Elkind. He explains, "Young children have to learn what I call a 'fundamental curriculum,'" which includes learning about colors, weights, and units.

One way children learn about these concepts is through experience and touching, which often happens when they play. Play, in addition to being a natural activity for young children, helps them learn social skills, promotes their emotional development, and allows them to exercise their creativity, says Bredekamp. Play can give children a chance to understand symbols by learning that words can stand for things, she explains.

High-quality early childhood programs structure activities so that child play leads to child learning. In Amy Wraga's classroom for 2-year-olds at the First Presbyterian Weekday School, she has arranged the room in centers. One center contains blocks, while others hold crayons, paint, and paper; secondhand adult clothes for dramatic play; books and a quiet area; manipulatives such as snap beads, games, and play dough; and pots and pans and toy appliances.

For the first hour and a half of the three hours that they are at the preschool, the children choose which center to visit and decide how long to stay there before moving to a different one. Children play alone or with other children. When allowed to decide what to play and with whom, children learn through their relationships with other children, not just with adults, says Bredekamp. In her class, Wraga explains, one goal of an activity may be for children to learn colors, but it is equally important to give children the chance to socialize with one another and learn how to communicate and take turns.

Providing an environment in which young children can learn these social skills is a primary aim of most early childhood education programs, adds Duerr. Young children believe they are the center of the universe, she explains, and always think they should go first in any situation. In today's society—which includes dual careers for parents, single parents, and a global economy—children need to learn how to get along with others, she asserts.

Although being cared for by a parent in the home is wonderful, Duerr says, group child care programs can have a positive impact on the socialization and development of children. After all, "you can't teach sharing and getting along with others unless you have other children around," she notes.

INTEGRATING TEACHING TECHNIQUES

While play is an important way for children to learn to get along with others and to investigate their environment, it shouldn't be the only method, experts say. People outside of the early childhood education field sometimes think that a preschool should either allow children to play or have students fill out worksheets and work with phonics, says Katz. "Neither is enough to engage the child's mind," she advises.

Katz encourages teachers to strengthen each child's natural disposition to investigate, hypothesize, and look for cause and effect by using a variety of teaching methods. Kuhlman agrees, saying that she has found that lesson planning based on what she and her coteacher observe about the kids' interests and behavior is the most successful teaching strategy they employ. The teachers look at the concepts and interests children are beginning to develop and build on those.

For example, in Kuhlman's class of 2½- to 5-year-olds at the Child Care Education Program at UNC–Greensboro, instruction is tailored to the needs of individual students and the class as a whole. One girl in Kuhlman's class is very interested in writing and in spelling words phonetically. The teachers encourage her interest and work with her on phonics. Meanwhile, when Kuhlman and her coteacher noticed that some of the older children in the class were starting to write, they organized an activity to make books. The younger children colored in theirs, while the older ones wrote and received guidance on spelling and choosing words.

CHILDREN CHOOSE THE CURRICULUM

Sometimes a child's interest in a topic captures the imagination of the other children and becomes a long-term project for the class. According to Duerr, a project can be initiated by anyone in the learning community, including a child, parent, or teacher.

Duerr cites an instance when a teacher was reading a book about how to plan a lesson around a medieval theme. A student in her class saw a picture of a sword in the book and asked to make a play one. Other students also became interested in swords and asked a variety of questions: Who used them? What is a knight? What was it like to live in a castle? What did people eat back then? The project became an in-depth exploration of medieval times. The class visited the library to find answers to their questions, read and compared Robin Hood legends, wrote their own Robin Hood play, and made candles for a medieval feast.

Duerr, who was trained as an elementary school teacher, emphasizes that in preschool programs, the ideas flow from the students to the teachers, and the teachers help to guide student inquiry. In later grades, she explains, curriculum often originates with the teacher. In contrast, educators of younger children rarely plan lessons more than a short time in advance. Teachers in her school meet weekly to review where they are, discuss whether interest is waning in a project, and explore how they can progress from the work students are pursuing to activities that challenge the students to grow intellectually and socially.

ASSESSING LEARNING

When learning is student driven and its goals are to nurture children's social, emotional, and intellectual skills, assessment becomes a difficult task. Duerr explains that early childhood educators have inherited the idea of measuring young children's learning from elementary and secondary educators. "Our first goal is to make sure children can get along with each other," Duerr says, because they can't learn otherwise. "But you can't assess this goal by assigning a number to it."

Teachers at her school collect children's work, take pictures, and record children's voices to create portfolios for each child. "You can include a child's first attempts at drawing circles," explains Duerr. "Later you can see that she has progressed to drawing letters and to trying to write her name."

MAKING PARENTS PARTNERS

In addition to providing a record of a child's development, portfolios are an effective way to involve parents in the education of their children, Kuhlman has found. She maintains a portfolio on each child with teachers' notes and samples of the child's artwork. Parents can provide important information to teachers about the child's development when they review the portfolios together, she explains.

Kuhlman encourages parents to take the portfolios when their child leaves her classroom and to review it with their child's next teacher. By passing a portfolio on, Kuhlman can ensure that the child's experience in her class is not lost when the child moves on to grade school or to another teacher, she says.

Because young children are dependent on their parents, teachers need to build strong relationships with parents, early childhood educators say. "The initial caring and loving relationship children receive is the foundation for other relationships as kids grow older," says Bredekamp.

Teachers should always look at the experiences each child has had, asserts Duerr, and build on his or her skills.

Kuhlman and her coteacher also encourage parents to drop by the classroom to have lunch with their children and to participate in activities, such as telling stories to the class. They created a board where they post a review of what the children participated in each day and include comments about what individual children did. "We include comments such as, 'Matthew was interested in this topic today,' so that child's parents can talk to him about it at home."

ENSURING HIGH-QUALITY PROGRAMS

While many early childhood programs reach out to parents and provide safe, nurturing, and educational experiences to young children, finding out if a program is of high quality can be difficult. "Good facilities have the same elements: trained staff, a good learning environment, and good learning materials," says Elkind. However, programs vary from state to state because state day-care requirements differ so widely.

For example, NAEYC recommends that for programs with children under the age of 1, there should be one adult present for every three children. However, because staffing requirements are usually mandated by states, this number varies across the United States. Idaho requires only one adult for every 12 children under 1 year old, cites Bredekamp.

While the creation of national standards for early childhood education is not a priority right now, says Bredekamp, NAEYC offers a voluntary accreditation program that she hopes will serve as a benchmark by which states and individual programs can compare and measure their standards.

NAEYC's National Academy of Early Childhood Programs, which administers the accreditation system, lists characteristics of high-quality programs. The characteristics address staffing; the child's cognitive, social, emotional, and physical development; and communication among parents and staff, among other factors.

NAEYC's voluntary accreditation program assesses the "quality of interaction between teacher and child" says Duerr. In contrast, Pennsylvania's license requirements for day-care facilities pertain primarily to health and safety issues. The commonwealth's Department of Welfare checks the temperature of the room and the water, explains Duerr. When Duerr and her colleagues at Penn State's Child Development Laboratory decided to participate in the NAEYC accreditation process—which includes a self-study component—they viewed it as an opportunity for self-improvement. Going through the process gave them the impetus to make changes they were already considering, she says.

For example, mixed-age grouping is not required for NAEYC accreditation, but thinking about their school's philosophy made them realize that the way they were grouping children was not necessarily best for children. "We asked ourselves, Why do we move kids to different classes at arbitrary ages?" says Duerr. Now the children are placed in two groups with different developmental needs: infants and toddlers who are between 6 weeks and 3 years old, and preschool children who are between the ages of 3 and 6 years.

Based on the experiences at her school, Duerr believes that accreditation should be pursued by every day-care facility in the country: "It is the one assurance of quality that most people recognize and respect."

TEACHERS GROWING AS PROFESSIONALS

If accreditation can tell parents that a program is of high quality, Kuhlman says that she would like to see a standard for teachers so that a parent who walks into a classroom knows that the teachers have a certain level of knowledge, acquired through experience, education, and professional development.

For her part, Wraga has found that professional development opportunities have helped her grow as a teacher. To maintain accreditation under Georgia's standards for early childhood education, teachers and aides in her school are required to attend 20 hours of professional development each year. Wraga usually attends the state's national conference on early childhood education to hear nationally known educators speak, as well as attending classes at the University of Georgia. Classes she has taken range from how to incorporate special education students in the classroom to CPR training, from how to arrange the classroom to preventing infectious diseases.

While she finds the content of classes helpful, the most important benefits to Wraga arise from meeting fellow teachers at conferences and in classes. "The more you interact with other people who do what you do, the more you can exchange ideas," she explains.

Despite an increased emphasis on professional development, many teachers of young children remain frustrated about the lack of opportunities to advance in their careers. Duerr says she has "wrestled with the dilemma that you can't move up the career ladder and stay in the classroom as a teacher." In order to progress in their careers, many teachers assume administrative duties. "I've had almost 20 years of experience in this field," notes Duerr, "but as a teacher I'd still be making $20,000 a year."

In fact, concerns about compensation and career paths are identified as the biggest problems in the field, say experts. With the demands on early childhood educators, it frustrates Kuhlman when people say "it's just babysitting." She explains that working with young children requires an understanding of child development; a knowledge of teaching, assessment, and classroom management strategies; and the skills to work with the child's family.

APPLICATIONS FOR K–12 EDUCATION

Despite their struggle for recognition, early childhood educators point to a long history of educational success and innovation. "Historically, the greatest innovators in education—[Maria] Montessori, [Jean] Piaget, and others—have worked in early childhood education," maintains Elkind. "We have a tremendously powerful legacy and a strong foundation on which to build."

"There is quite a bit to learn from early childhood education experiences that can be 'pushed up' to later grades, instead of the classic pushing down," asserts Katz. For example, Duerr relates how her local school district is investigating forming two charter schools: "In their plans, they talk about the 'innovative teaching strategies' they plan to use, such as focusing on the individual child's needs and interests and placing the teacher in the role of a guide or mentor. This is what we already do in early childhood education." In the meantime, early childhood educators do not plan to wait for their colleagues who teach older children to catch up with them, even if that means a bumpy transition for children leaving preschool. "It's important to use what we know now," Lilian Katz says. "If someone told you there would be a famine in three years you wouldn't prepare by practicing being hungry for three years. You want a good diet on a steady basis."

SUPPORTING CHILDREN BY SUPPORTING FAMILIES

KATHY CHECKLEY

A father spends an afternoon at his daughter's child care center and learns that playing house helps build her math skills. Setting the table with four cups, four plates, and four knives helps his daughter understand what *four* is, the father is told. He's given additional activities designed to further develop her math skills, through play, at home.

A group of elementary school teachers conducts a workshop designed to help parents build their children's interest in reading. Through role-play exercises, parents discover how to read a story and learn about the kinds of questions children might ask about a book. The parents and teachers then prepare a variety of responses to those questions.

An administrator wants to make life a little easier for the families of the children enrolled at her child care center, so she offers additional services. For example, parents can buy postage stamps, rent videos, drop off dry cleaning, and order take-out meals—all at the center. Instead of running to the post office or making dinner, she reasons, parents can spend the time they save with their children.

These are examples of the many ways early childhood educators are striving to meet what has become their dual mission—to involve parents in schooling while also supporting the family. This "family-centered"

This article was originally published in the Winter 1998 issue of ASCD's *Curriculum Update* newsletter.

approach, say experts, acknowledges what research has revealed—that if children are to be truly successful in school, their parents must be involved in their education. And parents are more likely to become involved, these experts contend, when schools consider the needs of the family, as well as the child.

THE FAMILY-CENTERED APPROACH

"When I entered teaching," says Phyllis Jack-Moore, "I had the attitude, 'I'm the expert and I'll tell you how I'm working with your child.' Now I realize that what parents and I can do together benefits the child far more than anything I could do alone."

An early childhood educator for almost 30 years, Jack-Moore says she has also come to realize that stresses on families are visited on teachers. Therefore, providing for the well-being of the family enhances the educational environment both at home *and* at school.

This perspective guided Jack-Moore as she helped establish the Campfire Family-Centered Child Care Center in Ft. Worth, Tex., four years ago. From the very beginning, she says, "we wanted parents to view the center as part of the extended family. So we asked, What can we do that would help parents?"

"Anytime I made a decision as a teacher I would ask myself, Is what I want to do family-centered?" says Melinda Weiler, one of the first teachers hired at Campfire.

Weiler is now the family services coordinator, and that family-centered mind-set governs how she and other Campfire teachers determine what services to provide to families. In addition to stocking items such as stamps and snacks for parents to purchase, the center also offers parents many opportunities to learn and become involved in their child's education. For example,

• Teachers at Campfire conduct workshops on everything from child development to parenting skills.

• Parents can attend family forums to discuss the challenges that confront them and brainstorm ways the center can help them meet those challenges.

• Parents and teachers meet twice a year to set learning goals for their children. These goals can include what families may be focusing on at home. If, for example, a parent is trying to help her child become more responsible at home, teachers can mirror that focus in classroom activities.

• Teachers share their curriculum with parents and discuss ways parents can extend the learning at home.

Through such activities, parents know that the school really wants them to be involved, says Weiler. "There isn't a we vs. them feeling here." She adds that she and other Campfire staff have learned that "the more we support parents, the more they support us."

HELPING PARENTS HELPS CHILDREN

"If you really want to help young children, help the parents," asserts Sharon Darling, president of the National Center for Family Literacy (NCFL). This is especially true, she says, for those children whose families are living in poverty. These are the parents who "may have given up on life—and that colors the expectations they have for their children," Darling explains. "We have to help these parents learn that they can learn." And in doing so, these parents will then "be hungry for activities that will help their children learn."

It's through family literacy programs that parents discover the student within themselves, says Darling. Through such programs, parents acquire basic skills and become "equal partners" in their children's education.

An important component of literacy programs is the focus on parent-child interactions, through which parents learn how their children learn—and how they can support that learning. "We need to teach some parents what they need to do to help their children develop," says Bonnie Lash Freeman, a training specialist at NCFL.

One effective way to do this, she says, is to teach parents how to "do observations." Ask parents to watch their child engaged in an activity at home, she advises. Have them describe, in an essay, what they see, and then have parents compare their observations to child development charts. "Parents begin to see where their children are supposed to be," says

Freeman. "This is reaffirming to parents and helps them to develop appropriate expectations."

Parents also need to talk with one other about what they observe, Freeman notes. Through such debriefing sessions, parents learn to support one another as they make learning "part of the daily home routine."

But start slow, Freeman advises. Debriefings should be conducted only after trust has been established. Start with private conversations between parents and staff, through which staff "catch parents being good." Then, introduce journal writing as a form of dialogue between a parent and a staff member. Begin whole-group discussions by asking parents to respond to learning scenarios, discussing possible strategies they could use to meet the challenges posed in the scenarios. Then, graduate to whole-group conversations and ask parents to identify how other parents in the program are successfully encouraging their child's learning.

This process, says Freeman, helps parents "learn to articulate specifically what they see" as their children grow and develop. Such an experience, she explains, also encourages parents to think about themselves as learners.

The process also communicates to parents that they are as important as the child, asserts Darling. Giving parents such a vote of confidence is a highly successful approach, she maintains, pointing to recent NCFL studies that show that when parents realize success in literacy programs, their children enter kindergarten ready to learn. It's just clear, Darling states: "The primary predictor of how a child will do in school is the educational attainment of the parent in the home."

BREAKING DOWN BARRIERS

"By fostering a greater sense of family and setting expectations for parental involvement, early childhood educators are setting up a lifelong pattern of involvement," says Parker Anderson of the National Association for the Education of Young Children (NAEYC). When educators help parents see their roles and responsibilities early on, "this sense of responsibility will continue throughout the child's education," she states.

Anderson concedes that parent involvement is still only a dream for many caregivers and teachers. But, says Anderson, assistant director of

NAEYC's National Institute for Early Childhood Professional Development, part of the problem may be in how teachers seek parental support.

"Many teachers simply say, 'Oh, our parents won't get involved,'" basing their assertions on poorly attended functions that were advertised in rather traditional ways—through printed flyers, notices on bulletin boards, and so on. "There are more effective ways to get families involved with what we're doing," Anderson asserts.

Karen Mapp, program director at the Institute for Responsive Education, agrees. "Many parents have a desire to be involved," she says, but a key factor in turning that desire into action "is how the school relates to parents."

Mapp documented the success of one school's parent involvement effort in the September/October 1997 issue of the *Harvard Education Letter.* Mapp writes that the staff at the Patrick O'Hearn Elementary School in Boston "use a well-executed process of 'joining' with families." ("Joining" is a term Mapp borrows from her background in marriage and family therapy. When a counselor works with a family, she explains, that counselor must "join" with each member of the family, finding common ground so everyone feels equal.)

Staff members at O'Hearn, says Mapp, work hard to ensure that families know that any type of involvement is truly appreciated—"whether it be reading to a child at home, donating a book to the school library, or being active in school governance."

But first, Mapp notes, the teachers had to get parents to the school. What they found most effective, she says, was to begin a family outreach program. "A core group of parent volunteers started by visiting parents whose children were new to the school to welcome them and answer questions." Through the family outreach efforts, more parents learned about O'Hearn events—plays, evening open houses, breakfast gatherings, and so on. Once parents started attending those events, says Mapp, "the barriers between parents and staff were slowly but surely broken down."

HELPING TEACHERS EMBRACE PARENTS AS PARTNERS

"It's important for teachers and caregivers to consider parents as resources, to listen to them and get creative ideas," says Elena Lopez, associate director of the Family Research Project at Harvard University. But to do so, teachers and caregivers need better training. "Training should be more comprehensive and focused on helping teachers understand family dynamics and child development," she states. Teachers also need to learn more about effective home-school communication: how to involve parents in their children's learning, how to tap parents' skills, and how to see families as allies.

Lopez's view is supported by a series of four papers published by the Family Research Project. Called *Families Matter*, the papers champion family-centered child care and the idea that early childhood education must focus on family, as well as child, development.

Moreover, training should help teachers see that they aren't "learning how to change parents, but rather how to change themselves to work effectively with parents," write Lisa Lee and Ethel Seiderman in *The Parent Service Project*, one of the four papers in the *Families Matter* series. It's important that teachers arrive at this understanding, contend the authors, because early childhood programs are enriched when parents and teachers share skills and expertise.

NCFL's Sharon Darling agrees, pointing out that parents and caregivers, after all, have the same goal—to do what's best for the child. When educators talk about parent involvement, she notes, they don't offer many specifics. What teachers need to learn, says Darling, is how to say to parents: "We want to help you achieve your goals. We want to help you help your child."

For more information on the National Center for Family Literacy, call 502-584-1133 or visit their Web site at [http://www.famlit.org]. The Families Matter *series of papers is available from the Harvard Family Research Project. Call 617-495-9108. The e-mail address is [HFRP@hugse1.harvard.edu]. The Web site address is: [http://hugse1.harvard.edu/~hfrp].*

DEVELOPMENTAL LEARNING: JOYFUL NOISE

LARRY MANN

As director of the Flagstone Child Development Center in Alexandria, Va., JoAnn Barney has many concerns—the safety and well-being of dozens of children, the expectations of parents, the school budget, enrollment, staffing, materials, and schedules. But one thing that would stop her in her tracks, she says, would be *silence*. "Children are born to be noisy, curious, and inquisitive," Barney states emphatically. "When I hear joyful noise, I know my staff are doing a good job."

Barney's contention is supported by the National Association for the Education of Young Children (NAEYC). The first item on their list of 10 signs of a great preschool is that children spend most of their time playing and working with materials and other children. They do not wander aimlessly, and they are not expected to sit quietly for long periods.

"Play *is* academic," Barney explains. "With young children, play is the avenue to learning." Through play, children learn colors, numbers, and the alphabet in the context of the reality of their world, says Barney.

At Flagstone, which is accredited by the NAEYC, the role of the teacher is to be ready with learning opportunities through play. "As children and I play with blocks," says teacher Annie Hitselberger, "I ask questions about colors and names of shapes, about what is taller and shorter, or about balance. We look for learning opportunities in everything we do." Teachers also track the progress of the child and hold parent conferences on goals and objectives according to the child's internal time table.

DELIGHT IN LEARNING

Recently, the Flagstone children went on an outing to a nearby restaurant. Touring the cooking, washing, and serving areas, the children

This article was originally published in the Winter 1998 issue of ASCD's *Curriculum Update* newsletter.

observed the various roles of restaurant employees. Upon returning to Flagstone, some of the preschoolers gravitated to their classroom housekeeping center, with its small dinner table and chairs, dishware, kitchen sink, and toy oven. While some played the roles of customers, others brought menus and wrote down orders, cooked pretend food, and served it as graciously as preschoolers can. Others took up cleaning and dishwashing. "A total developmental program," observes Barney, "includes academic as well as physical and emotional experiences. We are about finding the delight in learning through play."

Having been involved with early childhood education for more than 30 years, Barney remembers the formal, structured programs of the 1960s. "We saw ourselves as teachers who were going to fill the empty vessels of children's minds," recalls Barney. "But now my philosophy is to start where the child is, because we know that children come with a wealth of knowledge and experiences. If children are not interested in your lesson plan, I think you should throw it out, no matter how good it is," Barney insists. "Forced education is not enjoyed education; without choices, children do not learn to take responsibility for their decisions."

CHOICES

Children in Hitselberger's class have lots of choices. Her 3- to 4-year-olds learn that their classroom is organized by centers: housekeeping, science, writing, art, sensory exploration, computers, and books. Greeted with choices and new activities every day, children begin playing at activity centers when they are ready. "No child is forced to do anything lock-step with others," Hitselberger explains.

Audra Blazey, coteacher with Hitselberger, points out that the most important thing for children to learn in their senior preschool class is to take responsibility for making choices. "When the children come in each morning, they are responsible for hanging up their coats and choosing a learning center." By doing this, they learn self-direction, she says. "In a developmental preschool, the freedom to choose alternatives is very important."

To help children learn social skills, Blazey and Hitselberger use a daily activity called *circle time*. Seated in a circle with a teacher, the children learn the give and take of group conversations. In this more structured activity, children learn vocabulary, discuss the theme for the week, and share ideas. "At the beginning of the year, children are not very good at this," Blazey observes. "But with daily experience, children get used to the schedule, and learn to control themselves. Last week they enjoyed a discussion about bears, sharing what they knew about hibernation and telling why they think bears need to sleep for so long."

Once a week, Miss Ashley, the music teacher, appears with an irresistible collection of rhythm instruments. For all the children who want to join in, Miss Ashley leads them in favorite songs, chants, and rhythms, helping them hear the rhythms in music. "Just participating is more important than getting it right," Blazey explains. "Learning how to listen has to be a risk-free experience."

In handling discipline problems, Flagstone teachers completely avoid the practice of *time out*. Because there are two teachers with each group, one of them can always sit with a child to talk about the incident, a strategy they feel is more helpful to children than punishment. Often, they need only redirect a child's attention away from problems. For appropriate behavior, these teachers affirm children's efforts with expressions such as *good job* or *good work*. They do not say *good boy* or *good girl*.

"We are building their confidence and acceptance of themselves," Barney says. She recalls an incident from earlier that day. "I was watching a little guy painting. First he brushed a big patch of orange across his paper. Then some yellow, and then green. He just wanted to enjoy the colors. Then, he noticed a toy truck nearby, and I watched to see what he would do. He picked it up and ran the truck over his colors. 'Look— tracks!' he said. 'Railroad tracks.' Then he made the tracks go around in a circle. 'No, a speedway,' he said. Do you see how many other experiences he's associating with painting?"

"Then I asked him if he wanted me to write this down—something we do for the parents. And he said, 'Right here,' pointing to a corner of the paper. 'Write: Many Beautiful Colors. And I put tracks on it. First they were railroad tracks. Then they got to be speedways.' As I finished writing this, he said, 'One more thing,' and he smeared some of the colors with his hands. 'Now it's perfect.'

"So you see," Barney smiles, "we are not critical of their attempts. All children should leave here with the feeling that there isn't anything they can't try—that they can go out and just do it, believing in themselves and accepting their level of achievement."

For NAEYC's list of 10 Signs of a Great Preschool, direct your Web Browser to <http://www.naeyc.org/eyly/1996/eyly9601.htm>.

NOT YOUR TYPICAL PRESCHOOL CLASSROOM

ANGELIKA MACHI

A little girl sits on the floor in the block area, quietly constructing a small house with Legos, while three of her classmates stand in the housekeeping area, discussing what to "cook" for breakfast. Across the room, a group of children sit at a table, enjoying their discovery that mixing flour, salt, and water together resulted in a batch of modeling dough. Suddenly, a bell rings—it is clean up time. A noisy bustle ensues as toys are placed on shelves, baby dolls are put in their cribs, and play dough is rolled up and stored away. When the room is clean, children head to the bathroom to wash their hands. Soon everyone is seated at the lunch table, where dishes are passed back and forth and food is spooned onto plates.

MAKING A DIFFERENCE

The preceding scene is typical of most preschool classrooms. However, this is *not* just any early childhood classroom. It is a Head Start class-

---

This article was originally published in the Winter 1998 issue of ASCD's *Curriculum Update* newsletter.

room. Many of these students live in public housing and depend on monthly welfare checks for their food and clothing.

Since 1965, Head Start has been providing services to low-income children and their families. Currently, there are more than 42,000 Head Start classrooms in operation throughout the United States, the District of Columbia, Puerto Rico, and U.S. territories. The Administration for Children and Families (ACF), a division of the U.S. Department of Health and Human Services, which manages all Head Start programs, reports that in fiscal year 1997, almost $3.6 billion was appropriated for Head Start, with an enrollment of approximately 793,800 children. For fiscal year 1998, more than $4.3 billion has been appropriated, with an estimated enrollment of more than 828,000 children.

Services provided to Head Start children and their families focus on the following four areas:

• *Education.* Meeting the needs of every child while fostering intellectual, social, and emotional growth is the major goal in each classroom. Basic skills such as social skills, self-help skills, and personal hygiene are taught, as well as encouraging learning through play.

• *Parent Involvement.* Parent involvement is considered an essential component of Head Start, with parents volunteering in the classroom, attending parenting classes, and serving on policy councils and committees. This involvement helps to empower parents with the knowledge and skills needed to nurture their children's learning and growth outside of the classroom.

• *Health.* The elements of a healthy lifestyle, such as eating nutritious foods and staying up-to-date with immunizations and dental checkups, are continuously enforced.

• *Social Services.* Head Start children and their families have a variety of social services at their disposal, including community outreach, family needs assessments, referrals, and crisis intervention.

CONTINUING THE BENEFITS

The services and experience that children obtain through Head Start allow them to enter public school with the skills they need to succeed. Sarah Greene, chief executive officer of the National Head Start Association in Alexandria, Va., consistently hears from teachers and principals who state that they see significant differences between those students entering school who have been actively involved in Head Start, and those who have not. The most obvious difference, says Greene, is that former Head Start students "enter school ready to learn."

Unfortunately, the benefits of Head Start tend to drop off as a child progresses through public school. One explanation for this "fade-out effect" is the "lack of continuity in philosophy, methods, services, and environment that exist[s] between Head Start and public schools," according to the 1996 report *Head Start Children's Entry into Public School.* To address this problem, Congress authorized funds in 1991 for the Head Start Transition Project Act, which assists students and their families in making a successful transition from Head Start to public school by continuing the services in the four target areas—education, parent involvement, health, and social services—from kindergarten through grade 3. The Act also allows Head Start programs to work more closely with schools in the same community to ensure that the transition between the two runs smoothly. Though the final data for this project are still in the process of being collected and compiled, a midpoint review revealed that extending Head Start services beyond preschool is beneficial to those children and their families who are involved in the program.

Thirty-two years ago Head Start began as an innovative program geared to meet the needs of low-income children and their families. Today, Head Start's services are successfully meeting those needs, and, as Greene states, continues to be "a program that allows *everyone* to participate."

INCLUSION

---◆---

MAKING SCHOOLS MORE INCLUSIVE

SCOTT WILLIS

When teacher Nancy Brant was a college student, she visited her 10-year-old brother at his school. Because her brother had Down's syndrome, he was taught in the basement of the elementary school, Brant recalls, in a room "so hot you could hardly breathe." His teacher was kind but kept him busy doing simple tasks to help other children. "I don't think he was ever challenged," Brant says sadly. In time he was allowed to graduate, but he never took part in regular classes.

Years later, memories of her brother's experiences spurred Brant to find a better solution for another child. As a 6th grade teacher at Miller Middle School in Marshalltown, Iowa, Brant willingly accepted a girl with Down's syndrome into her classroom. To make the placement work, Brant found ways to modify both instruction and assessment for the girl. Brant gave her simpler spelling words, for example, and tested her orally to circumvent her poor handwriting. With the girl's permission, Brant held an open discussion with the class about ways to include her, emphasizing how brave she was to face the challenges of a regular classroom. The other children in the class "included her fine," Brant reports with satisfaction.

The difference between the way Brant's brother and her student with Down's syndrome were taught reflects a new philosophy in how public schools should serve children with disabilities. Today, many educators believe these children should be included in regular classrooms far more

---

This article was originally published in the October 1994 issue of ASCD's *Curriculum Update* newsletter.

than in the past, and that special education must become more integrated with general education.

Who are the children in special education? According to government statistics cited in *Winners All: A Call for Inclusive Schools*, a report published by the National Association of State Boards of Education (NASBE) in 1992, nearly one-tenth of all U.S. students aged 6–21 receive special education services. About one-half of those students have learning disabilities; one-quarter of them have speech or language impairments. The rest are mentally retarded, emotionally disturbed, or have hearing, visual, orthopedic, or other health impairments. These include cerebral palsy, muscular dystrophy, autism, and Down's syndrome.

In the past, many students with disabilities have been taught in a separate setting for all or part of the school day. Advocates of more inclusive schooling, including organizations such as The Association for Persons with Severe Handicaps (TASH), NASBE, and ASCD, are urging educators to try much harder to include these children in regular classrooms at their neighborhood schools. Rather than moving children to services, as in the past, educators should move services to the children, they say.

Beyond Access to Outcomes

In 1975, the U.S. Congress passed P.L. 94-142, a law that guaranteed all children, regardless of disability, a free and appropriate public education. At that time, many children with disabilities were excluded from public schooling—as many as one million, according to NASBE. The new law specified that these children were to be schooled in "the least restrictive environment," to the maximum extent appropriate. It also required that educators develop an individualized education plan (IEP) for each student in special education. As amended, this law is now known as the Individuals with Disabilities Education Act (IDEA).

In response to the federal law, most states have created "categorical" programs that serve children based on their type of disability—and that tie funding to the number of children in each category, experts say. Because children with disabilities are so diverse, most school districts provide a "continuum" of services for them. At one end of the continuum—the least restrictive—are regular classrooms. The next option is resource rooms for part-day pullout programs. Next come self-contained classrooms; then separate schools for children with a particular disability, such as mental retardation or behavior disorders. At the other end of the continuum are residential schools (typically private), followed by institutions and hospitals.

Unfortunately, many states have not considered the regular classroom part of the special education continuum, says Virginia Roach, deputy executive director of NASBE. Many children with disabilities have been placed in separate buildings or isolated wings. Moreover, under existing funding provisions, many of these students would lose supports and services if they were placed in a regular classroom. Thus, funding creates a powerful incentive to keep a separate system to educate them.

To comply with the law, educators should *presume* a child with disabilities will be placed in the regular classroom—with supplementary aids and services if needed, reformers say. Yet, in many school districts, a child identified as having a particular disability is automatically assigned to a certain separate program, says Frank Laski, acting executive director of TASH. Rather than upholding "a strong preference and presumption for regular education," in many cases educators do not even consider that option, he says.

How have these rigid practices affected individual children? For many, they have meant long bus rides to a "center" for children who share the same disability, as well as the stigma of being labeled and treated differently from other children, and isolation from the life of their neighborhood.

When Tiffany Robson, who has multiple disabilities due to a rare chromosome abnormality, was in kindergarten, she did not attend her neighborhood school in Port Coquitlam, British Columbia. Instead, she rode a bus one hour each way to a special program. Because her school was so distant, her mother, Karen Robson, could not meet with Tiffany's teachers as often as she wished. Perhaps most distressing, Tiffany did not have a chance to form friendships, as she lived far from her schoolmates and was away from her own neighborhood from 8 a.m. to 4 p.m. Karen Robson attests to "the stigma attached to the bus that picks up all the kids with challenges." The bus was a constant reminder that her child—and her family—were different, she says.

Unfortunately, the drawbacks of separate programs are not offset by clear benefits. Reformers emphasize that these programs cannot be justified by their educational outcomes, which have been poor. According to

Roach, special education has too often consisted of watered-down skill-and-drill instruction, only loosely related (if at all) to students' IEPs, using the same instructional methodology as in regular education. The dropout rate has been twice that of regular education, and post-school outcomes have been grim.

Special education has done a good job in providing access to many children who hadn't been schooled before—those with cerebral palsy, for example, says Lynn Malarz, director of professional development for the Council for Exceptional Children (CEC). But special education has not done well by students with mild to moderate disabilities, she says. As adults, these students have low rates of employment (usually in menial jobs) and high rates of drug addiction and criminality. "It's taken us 20 years to gather those statistics," Malarz says, and the picture they paint is bleak. "What we thought was going to produce a better quality of life [for these students] sometimes hasn't even kept the kids in school."

Special education is dysfunctional, overgrown, and "incredibly bureaucratic," says Joy Rogers, a professor of counseling and educational psychology at Loyola University. Too often, children in pullout programs fall farther and farther behind, while missing instruction in the regular class. "In some cases, what they miss is more important than what they get," Rogers says.

Furthermore, grouping children with like disabilities can be counterproductive, many experts point out. When children with communication disabilities, for example, are grouped together, "the role modeling for language is extremely poor," Malarz says. Similarly, children with behavior problems learn from each other ways to misbehave.

Special education has also been criticized for placing more emphasis on complying with the law than on ensuring good outcomes for students, says Doug Fuchs, a professor of special education at Vanderbilt University. According to critics, federal and state officials have failed to encourage a quality-driven system. "Federal monitors would swoop down on a school district and demand to see students' IEPs," Fuchs says, "and if they were up to date, the district was deemed okay." Regulators didn't inquire into students' progress—or lack thereof.

Fragmented categorical programs have not been very helpful, according to Margaret Wang, director of Temple University's Center for

Research in Human Development and Education. In large urban schools, more than half of the children may receive pullout services, Wang says, turning classrooms into "Grand Central Station" and teachers into dispatchers. The basic problem, she asserts, is that educators have focused on what's wrong with the children. Instead, they should change the learning environment to allow these children to succeed.

A BETTER ENVIRONMENT

In what ways does inclusive schooling provide a better environment for children with disabilities?

Inclusion benefits these children both academically and socially, advocates argue. The regular classroom environment bolsters their academic progress, because they are held to higher expectations, exposed to more challenging content, and inspired by the example of their nondisabled peers. They benefit socially because they can see models of appropriate social behavior and make friends with children from their own neighborhoods.

Benefits of this kind have been demonstrated in the case of Tiffany Robson, who is now a 4th grader at Kilmer Elementary School in Port Coquitlam, B.C., an inclusive school. Although Tiffany has multiple disabilities, including vision and hearing impairments, she is fully included in a regular classroom, assisted by a full-time aide. She studies modified lessons that parallel what the other students are learning. Tiffany is making satisfactory academic progress, her mother, Karen Robson, says, and she now has many friends.

Karen Robson "can't express enough" the advantages of being able to walk Tiffany to school—where she sees other children welcoming and helping her daughter—and being able to talk daily with Tiffany's teacher and aide. She now has a sense of belonging to the community, she says.

An increasing number of schools are finding inclusion of this sort feasible, experts say. Moreover, recent federal court decisions have sided with parents who want their disabled children taught at the neighborhood school, leaving schools that are not inclusive vulnerable to legal challenges.

"Our feeling is that for children with disabilities, more often than not, the continuum of services has been weighted toward segregated,

Inclusion and the Disruptive Child

Even some educators who support inclusion have reservations about including children who are so disruptive they detract from the education received by the rest of the class. According to NASBE, about 9 percent of children in special education have serious emotional disturbances. Deciding how to serve these children poses a challenge for inclusive schools.

James H. Boyd Elementary School in Huntington, N.Y., has had "excellent success" with including students who are physically disabled, learning disabled, blind, and hearing impaired, says Principal Allan Vann. But students who are emotionally disturbed—and disruptive—have been more problematic, requiring "tough balancing acts" between the rights of the individual and the rights of the group. If a child throws a book or shouts an obscenity, the teacher must struggle to restore a positive atmosphere, and the "teachable moment" may be lost forever, Vann says. Some children who are less severely emotionally disturbed can be mainstreamed for one or two subjects—math or science, for example—but they can't handle a regular classroom for six hours, Vann says.

"Clearly, some students don't belong in regular classes," because teachers don't have the wherewithal to provide for them, and they cause problems for other students, says Peter Idstein of Wilmington College. Idstein has written about his difficulties, in his former role as an elementary principal, in trying to move a child from the regular classroom to a more restrictive placement. The child in question would scream, throw furniture, talk to himself, hit other children and lick their faces.

"Nobody seems to care very much about the other kids in the classroom," Idstein says. "There are kids on the receiving end of these behaviors." Federal law is focused on the rights of children with special needs, he notes, and there is no formal balancing of competing concerns. "Nondisabled kids stand without advocates," he says.

Concerns about disruptive children are valid, says Theresa Rebhorn of PEATC, but there are steps educators can take to include these students successfully. For example, they can develop a behavior management plan that all staff members participate in; provide an aide for the child who gradually "fades" over time as the child's behavior improves; find a peer buddy; or allow the child to take "time out" when necessary—to sit quietly or talk with a counselor. Children who are disruptive can also benefit from seeing appropriate behavior in the regular classroom, Rebhorn says.

Not everyone agrees that good behavior is contagious, however. Inclusion advocates overstate the positive effects of role modeling on disabled children, says Jim Kauffman of the University of Virginia. Many of these children don't have the subskills they need to benefit from modeling, he argues: they don't retain what they have observed, don't know when to produce the behavior, and aren't motivated to do so. And children are often attracted to bad role models, he adds: overly aggressive children gravitate toward aggressive models, for example.

Maintaining Options

Shutting down the more restrictive options for disruptive children would be doing them "a terrible disservice," says Jo Webber, president of the Council for Children with Behavior Disorders (CCBD).

Webber's organization represents children who are emotionally disturbed or who have disorders of conduct, attention, or personality—children who tend to "act out" and are prone to violence. These children are often taught in resource rooms, sometimes with some mainstreaming. The "tougher kids" are placed in self-contained classrooms, separate schools, or psychiatric hospitals. Children with behavior disorders are "hard to tolerate in the regular classroom," Webber says. If they are placed there, "that's going to last a week or two, until somebody gets hurt," she predicts.

The CCBD supports a full continuum of services, Webber says. "Our kids have failed in general education already," and "dumping them back in is one of the worst things that could be done." As for providing these students the support they need to function in a regular classroom, Webber says, "I'm not sure what that support would be." The presence of a full-time aide would probably embarrass them and "set them off," she says. Most of these children need a therapeutic setting, which is typically segregated.

Webber is worried that including these children may backfire. If there is too much inclusion of disruptive children, "general education will blow a gasket," she fears, and, in the backlash, these children will be put in even more segregated settings than at present.

Inclusion of disruptive students is "potentially a real issue," says Douglas Biklen of Syracuse University. But "saying you believe in inclusive education is like saying we should stamp out racism," he maintains: it doesn't mean you can accomplish the goal overnight or know all the ways to root out problems. Rather, it's a statement of one's ideals. The difficulty of attaining those ideals "doesn't lessen the importance of staking out your educational philosophy," he asserts.

self-contained settings," says Theresa Rebhorn of the Parent Educational Advocacy Training Center (PEATC) in Alexandria, Va. Inclusion "tries to help balance the continuum more." When students with disabilities are placed in regular classrooms, they benefit from better modeling of learning, behavior, and language, Rebhorn says.

Many inclusion advocates emphasize that higher expectations prevail in regular classrooms. In special education, the "normal baseline" has become more and more remote, says Roach, because teachers are "so far removed from what normal development is." For example, 4th graders may still have nap time.

"A lot more learning goes on in a regular classroom," Rebhorn states bluntly. In special education, a teacher's focus becomes "very, very myopic," she says. To make her point, she describes a visit she made to the center where her local school district proposed placing her daughter, who has severe disabilities. Although the center had a good teacher-to-student ratio, Rebhorn "didn't see a lot of education going on." One 6th grade class of three students was deep in a lesson on the difference between messy and neat—although the students had physical, not mental, disabilities.

Upholding high expectations is a must, because educators initially have very little idea of what a disabled child can achieve, says Douglas Biklen, a professor of special education at Syracuse University and author of *Schooling without Labels: Parents, Educators, and Inclusive Education.* Some educators feel confident stating limits, Biklen says, but he believes that doing so is irresponsible. Over the years, there has been "a dramatic transformation" in expectations for the disabled *and* in their performance, he says.

Inclusion also brings benefits for nondisabled students, advocates claim. By interacting with their disabled peers, nondisabled children become more tolerant and learn to appreciate human differences. In inclusive classrooms, nondisabled children may also benefit from instruction that is more individualized and from increased staffing. "An aide doesn't just 'velcro' herself to the child with a disability," Roach points out; "she's there to support the entire class."

Through inclusion, nondisabled children learn to "understand and accept children with disabilities," Rebhorn says. Rather than feeling overwhelmed when they encounter these children, they come to see how disabled children are "more like them than not like them," she says. This happens because their disabled peers "aren't visitors; they're part of the class, and they share that common identity."

The benefits of fostering greater familiarity with the disabled go far beyond relations at school, experts say. If a child with mental retardation, for example, grows up knowing her age-peers in the community, other children will know how to get along with her, without fear, Rogers says. Ultimately, this familiarity may mean that she is more employable as an adult and better able to participate in the community.

Regardless of how they feel about inclusion, however, many regular classroom teachers feel ill-equipped to teach children with disabilities. After all, they are not certified in special education. Yet, some experts say, special education teachers do not draw on a separate knowledge base.

According to Wang, strategies for teaching children with disabilities do not "tie to labels." In other words, no scientific data suggest that one should teach students with learning disabilities differently from those in Chapter 1 programs, for example. "Good instruction is good instruction," Wang says. Children who are not doing well in school need *intensive* instruction—a different amount, not kind, of help. The belief that special educators draw upon "some kind of mysterious knowledge base" is "a misconception we have created in 20 years of special ed," Wang says.

Other experts, however, say special education teachers provide help that is significantly different. Teachers in general education and special education may use many of the same strategies, says Ellen Schiller of the U.S. Department of Education's Office of Special Education Programs. A good special education teacher, however, will provide instruction that differs markedly in its explicitness and pacing, in the way it scaffolds the curriculum, and in its degree of corrective feedback and reinforcement. "The intensity is much different than what general education kids would get," Schiller says.

Special education hasn't used the knowledge at its disposal—the scores of strategies developed over time by researchers and teachers in the field, says Fuchs. This failure has stemmed, in part, from lack of leadership to underscore that special education is there to *teach* these children, to shore up their skills. Thus, to curtail special education based on its record would be "somewhat precipitous and premature," Fuchs says. It *can* do a good job.

DOES FULL INCLUSION GO TOO FAR?

While most educators agree that schools should become more inclusive, controversy rages around the notion of "full inclusion" of children with disabilities. According to Fuchs, advocates for children with severe mental retardation typically support full inclusion, because they are more concerned with socialization than with academic progress. Advocates for children who are learning disabled, blind, or deaf tend to be staunchly opposed.

Muddying the debate, "full inclusion" appears to mean different things to different people. To some, it means full compliance with the IDEA; if this goal were achieved, "we would see almost all [disabled] children participating in the regular classroom to a much greater extent than they now do," says Laski. For others, "full inclusion" means placing literally every child in the regular classroom full-time.

Biklen, who describes himself as an advocate of full inclusion, would like schools to provide "a range of options that are always integrated." Speech therapy, for example, can be provided in the regular classroom (rather than in a pullout setting) if the teacher consults with an expert and uses "integrative therapies," he says. In light of the goal of such therapy—to help students communicate better in the classroom—such an approach makes sense, Biklen believes. But he doesn't think educators should be "so doctrinaire as not to allow a kid to see a specialist now and then."

Some full inclusionists, however, want to scrap the continuum of services entirely. As long as placement options other than the regular classroom exist, educators won't have to restructure general education to accommodate all children, says Mara Sapon-Shevin, a professor of education at Syracuse University. The continuum provides a "default option," she says: children who challenge the system are simply removed from it, so the system itself doesn't have to change.

"We need a continuum of *supports*," not of placements, Sapon-Shevin asserts. "Everybody gets in the pool, whether or not they can swim," she says. "But some kids stay in the shallow end; some have a flotation device; some have a raft."

The belief that certain children can't be included in the regular classroom is based on a false assumption of lockstep instruction, Sapon-Shevin says. But by using strategies such as "multi-level" instruction, learning centers, and cooperative learning, teachers can accommodate all students.

Not surprisingly, the notion of scrapping the continuum of placements disturbs many in the special education community. The Council for Exceptional Children, for example, "believes that a continuum of services must be available for all children," although it supports inclusion "whenever possible," according to a policy statement.

One expert who disagrees vehemently with full inclusion is Jim Kauffman, a professor of education at the University of Virginia and co-editor of the book *The Illusion of Full Inclusion*. Unlike the "full inclusion extremists," Kauffman believes schools should include only those disabled students "for whom it's appropriate."

Kauffman has many concerns about overzealous inclusion efforts. First, he believes it is impossible to give *all* children a truly appropriate education in neighborhood schools and regular classrooms. Many children with emotional and behavior disorders need "a much more structured, predictable environment than you can possibly arrange in a neighborhood school," he says. Similarly, children with severe disabilities may need a school organized to serve their needs for physical therapy and training in life skills. Some advocates have gotten "carried away" thinking that regular classrooms could be made truly appropriate for all students, Kauffman says. "The rhetoric has gotten ahead of our knowledge."

Second, moves toward full inclusion limit the choices of parents of disabled children, Kauffman says. If the continuum of placements is curtailed or abandoned, then "parent options are severely restricted." Third, the inclusion movement puts primary emphasis on place, as if there were something magical about it, he says. Special education needs to transform the instruction it offers, not *where* it's offered. "It's what goes on there that's important."

Kauffman is also concerned that some districts may be moving toward full inclusion as a way to save money through reducing expensive special education services. Yet to provide truly appropriate education, inclusion will cost far more, he asserts: More teachers will be needed to provide the same intensity of instruction when disabled students are dispersed throughout the school or region. Given the current fiscal situation in many districts, it is probably not feasible to do inclusion right, he believes. (Other experts, however, claim that inclusion would yield substantial savings in busing and building maintenance costs, which could be reallocated for staff and support services.)

OTHER CONCERNS

Kauffman is not alone in his concerns. Skeptics cite other potential dangers of inclusion: Disabled children may not get enough specialized attention in regular classrooms, and they may miss out on instruction in life skills. Nondisabled children may get less attention from the teacher, and the pace of their instruction might be slowed down. Regular classroom teachers may not be given enough support to cope with the diversity of students and the demands of those with special needs.

This last concern, in particular, has prompted the American Federation of Teachers (AFT) to call for a moratorium on full inclusion policies, urging that policymakers put more time and thought into balancing the needs of special education and general education students.

The AFT's concerns are not based on prejudice, says Beth Bader, a policy analyst for the union. Instead, they stem from calls the AFT has received from teachers and parents across the United States, who tell of districts moving to inclusion precipitously, without adequate planning, and misleading teachers about the support they will receive.

The AFT has "no problem" with each child's right to a free and appropriate education in the least restrictive environment, Bader says. However, the union has "a big problem" with full inclusion. Even with supports and services, not all children with disabilities can be integrated into the regular classroom, Bader says. The AFT wants to preserve a continuum of placements, to ensure the best education for *all* children.

Students who are severely emotionally disturbed or medically fragile, for example, may require tremendous amounts of attention—and may even pose a danger to others, Bader says. Would their presence in a regular classroom be fair to other children? The AFT also has concerns about unreasonable demands on teachers to perform medical procedures, such as inserting a feeding tube or catheter.

Advocates for students with learning disabilities also object to full inclusion. Children considered learning disabled (LD) are a heterogeneous group, says Justine Maloney, legislative chair for the Learning Disabilities Association of America (LDA). Most LD children are of average intelligence, yet many have great difficulty learning to read, while others have "no sense of math." Many have a very short memory span; they are often disorganized; and some are hyperactive or easily frustrated. According to the LDA, in 1990–91 more than two million children in U.S. public schools were identified as having learning disabilities—more than half of all students considered disabled.

According to the LDA's official position statement on inclusion, "the regular education classroom is not the appropriate placement for a number of students with learning disabilities who may need alternative instructional environments, teaching strategies, and/or materials that cannot or will not be provided within the context of a regular classroom placement."

"There will always be some students who aren't able to survive and grow in the regular classroom," says Ann Kornblet, LDA's president. A regular class of 25 to 30 students may not be a good setting for a child who has difficulty processing information, Kornblet says. The surroundings would simply be too distracting.

Yet schools and districts are moving LD students into regular classrooms, Maloney says—all the more readily because these children are seen as only mildly disabled and therefore the "easiest to move." Maloney finds such thinking dangerously flawed. "If somebody can't swim, it doesn't matter if they're 5 feet or 50 feet from the shore," she says. "If they don't get the help they need, they're going to drown."

Naomi Zigmond, a professor of education at the University of Pittsburgh, has studied the inclusion of students with learning disabilities in regular classes. She considers them "the hardest students to do good full inclusion with."

One of Zigmond's studies examined four elementary schools in Pennsylvania that moved LD students into regular classrooms full-time.

(These students had formerly been taught in self-contained classrooms and resource rooms.) On the surface, all went well. Teachers adjusted to the change, and "everybody was happy." However, "for students with learning disabilities, this was not a better arrangement in terms of academic achievement," Zigmond found. Educating these students in the regular classroom yielded academic results "just as disappointing" as those produced by their previous placements.

Another study examined five elementary schools implementing full inclusion for LD students (with in-class support). This study found that LD students received extra help, but they seldom got the kind of "relentless, intensive" instruction they needed to make real progress.

On the basis of her research, Zigmond believes that inclusion is "much harder than we think it is, if the goal is academic progress." The challenge, she believes, is to find ways to provide both inclusive education and the intensive remedial instruction LD students need.

The deaf community has been outspoken against full inclusion policies, vigorously defending the maintenance of separate schools for the deaf. Because deaf children communicate by sign language, the regular classroom is an "unfriendly environment" for them, both pedagogically and socially, says Oscar Cohen, executive director of the Lexington School for the Deaf in Jackson Heights, N.Y.

Cohen bristles at the assertion made by some inclusion advocates that providing an interpreter for a deaf child "evens the playing field." Because the student still can't communicate with classmates or the teacher, and does not have full access to the school community, such an approach "shortchanges" the deaf child, he says.

No research exists that shows inclusion is effective for deaf children, Cohen says. But he believes it ought to be an option. In exceptional cases, some deaf children go to regular schools, he says—to take AP courses, for example. If they come from a supportive family, they can deal with the isolation. However, inclusion *won't* work for many deaf children, he emphasizes.

Full inclusion advocates are like zealots, Cohen says. "This idea of one-size-fits-all is either misguided idealism or cost cutting," he believes. Advocates for the deaf community will keep placement options open only with a fight—"and we're fighting," he says.

MAKING IT WORK IN PRACTICE

If a school or district decides to make greater inclusion of students with disabilities a goal, what does it take to meet their needs in regular classrooms? First and foremost, general and special education teachers must work much more closely together than in the past, experts say. In many cases, special education teachers act as consultants to regular classroom teachers, or co-teach classes with them that include children with disabilities.

At Miller Middle School in Mashalltown, Iowa, co-teaching is the norm, explains Principal Brad Clement. The impetus for change came when educators at the school realized that they couldn't meet all students' needs through pullout programs. "We had more kids with needs than we could serve that way," Clement says. (The school still provides a separate program for the most profoundly disabled children, and pullout programs for children with skill deficits.)

When the idea of co-teaching was first proposed, Clement was surprised at the number of teachers willing to try it. Teachers were surveyed about what subjects and grades they would like to co-teach, and with whom they were willing to work. The collaboration between regular education and special education teachers has allowed a professional dialogue that wasn't possible when they were segregated, Clement says.

Co-teaching is "very, very positive," says Linda Stephens, who teaches at Miller. Students think they're "lucky" to have two teachers, she says, and the stigma of receiving special help has been removed. Moreover, she believes disabled children are getting more attention, feedback, and monitoring than before. The teachers also benefit: they can share strategies and quickly head off misbehavior.

Children with disabilities "feel much more a part of the class," Stephens says. They also benefit from hearing class discussion. Expectations for them are high (even if modified). And these students come to realize they can hold their own—when a nondisabled peer says, "I agree with what Linda said," for example.

In regular classes, children with disabilities "see the good thinkers and readers—it forces them to really apply themselves," says Peggy Lynch, who co-teaches with Stephens. Although Lynch used to be very protective of her class and hated to be observed, she "loves" the co-teaching arrangement. It's more demanding, she says, but "the rewards far outweigh the extra work."

Students with disabilities are now getting much more assistance with their regular classwork, says Sue Merryman, a special education teacher at Miller who co-teaches five classes. "The kids don't even know they're in special education anymore," she reports. Moreover, co-teaching allows special education teachers to have a wider impact, Merryman says. While she used to work with only about 20 students daily, Merryman now interacts with more than 150, giving the district more for its money.

Parents have been very accepting of the co-teaching arrangement, teachers at Miller say. In fact, most parents of Miller students *want* co-taught classes for their children, because those classes have more adult support. And a recent survey showed that 80 percent of students prefer them, Merryman says.

MODIFYING THE CURRICULUM

For many disabled children, teachers must modify the curriculum to suit their needs and abilities. Modifying the curriculum requires "a real shift in the teacher's mindset," says Sarah Husband, who teaches at Kilmer Elementary School in Port Coquitlam, B.C. Teachers are so driven by the curriculum, she says, that they are stymied if it isn't relevant for a particular child.

For students with disabilities, teachers typically provide a "parallel curriculum"—lessons related to what the other students are learning but pitched at a simpler level. For example, in an 8th grade science class studying mitosis, a disabled child might be drawing cells. Or, in a math class, if other students are learning the concept of scale, a disabled child might be doing simple measuring.

Teachers can also have children with disabilities do part of an instructional task, says Biklen. They might be able to "keep up" with some aspects of the regular lesson. Educators are frequently surprised at the skills these students can demonstrate if given the opportunity, he says. "The stereotyped image of a child slumped over a table, unable to communicate, getting nothing out of a calculus class is *not* what we're talking about," he emphasizes.

In general, teachers should use a variety of instructional styles and media, Biklen says. "The strategies needed to make inclusion work are those historically associated with good schooling," he asserts, including experiential learning, group work, projects, and the teaching of inquiry skills. Inclusive classrooms are the most exciting, he says.

In teaching to the middle, teachers have always known they're losing kids, says Sapon-Shevin. Instead, teachers need to provide instruction that accommodates students at all ability levels. If teachers design a rich set of activities around a topic, they shouldn't have trouble selecting which are appropriate for different learners, whether they're gifted, ESL, or have cerebral palsy, she says.

Inclusive instruction is hands-on, participatory, active, and cooperative, Sapon-Shevin says. Innovations such as whole language, authentic assessment, and critical thinking are "part and parcel of inclusion," she asserts.

Many teachers use cooperative learning as a vehicle to include children with disabilities. "You really can't do inclusion in a competitive classroom," Sapon-Shevin says. Inclusion has been successful in the Winooski, Vt., schools, in large measure because teachers use cooperative learning, and because nondisabled students have been trained as peer tutors, says Richard Villa, an education consultant from Colchester, Vt.

Nondisabled students also act as advocates for their disabled peers, helping to plan accommodations for them, he says.

Teachers can also integrate instruction in life skills, Villa says. In many segregated programs, disabled students don't really *learn* life skills because they don't practice them in a real context, he says. Through inclusion, students can really do practical tasks, such as counting milk money or working in the cafeteria.

Of course, teachers must also modify assessment for some students with disabilities. Common modifications include giving oral tests, multiple-choice tests, or a limited number of problems, experts say.

WHERE TO BEGIN

How can a school or district best become more inclusive? Start a working group, Sapon-Shevin suggests—one that includes teachers from both regular education and special education, administrators, parents, and some students. Read the literature on inclusion and visit schools that are inclusive, she advises.

From many interviews with teachers and administrators, Roach has learned that teachers do not find pre-training that poses "what if" scenarios to be helpful. What they *do* find helpful is to see an inclusive classroom in action. "Teachers say, 'Until the kids are in the classroom, you don't know what you're dealing with,'" Roach reports. After the children are there, teachers need time to brainstorm solutions to any problems.

Administrators need to provide teachers with planning time and with opportunities to learn new teaching strategies, such as cooperative learning and peer coaching, Roach says. And administrators themselves need training. Her interviews have revealed that it's the building principal who "makes it or breaks it," she says.

Mike Snow, principal of Copeland Manor, an elementary school in Libertyville, Ill., offers advice for other principals. "You've got to get the teachers accepting of the idea," he says, by providing them with literature and workshops about inclusion, and opportunities to visit those who practice it. And principals must *show* their support, he says, by going into classrooms, working with the children, and handling discipline problems. "Teachers really try," Snow says, "but there's a lot of frustration." When problems arise, principals must help teachers brainstorm solutions and put them into practice.

Those with experience in moving to inclusion "unanimously" advise others not to move too fast, Roach says. She suggests starting pilot programs in a couple of schools, or beginning with kindergarten and "bumping up" the program year by year.

THE WAY OF THE FUTURE?

Many advocates are hopeful that inclusion will become more widespread. Roach hears more and more about districts moving toward inclusion, and some states are revamping their funding formulas to make them "placement neutral," she says. Pennsylvania, for example, now reimburses school districts for a fixed percentage of their students—providing no financial incentive to label and segregate children.

The national debate about inclusion is an indication of changing attitudes, Biklen says. He is "extremely optimistic" that pressure for inclusion will continue to mount, as educators develop models of what's possible and expectations are raised. As eyes are opened, there will be "no turning back," he says.

Whether inclusion will be the way of the future is "yet to be seen," says Malarz. At present, inclusion is practiced only in scattered places, she notes, and it is "not a given" that inclusion will become more widespread. In places where it starts and isn't successful, people will pull back, she predicts.

Malarz's hope is that special education will become more integrated with general education. Too often, the attitude of regular classroom teachers has been: "Those are *your* kids." All educators need to realize "it's *our* kid—it's the school's child," she says. That change would be "a big step."

INCLUSION GAINS GROUND

SCOTT WILLIS

Inclusion is on the rise. Spurred by changing public attitudes, court cases, and the work of advocates, inclusion of children with disabilities in regular classrooms is becoming increasingly common in schools across North America. Yet experts differ on whether inclusion is proceeding in ways that best meet children's varied needs.

All agree, however, that more and more children with a wide array of physical and mental disabilities—such as autism, Down's syndrome, mental retardation, blindness, and learning disabilities—are taking part in

---

This article was originally published in the December 1995 issue of ASCD's *Education Update* newsletter.

regular classroom life with their nondisabled peers. "The momentum has picked up dramatically," says Richard Villa, an inclusion consultant from Colchester, Vt. (Villa is co-editor of the ASCD book *Creating an Inclusive School*, which was mailed to comprehensive and premium members last month.)

The movement to place children with disabilities in regular classrooms is "a national trend," affirms Virginia Roach, deputy executive director of the National Association of State Boards of Education (NASBE). Inclusion efforts are under way in virtually every state, she says.

In New York State, for example, inclusion is making rapid headway. According to Philip Ellis of the New York State United Teachers union, an annual survey of union local presidents shows a steady increase in inclusion activities. In 1993, 60 percent of survey respondents reported inclusion activities in their districts. In 1994, that figure had climbed to 75 percent. By 1995, it had reached 83 percent.

Inclusion "has just exploded across the country," says Beth Bader of the American Federation of Teachers. At first, inclusion was "pushed" by the disability community, she says—but now it is also being promoted by school administrators who want to check the mounting costs of special education.

In this rapid change, some experts see reasons to celebrate; others find cause for concern. Advocates of inclusion point to benefits for disabled children—higher expectations, better socialization—and for nondisabled children, who learn to accept human differences. Critics of inclusion efforts, however, say both teachers and students are being hurt in the rush to embrace inclusion. Teachers complain that they are excluded from planning and given inadequate resources, Bader says. In some cases, teachers have been given sole responsibility for a class of 30 children, more than 10 of whom have disabilities. Such circumstances are "a recipe for disaster," she warns.

ENOUGH SUPPORT?

Ideally, when children with disabilities move to regular classrooms, their teachers receive support in the form of training, help from a special education teacher (consulting services or coteaching), instructional aides, and so on. Of prime importance is collaboration with specialists. Inclusion is forging "a very different relationship" between regular education teachers and special education teachers, who now often work in teams, says Douglas Biklen of Syracuse University, author of *Schooling Without Labels.*

Inclusion works well when there is "true collaboration" between general education and special education teachers, says Theresa Rebhorn of the Parent Educational Advocacy Training Center in Fairfax, Va. When these teachers have "a full and equal partnership" and plan lessons together, that's "an excellent scenario" for inclusion, she says.

Rebhorn's own son, who has a learning disability, is in a class of 29 students, 13 of whom have learning disabilities. This statistic initially caused Rebhorn some apprehension. But the general education and special education teachers team teach, and "it works beautifully," she reports. The teachers' efforts to individualize instruction are "a really, really collaborative endeavor."

Many experts and teachers are protesting, however, that teachers are not getting the support they need. In New York State, for example, "the overwhelming majority of school districts don't provide staff development prior to placing children with disabilities in general education classrooms," says Ellis, basing this conclusion on the union's survey of local presidents. And in 1995, only one-third of respondents who said that training *was* provided deemed the training adequate.

Moreover, teachers are sometimes not even informed of students' disabilities, Ellis says. Although teachers need to see children's IEPs to modify instruction and testing, IEPs may be withheld from them. "Teachers are operating in the dark."

In many cases, children with disabilities are moved from resource and self-contained classrooms into regular classrooms, and the necessary supports do *not* follow the children, says Doug Fuchs, a professor of special education at Vanderbilt University. Regular education teachers are "left holding the bag," he says. "What's happening is not what any advocate had in mind."

Maintaining needed supports for disabled children in the regular classroom is "an enormous task," Fuchs says—one that requires a degree of commitment, communication, and skill that he doesn't see in many schools. Both teachers and children are losers, he believes.

Special education teachers suffer, Fuchs says, when their 18 or 19 students are dispersed among 10 classrooms. How can a special education teacher check on his or her charges and collaborate with all of their teachers? he wonders. Such a feat would be nearly impossible, even for "a bright, energetic one on roller skates."

Inclusion is "happening nicely" in wealthier suburban and rural districts, where there are fewer children with disabilities and educators are "really trying" to make it work, Bader says. But where budget cuts are driving inclusion, "awful things are happening." Some districts are "dumping" disabled children "wholesale" into regular classrooms, she claims. This practice aggravates discipline problems, when children with behavior disorders are returned to regular classrooms. "A backlash is building up among parents of nondisabled children," who feel that their children's education is being compromised, Bader says.

Some experts even question "successful" instances of inclusion. When people say inclusion efforts are "successful," they seldom mean that students with disabilities are making gains in academic achievement, says Jo Webber of Southwest Texas State University. Usually, "success" means that disabled students have been placed in regular classrooms, their behavior is not unduly disruptive, and teachers are not unhappy. Webber is concerned at the lack of documentation for improved academic achievement—or even gains in social skills.

"I do not see evidence of inclusion programs strengthening [students'] academic achievement," agrees Fuchs—although he concedes that the same could be said of many special education programs. Inclusion advocates are savoring placements in general education classrooms as a "victory," Ellis says. Few are asking—yet—what kind of education disabled children will receive there.

SUCCESS STORIES

Some experts believe concerns about inclusion are overblown. The attitudes of teachers and administrators who have experienced inclusion are "overwhelmingly positive," Villa asserts.

Inclusion has been most successful where it has been part of broad reform of general education, Villa says. In many schools, the presence of children with disabilities has sparked other reform initiatives, such as team teaching, peer teaching, cooperative learning, authentic assessment, multiple intelligences, and thematic, interdisciplinary instruction. Inclusion works best in certain school environments, Roach adds. It tends to thrive where there are strong lines of communication and a culture of innovation and reform. "School reform and inclusion are synonymous," she believes.

Inclusion "changes the business of how we do school," Villa says. "If you can send children who challenge the status quo somewhere else, you don't have to change." Through inclusion, teachers are collaborating and gaining new skills—and the benefits are accruing to all children.

Despite the controversy, Villa expects inclusion to become even more widespread.

"I don't think there's any going back," he says. "The rationale for it is so compelling." Rebhorn agrees. "There are too many success stories, too many parents who want this for their kids, too many educators who believe in it—I don't think we'll go back to segregation."

"As a parent, I feel a sense of urgency and 'just-do-it,'" she adds. Children with disabilities "do not have a day to waste."

◆

FACING THE CHALLENGES OF INCLUSION

SCOTT WILLIS

Across North America, regular classroom teachers are facing a new challenge: teaching children with disabilities. With varying degrees of support from special educators and administrators, teachers are striving to

This article was originally published in the January 1996 issue of ASCD's *Education Update* newsletter.

meet the needs of students with physical, mental, and emotional disabilities—students who, in the past, were taught in settings other than the regular classroom.

Teachers are seeking—and finding—ways to make inclusion work, experts say. Until recently, educators were caught up in debating the pros and cons of inclusion, says Richard Villa, an education consultant from Colchester, Vt., and co-editor of the ASCD book *Creating an Inclusive School.* Now teachers are asking, "How do I do it?"

The answers are not simple. "What we're asking teachers to do is so dramatically different," Villa says. "We're asking them to feel uncomfortable and incompetent for a while." Teachers are far more likely to accept inclusion, he notes, if they get strong administrative support.

Administrators can support teachers in their inclusion efforts, Villa says, by providing them with training, listening to their concerns, helping them solve problems, adjusting schedules so they can collaborate, and giving them feedback. Administrators can also make sure teachers get the resources—technological, material, and human—that they need to make inclusion work.

The resources issue is a major bone of contention between inclusion supporters and skeptics. What kinds of resources for inclusion should teachers reasonably expect?

Besides support from the principal, teachers need one-on-one aides, consulting support from disability specialists, and coteaching arrangements, says Beth Bader of the American Federation of Teachers. With such support, a teacher might be able to handle two or three children with disabilities, she speculates. Planning for inclusion should start a year before children's placements are changed, and teachers should be asked to volunteer to move to inclusion, she adds.

Although teachers' unions are protesting the level of support teachers are receiving, which they consider inadequate, some experts believe educators may overestimate the amount of support needed to make inclusion work well.

When administrators implement inclusion, they sometimes provide a very high level of support "to keep the regular staff appeased," says Douglas Biklen of Syracuse University, author of *Schooling Without Labels.*

For students with severe disabilities, "the support services are very substantial—sometimes unnecessarily so," he says.

Biklen cites the example of a student with autism who was placed in a regular classroom. Three adults worked with this student: the regular classroom teacher, a teaching assistant, and a full-time special education teacher (who also served two other students with less severe disabilities). Biklen finds this degree of support excessive. The consulting teacher could have been present for just part of the day, to help adapt the curriculum, he says. The modified curriculum could have been taught by the regular classroom teacher or by the assistant.

One-on-one aides may also be excessive, according to some experts. Although teachers often lobby for instructional aides to work with disabled students, aides can actually be a barrier to inclusion, Villa believes. Aides who act as a "hovercraft" can hinder disabled children from interacting with their classmates. Aides should be "general classroom assistants" who work with nondisabled children as well, Villa advises. They shouldn't just "velcro" themselves to children with disabilities.

Although concerns about support for inclusion are legitimate, some teachers may have more support at their disposal than they realize, experts say. Teachers' colleagues and students may be untapped resources.

Conferring with colleagues may be more useful than training that provides general information about disabilities, says Virginia Roach of the National Association of State Boards of Education (NASBE). Teachers with experience say that "Special Ed 101" courses are not very helpful, she reports. Instead, teachers say they need "opportunities to work with other professionals to brainstorm and problem solve around specific kids." Sometimes the solution may require training in general education techniques such as team teaching or cooperative learning, she notes.

Students are "the most underused resource" for supporting inclusion, Villa says. Nondisabled children are very creative in devising lesson modifications, physical accommodations, and behavior interventions for their classmates with disabilities, he says. One 1st grade teacher, for example, asked her students how to modify a lesson for Molly, a classmate who was deaf and blind. Within 10 minutes, the class had generated more than 60 ideas, Villa says.

GARNERING SUPPORT

Despite these potential resources, some teachers with disabled students simply don't get the support they need to make inclusion work well. How can these teachers cope?

According to Villa, they should create a support team that includes the child, the child's parents, colleagues who have experience with inclusion, and other interested parties. Teachers need to "reach out to people with expertise and experience," he emphasizes. Teachers who lack support should begin by "opening up lines of communication with the parents," Roach says, because parents act as "a conduit" between general and special education. Then teachers should "sit down and problem solve with fellow teachers," brainstorming ways to address specific issues, she suggests.

"Teachers are truly in the middle," says Bader, because they have "no rights in the law or regulations." Teachers need to enlist their unions to pressure school districts to provide adequate support, she asserts.

According to Philip Ellis of the New York State United Teachers Union, teachers who are provided insufficient resources should lobby district administrators for "supports and services as stipulated in federal regulations." Teachers' requests should be specific, he advises. For example, they could ask for opportunities to observe classrooms where inclusion is thriving; for a reduction in class size of 10–15 percent; for staff development training during the summer; or for paraprofessional assistance.

"Teachers have to be the ones to say, 'This is what we need,' and they ought to be able to get it"—whether they need information, training, or an aide, says Theresa Rebhorn of the Parent Educational Advocacy Training Center in Fairfax, Va. Teachers should unite with parents and be demanding, she says.

According to Jo Webber of Southwest Texas State University, a teacher who feels unsupported should tell the principal, "My heart's in the right place—I'm willing to accept this child in my classroom—but I need to plan with an administrator and a special education representative." During such planning, a fundamental question that must be answered clearly is "What do we want this child to learn?" From that answer should flow decisions as to necessary resources, support options, outside agency involvement, and the need for an oversight committee, Webber says.

While holding high expectations for their students, teachers should not hold unrealistic expectations for themselves, Roach cautions. Often, teachers feel tremendous pressure to "fix" their students with disabilities—to bring them to grade level. That's not what's expected, she emphasizes. "Parents expect appropriate programming, but they don't expect the teacher to ameliorate the disability."

Even after the resources issue has been addressed, educators "still haven't dealt with the fundamental issue," Biklen believes. "The real challenge is to get all educators to have an open mind about the education potential of children with disabilities," he maintains. It's universally accepted that nondisabled children need a good education, but disabled children may be seen differently. It's "terribly important" that society come to see a child with autism, cerebral palsy, or Down's syndrome, for example, as "somebody who desperately needs a quality education," he says.

INTEGRATING THE CURRICULUM

◆

INTERDISCIPLINARY LEARNING

Scott Willis

Four teachers at York High School in Yorktown, Va., decided last year to make some connections among their subjects—science, algebra, geography, and English—for their 9th grade students. Using a common planning period to collaborate, the teachers began modestly with an assignment to summarize earth science articles that strengthened students' knowledge of science as well as their writing skills.

Later in the year, the teachers launched an interdisciplinary project focused on the winter Olympics in Albertville, France. In small groups, students were presented with a problem related to one aspect of hosting the Olympics—providing transportation, food, lodging, entertainment, or security. The groups wrote proposals setting forth their solutions, drawing on what they had learned about the geography of the region and applying science knowledge and math skills.

In another effort to make the disciplines mutually reinforcing, Margie Williams, the English teacher, taught vocabulary that students would soon encounter in their algebra and earth science classes. "We knew it had to be beneficial for them to see [the vocabulary words] more than once" and in different contexts, she says. Her English instruction did not suffer, she adds—she actually taught *more* vocabulary than in the past. And when students came across the words again in other classes, "they felt good about being prepared."

This article was originally published in the November 1992 issue of ASCD's *Curriculum Update* newsletter.

These efforts at York High School reflect a growing interest among educators in providing instruction that cuts across the disciplines. Teachers throughout the country are exploring ways to transcend rigid discipline boundaries, observers say.

The trend toward interdisciplinary instruction is "a great movement on many, many fronts, including colleges, national organizations, and state education departments," says Heidi Hayes Jacobs, an education consultant and adjunct associate professor at Teachers College, Columbia University. A nationally recognized expert on the topic, Jacobs edited ASCD's *Interdisciplinary Curriculum: Design and Implementation.*

"Across the country you'll see an incredible increase in the number of teachers who are bringing units of study together sensibly," she says. "It's very widespread."

In K–12 education, the most interdisciplinary activity is seen in the early grades—where "whole language" provides a vehicle for integrating the subject areas—and in middle schools, where teaming has a strong foothold, experts say. Far less is happening at the high school level, where the disciplines are more entrenched and teachers see themselves as subject-area specialists.

The ramifications of linking the disciplines are so far-reaching—with implications for curriculum, assessment, teachers' roles, and the structure of the school day—that Jacobs sees the ferment of activity as "a major restructuring phase in American education."

A RANGE OF APPROACHES

Interdisciplinary instruction can take a variety of forms, experts say, from better coordination between disciplines to a total blending of them.

The simplest approach—sometimes called "parallel teaching"—leaves the disciplines intact but realigns content within them so that related topics are taught concurrently. For example, students read *The Diary of Anne Frank* in English class while they are studying the Holocaust in world history. Or they study statistics in math class while they are learning about demographics in social studies.

This approach offers a relatively easy way for teachers to begin linking the disciplines, Jacobs says. As a group, teachers scrutinize what they teach and when they teach it, looking for needless repetitions, gaps, and "natural" places for integration. Then they make adjustments so that topics are mutually reinforcing. "All the teachers need to be participating here," she recommends.

A more ambitious approach is for teachers—individually or in groups—to create interdisciplinary units organized around a theme, problem, or project. This approach requires a much greater investment of time by teachers, but the potential for making meaningful connections across disciplines is much richer, experts say. In this approach, discipline-based and interdisciplinary instruction co-exist.

The most sweeping approach—sometimes called "integrated" instruction—is to blend the disciplines entirely into thematic or problem-based pursuits. Instead of studying subjects, students might consider a question such as "Is war ever justified?" from the perspectives of history, literature, and science. In a fully integrated approach, "you're not quite sure what class you're in," says Pat Wasley, a senior researcher with the Coalition of Essential Schools.

Education consultant Susan Kovalik is an ardent advocate of this approach, which she calls "Integrated, Thematic Instruction" (ITI). In an integrated class, "you take the world the way it presents itself," she explains. Students take a place, event, or time and examine its environment, demographics, culture, and so on.

"You don't *ever* study things out of context," Kovalik emphasizes. Students still learn traditional content, she says, but they learn it in context, "used in a way in which it really exists." As a result, "kids never will say, 'Why do we have to do this?'"

WHY LINK THE DISCIPLINES?

Why does interdisciplinary instruction appeal to so many educators? Advocates claim it offers many advantages—first and foremost, that it mirrors the real world better than traditional, discipline-based instruction.

"The real world isn't divided into separate disciplines," says Suzanne Krogh, a professor of education at Western Washington University and author of *The Integrated Early Childhood Curriculum*. Young children are interested in the entire world around them, she says; it doesn't make sense to them to say "math" or "social studies." When instruction jumps from one discipline to another every 45 minutes, learning is fragmented unnecessarily.

Kovalik agrees. The disciplines are "contrived ways to give people information," she asserts. "The world operates as a whole."

In short, experts contend, the disciplines are artificial, and they slice learning into fragments that may never cohere. When students are taught solely through the disciplines, they believe that math is math, and social studies is social studies—and never the twain shall meet. The idea of applying mathematics to a social studies question, such as the changing demographics of cities, may never occur to them.

Interdisciplinary instruction, by contrast, "provides connections among subject areas so that students can better understand that their learning has application to real life, to real topics—that learning is not just isolated bits of fact in a vacuum," Krogh says.

"Setting aside people's notions of what kids need to go to college, why *would* you teach in disciplines?" asks Rick Lear, senior researcher for school design with the Coalition of Essential Schools. Although the disciplines have "intellectual coherence," they are not necessarily the best vehicle for teaching students about the world. "If they were, we'd have more kids who were interested in math and science, not daunted by it," he asserts. The disciplines can help us organize our thinking, but they should not be the focus of instruction, he believes.

The argument that teaching through the disciplines is efficient does not cut much ice with these experts. "Efficiency is dependent on effectiveness," Jacobs points out. In discipline-based instruction, the teacher "may very quickly get through material, but the kids may not have gotten anything out of it."

Wasley concurs that the disciplines are an efficient vehicle for coverage—not learning. Although discipline-based instruction has enabled teachers to plow through lots of content, "kids aren't coming out as competent human beings," she says.

A second major benefit of interdisciplinary instruction is its power to motivate students, experts say.

Interdisciplinary themes and projects capture students' interest, increasing their level of concentration, says Krogh. "Sometimes kids are really turned on by a particular theme," she notes. When that happens, "they're more inclined to learn the academic subject matter."

"The kids' attention seems to be riveted on these [interdisciplinary] activities," says Steve Schwartz, social studies supervisor at South Shore High School in Brooklyn, one of 20 high schools working with the American Forum for Global Education to deliver New York's 9th grade social studies curriculum in an interdisciplinary way. Students' attention is greater because "they know class A will impact class B and maybe class C," Schwartz says.

Also motivating is the higher reality quotient of interdisciplinary studies, experts say. Units organized around a problem, theme, or project generally present new information in the context of real-world applications. Students study fractions or research meiosis because a need for that knowledge has arisen—not because it might be useful at some vague future date.

"Kids are motivated by their perception of the relevance of a topic," Wasley says. "If they only do math in math class and never see any applicability, never engage in problems that serve a personal purpose, then they won't invest energy" in studying the subject. In discipline-based instruction, students often see no reason to take Algebra I except to take Algebra II, Lear notes.

Interdisciplinary instruction can also help teachers surmount the problem of the overcrowded curriculum, experts say.

"Interdisciplinary approaches offer a way of ranging over the disciplines without getting tangled in the maze of coverage," says David Perkins, co-director of Harvard's Project Zero. Through interdisciplinary instruction, teachers can "fold together perspectives from two or three disciplines" in the same lesson.

Interdisciplinary instruction can also help bring order out of the chaos caused by the "knowledge explosion," experts contend. Knowledge is growing rapidly, and schools can't just keep throwing more and more random facts at students, Jacobs points out. "Facts are like the chips in a mosaic," she says, and educators need to be very clear about the glue— the organizing principle—that's holding them all together. Interdisciplinary approaches can lend coherence to abundant facts by showing how they interrelate.

Choosing an Interdisciplinary Theme

Choosing a fruitful theme is critical to the success of an interdisciplinary unit, experts emphasize.

The theme or question chosen has to be broad enough that students can find an area of personal interest, says Pat Wasley of the Coalition of Essential Schools. "What is the relation between the elements in the garden?" will be a more productive question than something narrow, such as "What is soil?" A theme that is too broad, however, can be "a disaster," says Rick Lear, also of the Coalition, because, if everything fits into it, the theme becomes meaningless.

Education consultant Susan Kovalik suggests several criteria for choosing a good theme, in the form of questions teachers should ask themselves:

✦ What is so important about this theme that it will promote future learning?

✦ Does it have substance and application to the real world? ("Dinosaurs are dead," she notes, alluding to a popular theme.)

✦ Are relevant materials readily available?

✦ Is it meaningful and age-appropriate?

✦ Does it tie into other units, enabling students to make generalizations and have greater understanding? (Themes must relate to one another, she says. It is a mistake to think "You do fish for one month, then simple machines for one month." Themes should "flow" logically.)

✦ Is it worth the time needed to create and implement it?

Teachers need to guard against choosing themes that will "play well" with students but not yield much learning, warns David Perkins of Harvard's Project Zero. "Sometimes [units] are organized around trivial themes with no depth," he says. As an example, he cites the theme of "transportation," an arbitrary category that "doesn't boil down to much" as a means of integrating subject areas. "Evidence" is a better theme, he says, for several reasons:

✦ It applies broadly to a wide range of subject areas. The question, "How do we know what we know?" applies to all subjects.

✦ It discloses fundamental patterns. Discussion of "evidence" would lead to analytical concepts such as hypothesis, experiment, and deductive and inductive reasoning.

✦ It reveals contrasts and similarities. For example, evidence in math consists of logical reasoning; in science, experimentation; in literature, textual analysis and interpretation. Hypothesis and conjecture, however, operate in all subject areas.

Another important criterion of a good theme, Perkins adds, is that it fascinates students once they get immersed in it.

Students' reactions to themes can be difficult to predict, however. Six teachers at the Fryeburg Academy in Fryeburg, Maine, collaborated to develop units on evolution, power, discovery, and revolutions, says Jan Hastings, a music teacher at the school. When they taught the first unit, on evolution, the teachers were pleased. But "the kids hated it. They said, 'We don't want to hear about the same thing in every class.'" Hastings attributes students' resentment to the fact that they had never been asked to think about the same concept in every subject area before.

Suzanne Krogh of Western Washington University had an entire class reject her dinosaur unit. She canceled it, despite the time and energy she had invested in preparing it. "The teacher has to be flexible and listen to what children are interested in," she says. Themes that capture young students' interest include marine ecology, the planetary system, and space exploration, she has found.

To avoid student apathy or rebellion, interdisciplinary themes should arise from students' own questions and concerns, says James Beane of the National College of Education in Evanston, Ill. Themes and related activities should be "planned from scratch with kids," he believes, by surveying students or brainstorming with them. Such an approach taps students' interests and empowers them as learners.

Those who believe adolescents' interests are trivial or self-centered are simply mistaken, Beane says. Students have "tremendous concerns about the larger world," including such issues as world peace, the economy, racism, and protecting the environment. "They're very concerned about the future."

"We're not just saying to kids, 'What do you want to do?'" Beane emphasizes. Instead, the approach is tightly structured. Whatever themes are chosen should have "major self and social significance," he says.

Instruction has more power if teachers build the curriculum around what students see as relevant right now, agrees Gordon Vars of Kent State University. Vars sees no reason to be concerned if students cite trivial interests. In the hands of a good teacher, he says, even something frivolous can lead to serious study. If the starting point is Nintendo, for example, students' explorations can encompass science, math, social studies, psychology, English, and technology.

(box continues on next page)

Choosing an Interdisciplinary Theme (*continued*)

Krogh confirms that students don't necessarily want to study pop-culture fluff. Intrigued by differences between languages, her class of 2nd graders at an international school in Spain asked to study language roots. The students created charts of languages that evolved from Latin, studied linguistics and geography, and traced the influence of the ancient Romans.

Such enthusiasm comes as no surprise to Wasley. When teachers honor students' natural investigative qualities, students produce sophisticated works, she says. "People like to create their own learning tasks."

Yet another advantage of interdisciplinary instruction is the way it fosters collaboration among teachers.

"One of the strongest detriments to the professional growth of teachers is that they work in isolation," Wasley says. "Working together is a necessary benefit of doing integrative work." Teachers work closely together as they align the topics they teach or develop units that cut across disciplines. "In a thematic approach, the curriculum binds them together," she says.

When teachers collaborate to plan interdisciplinary instruction, "the process is almost as important as the product," says Joan Palmer, associate superintendent in the Howard County (Md.) Public Schools. Teachers who work together develop "a new understanding and respect for other content areas" and a "collaborative spirit," she says. The result is "positive networking throughout the school."

IN DEFENSE OF THE DISCIPLINES

Not everyone finds these arguments for interdisciplinary instruction entirely compelling, however.

One expert who has reservations about them is Grant Wiggins, director of programs and research at the Center on Learning, Assessment, and School Structure (CLASS). While he sees value in making connections across disciplines and is not opposed to the growing interest in interdisciplinary instruction, Wiggins rejects the notion that discipline boundaries are harmful and arbitrary.

"I don't understand this penchant" for breaking down discipline boundaries, he says. The contention that the disciplines don't reflect real life sets up "a phony contrast," he believes, because there *are* disciplines that operate in the world outside school.

Wiggins also rejects the argument that interdisciplinary instruction is, in itself, more relevant and hence more motivating. "Any thoughtful approach to curriculum is going to make things more contextualized and interesting," including discipline-based approaches, he says. Citing the case study method used at Harvard Law School, which is closely tied to the real world yet subject-specific, he argues that better attention to content and context can make discipline-based instruction as relevant and motivating as integrated instruction is touted as being. Moreover, interdisciplinary approaches sometimes fail to motivate students, he notes. "I've seen thematic approaches that leave the student cold."

Wiggins also worries that interdisciplinary teaching tests the boundaries of teachers' knowledge, requiring them to wade into topics beyond their area of expertise. Such efforts can be "a fun adventure or pooled ignorance," he warns.

The idea of interdisciplinary instruction is popular, Wiggins believes, because "it's a seemingly plausible response to a real, perceivable problem: dreary teaching of subjects." What is needed is better teaching of subjects, including the finding of meaningful connections between them, he says.

HOW IS LEARNING DIFFERENT?

Of course, the most fundamental question to consider in weighing the merits of interdisciplinary instruction is how it affects students' learning. Do students learn better when instruction cuts across disciplines—and, if so, how?

"We have known for a long time that students learn more, remember more, and apply knowledge more" when they are taught in an interdisciplinary mode, says Palmer. Students need to see the whole context of what they are learning, she believes. When they do, "they thoroughly understand; they're not just doing rote memorization."

Students' learning is richer when they are taught in an interdisciplinary mode because drawing connections between subjects requires students to do more higher-level thinking, says Ben Ebersole, a professor of education at the University of Maryland–Baltimore County and head of ASCD's Interdisciplinary Curriculum network. "You really have to understand things better to put them together," he says.

Interdisciplinary instruction yields more long-term learning, without sacrificing the basics, says Daniel Tanner of Rutgers University, co-editor of *Restructuring for an Interdisciplinary Curriculum*. Perkins "cautiously" agrees that an interdisciplinary approach could yield better retention, because the more "multiply connected" a piece of information is, the better it is remembered. He also believes that interdisciplinary approaches can foster more creativity and thoughtfulness.

Moreover, students gain two very important insights through interdisciplinary work, Perkins maintains. First, they learn how the disciplines can work in concert. "By and large, in conventional education, the disciplines are not shown to work together," he says, even though "many, many real-world endeavors" draw upon more than one discipline. Even within the professions, the boundaries between disciplines "are not as impermeable as they are in a typical school setting."

Second, students gain perspective on the disciplines: they get a broader view of the subject matter of each, and they learn "how it's done and what it's good for" in real life. This perspective comes more easily through interdisciplinary work, Perkins says, because the nature of each discipline is defined partly through its relation to the others; and the unique qualities of each come into sharper focus when the disciplines are compared and contrasted.

For example, many students have "a narrow, distorted view of the mathematical enterprise," Perkins charges. They see mathematics as a set of routines one can execute, with a limited range of applications: primarily, household budgeting and income tax returns.

Through interdisciplinary projects, however, students can see the discipline in a new light. In studying the Westward Expansion, for example, students could use mathematics to analyze the number of people involved, the miles they traveled, their food and water needs, and so on. By applying math in this context, students would learn the value of mathematical modeling, of using mathematics to characterize a situation—an application they don't typically experience in math class.

The project would also give students a new perspective on the Westward Expansion, he says, helping them conceive it as a mass movement, rather than seeing it solely through an individual participant's story, the way the topic is usually presented.

Sparking insights is the goal, says Wiggins. Good interdisciplinary instruction creates conditions for students to see connections spontaneously, "without having their noses rubbed in it," he says. Ideally, students will have "flashes of insight and meaning" when they "understand simultaneously something about each discipline and how each informs the other." For example, a student might get an insight into calculus from reading philosophy.

Suzanne Krogh of Western Washington University, who in 1987–88 taught 2nd graders at an international school in Barcelona, believes her students *did* learn better as a result of the thematic units she used—although that improved learning was not reflected on standardized tests. Her students learned more about the real world, did a better job of synthesizing learning into a meaningful whole, and became more reflective and motivated learners, she says.

HOW MUCH IS ENOUGH?

While experts agree on the value of making connections across disciplines, opinions differ regarding how much of the curriculum should be devoted to interdisciplinary studies. Most experts recommend striking a balance between integrated units and discipline-based work, to capitalize on the strengths of both approaches. Some, however, take a more radical position in favor of a fully integrated curriculum in which discipline boundaries are completely dissolved.

Perkins poses the "how much" question this way: Should the basic organizing scheme of the school day be a set of disciplines with cross-pollination, or cross-disciplinary enterprises with frequent focused dips into the disciplines?

"It's a very tricky question," he says, "because it's a values question as well as a pedagogy question." To answer it, educators must first decide whether they value "disciplinary expertise or flexible eclecticism" more highly—an issue not easy to resolve.

Deciding the question on pedagogical grounds is no easier. "It's not clear which [approach] would serve the learner best in the long run," Perkins says. "We don't know enough about brain research and the nature of learning to say" which approach would yield the most learning. "I could trump up arguments on both sides."

Other experts are more definite in their advice. Kovalik believes the goal should be to provide students with a totally integrated day. She worries that efforts to pursue interdisciplinary units will not go far enough for teachers to realize the potential of thematic studies.

Wasley agrees that the payoffs of fully integrated instruction are "a lot bigger" than those of a more modest interdisciplinary approach. "I don't have much confidence in disciplines," she says, adding that she doesn't see enough advantages to the disciplines to justify sticking with them.

Like most experts on the topic, Jacobs advocates finding a balance between the two approaches. "Let's get away from the rigidity of the disciplines, but let's not backlash and go to the other extreme," she advises.

Although she believes educators "haven't done the disciplines well," Jacobs doesn't want to abandon them. "I don't think it's a good idea to drop the power of what each discipline can offer," she says. The disciplines are "straightforward and focused." At their best, each offers a problem-solving method—such as the empirical method in science—and a body of skills that can be "very enabling" to students. "Some skills and perspectives are taught well through periodic visiting through the disciplines," she says.

The most effective schools deliberately provide students with a variety of experiences, Jacobs says. She uses an analogy to make her point: Learning through an integrated approach based on broad themes is like looking through a wide-angle lens; learning through the disciplines is like looking through a zoom lens. "You want the wide-angle lens, and you want the focus of the zoom," she says. "You see different things when you zoom in."

Wiggins agrees that the disciplines should not be abolished. A totally integrated approach is dangerous, he believes, because, over the long term, it "equips the student for everything and hence for nothing"—as would learning "athletics" without training in any particular sport.

Another expert who sees value in the disciplines is David Ackerman, superintendent of the Catalina Foothills School District in Tucson, Ariz., who has written on curriculum integration. "It's a long way from being demonstrated that [a fully integrated approach] offers students more than subject-based instruction," he cautions. For example, "it's not *a priori* obvious" that a thematic course in which a student learns some chemistry will be as effective as a first-rate chemistry course. And, he points out, in the work world, people do tend to have subject-specific knowledge.

Educators need to consider carefully which approach will best serve students, he emphasizes. They should ask, "What do kids need to know?" and then consider what curricular structure will help students get that knowledge most effectively. To decide whether an interdisciplinary approach makes sense, teachers should consider these questions:

• If I use an interdisciplinary approach, is there a reasonable chance my students will understand more insightfully?

• Will knowledge from one subject strengthen students' understanding of concepts in another?

• Will this approach enhance the learning of discipline-based concepts?

• Is the content an important part of my subject? Is it something I would choose to teach anyway?

A teacher should look for "cross-cutting ideas with hybrid vigor," Ackerman says. Topics from different disciplines should be integrated when "to treat those ideas in isolation can be weaker than having several teachers come at it from different angles."

COVERING OBJECTIVES

Some skeptics warn that interdisciplinary instruction could make it more difficult for teachers to cover all of their curricular objectives—that important content will slip through the loosely woven net of thematic instruction.

"In the past, that's happened," concedes Jacobs. Some teachers have chosen a theme and then presented "a collage of randomly selected activities" instead of a coherent unit—a shortcoming Jacobs has termed the "potpourri problem." To avoid that mistake, teachers need to structure connections carefully. Units can't be created whimsically, she emphasizes.

It's "absolutely not" more difficult to cover objectives, Krogh says. Teachers should make a list of objectives and then "find ways to put them under the umbrella of a theme." The process is not difficult, but it does require more organization up front, she says.

"Sometimes there's learning the kids need that doesn't fit under an integrative umbrella," Krogh notes, adding that math skills sometimes fall into this category. When that happens, teachers should "just admit it" and teach the content in some other way. "There's no point in being contrived about it."

Integrated instruction is "not a matter of throwing everything up in the air," says Wasley. Teachers still have curricular objectives, such as having their students read the classics or understand how the government works; and they don't stop teaching discipline-based skills. "When you integrate, you don't abdicate responsibility" to monitor what students are learning, she says.

Far from missing objectives, teachers using integrated instruction can reinforce them many more times than in traditional instruction, says Kovalik. "Teach in context and that's key," she urges. If students don't know how to divide, for example, teachers should teach them in a brief "skill shop" and than quickly "allow them to continue the application."

While Ebersole is confident that interdisciplinary instruction can be used to deliver essential learnings, he concedes that proof is lacking. "We need research and evidence that interdisciplinary teaching does not neglect mastery of essential concepts of the disciplines," he says.

OBSTACLES FACED

Not surprisingly, interdisciplinary efforts—which swim against the tide of tradition—face a number of obstacles. One that observers often mention is the lack of time teachers have to plan interdisciplinary instruction.

"The heart of this is to empower the teacher as a designer and writer of curriculum," says Jacobs. Yet teachers may have very little time to devote to those pursuits. (One way to skirt this problem is to use "off-the-shelf" interdisciplinary programs, some of which are excellent, observers say. However, experts caution that "importing" a unit may not work, because teachers will have no investment in the curriculum decisions made for them by the unit's authors.)

Another commonly cited obstacle is the structure of the school day, which is parceled into short blocks of time. Thematic instruction tends to flourish in longer time frames, which allow for in-depth investigations. Yet changes in school scheduling practices to allow more flexibility are coming at a slow rate. "We absolutely have to reconfigure the way we use our time," Jacobs insists.

Nor should it be assumed that teachers automatically know how to collaborate, experts say. Most teachers are accustomed to working solo, and they may find it difficult to give up autonomy to work with others, Wasley says. They can ease that transition through frank discussions and "contracts" that specify conditions such as "no talking behind a colleague's back," she suggests.

The territoriality of teachers can be another obstacle to change. Many teachers, particularly at the high school level, will fight to defend their subjects from what they see as encroachment. When teachers at Fryeburg Academy in Fryeburg, Maine, began to explore linking the disciplines, "the departments were very threatened," says Jan Hastings, a music teacher at the school. Major concerns included the need to stick to the prescribed curriculum and the obligation to prepare students for the next level of instruction.

Curriculum materials can also be part of the problem rather than the solution. In examining social studies curriculums, Jere Brophy of Michigan State University has seen many misguided attempts at integration. "People who put together these curriculum materials are systematically dreaming up ways to integrate across subjects," he says. Unfortunately, they often merely insert isolated language arts skills—such as alphabetizing state capitals—that have "no social studies value at all." Integration is a tool to larger ends, Brophy notes. Sometimes "the means become an end in themselves."

Students can also be obstacles. Some students, particularly older ones, "are highly resistant to seeing the art teacher in the same room with the science teacher," Jacobs reports. Once these students have had a satisfying experience with interdisciplinary instruction, however, they're typically delighted, she says.

MOVING FORWARD

Despite the obstacles, many states and districts are moving forward with interdisciplinary instruction, experts say.

In Colorado, the state department of education has started an "Interdisciplinary Core Academy" to help middle school teachers learn about interdisciplinary instruction, says Judith Gilbert, a senior consultant to the Colorado Department of Education. Teams of teachers attend the Academy and work to develop interdisciplinary units. Gilbert is impressed by the "tremendous amount of time" teachers will commit to this undertaking.

"Virginia is ready to move ahead with an interdisciplinary approach where people are ready for it," says Carol Rezba of the state's department of education. Rezba, who is helping develop a common core of learning for the state, says the common core "promotes an interdisciplinary approach" because the outcomes are common to all disciplines. That common thread "gives the opportunity to make connections and blur the boundaries" between disciplines. "We've spent a lot of time in our schools teaching minutiae," she says. "We have to help [students] see connections."

In Texas, state testing "is becoming much more integrated," says Jan Moberley of the Region 10 Education Services Center, which serves 80 Texas school districts. For example, social studies and science tests now bring in elements of writing, reading, and math. In response to the changes in assessment, instruction will become more integrated, she predicts. (And Texas is not the only state where assessment is becoming more interdisciplinary. "Several state exams have already shifted," says Jacobs, including the New York Regents exam, which now has interdisciplinary questions.)

Individual districts around the nation are also moving forward. "We threw out the [disciplines] at the elementary level," says Betty Shoemaker, K–8 curriculum coordinator for the Eugene, Ore., public schools. Now, the district encourages teachers to organize the curriculum around "major conceptual themes and strategic processes," she says. The themes include *communities, change, systems, power, interactions,* and *forms;* the strategic processes include reading, writing, listening, speaking, and so on. Over two-thirds of the teachers are actively involved in the effort, she says, creating their own materials and moving away from textbook-driven instruction. And, "by and large, parents love it."

New York City has also joined the movement. "The New York City board of education is pushing the whole city to go interdisciplinary," says Jaimie Cloud of the American Forum for Global Education. As a symbol of that intent, the discipline offices at the central board have been integrated, she says.

READY FOR CHANGE?

"We've erred in staying strictly in the disciplines," Jacobs says. As more and more educators work to correct that imbalance, it remains to be seen whether parents, employers, and college admissions officials will accept the move away from the traditional disciplines-only approach.

Some experts are optimistic that they will. "Teachers and principals think parents are less ready for change" than they really are, says Wasley. "Parents just want their kids to come home and say, 'We learned something great today.'" If students spend at least part of the school day learning in an interdisciplinary mode, these experts believe, the odds of that happening will be much greater.

TEACHING ACROSS DISCIPLINES

SCOTT WILLIS

In K–12 education, a field considered susceptible to fads, interdisciplinary teaching is notable for having held the interest of educators over time. After years of discussion and exploration, teachers remain attracted to the idea of integrating subject areas, for at least part of the school day, experts say. And many believe this interest is growing.

This article was originally published in the December 1994 issue of ASCD's *Update* newsletter.

Interest in interdisciplinary teaching is "a wave that is gaining momentum in the United States, Canada, and Australia," says Robin Fogarty of IRI/Skylight Publishing, author of *The Mindful School: How to Integrate the Curricula*. "It's definitely a trend, not a fad."

When done well, interdisciplinary units enhance and enrich what students learn, experts say. For example, if students learn about the Revolutionary War while they also read a novel set during that period, they will learn more history *and* gain a better understanding of the novel.

Curriculum integration has taken root most firmly in the early grades, says Joan Grady, a senior program associate at the Mid-continent Regional Educational Laboratory (McREL) in Aurora, Colo. "Many elementary teachers, in their self-contained classrooms, perforce do a certain amount of interdisciplinary teaching," Grady says. Teachers at middle schools—where team teaching and block scheduling are common—do "a fair amount" of it. At the secondary level, teachers are doing less across disciplines, but "there's interest out there," Grady asserts.

Over the past few years, the focus of debate has changed, says education consultant Heidi Hayes Jacobs, author of ASCD's *Interdisciplinary Curriculum: Design and Implementation*. Today, there is no longer as much discussion among educators about *whether* to blend the disciplines, as about when, to what degree, and how best to do it, Jacobs says.

What accounts for the continuing appeal of interdisciplinary education? The widespread interest is fueled by a number of forces, Fogarty believes, including brain research on contextual learning; state and provincial mandates that promote interdisciplinary efforts; the middle school movement with its emphasis on team teaching; and the whole language movement at the elementary level, which cuts across disciplines.

"Teachers are desperately looking for ways to engage kids," says Pat Wasley, a senior researcher with the Coalition of Essential Schools at Brown University and author of *Stirring the Chalk Dust: Tales of Teachers Changing Classroom Practice*. By breaking through discipline boundaries, teachers can make the curriculum more relevant and contemporary, she says, because they can embed knowledge and skills in real-life contexts, rather than teaching them from a dry textbook. Concepts from biology and social studies, for example, could be taught through a focus on bio-engineering—a topical focus that students would find interesting. This approach also helps students understand the real-world *need* for what they learn, which makes them willing to work harder.

CONCERNS ABOUT CONTENT

Despite its popularity, interdisciplinary teaching raises concerns among some parents and educators. The concern voiced most often is that moving from a discipline-based to a theme-based approach will cause important content to fall by the wayside. Especially at the upper grade levels, teachers fear that the "purity" of their disciplines will be lost in integrated units, Fogarty says. Teachers worry they won't be able to go into depth in their subject areas because they're trying to meet a thematic focus.

Another common concern is that, in integrated units, one discipline will be allowed to overshadow another. Liz Orme, who teaches at Montgomery Junior/Secondary School in Coquitlam, British Columbia, notes that the chronological framework of the social studies curriculum can "smother" the English curriculum, which is less concrete and sequential.

Teachers also worry that one subject will be used as a "handmaiden" to another. Math might become merely a tool of science, for example—no longer studied for its own sake. "English is used a lot as a tool," says Grady of McREL, who trains teachers in a process for developing "chunks" of integrated curriculum. In planning these "chunks," teachers often ask students to make presentations or write papers, but they neglect to include novels and poetry, she says.

Some educators say they have learned from experience that these fears are well-founded. Kathleen Roth, an associate professor of teacher education at Michigan State University who also teaches 5th grade science, was dissatisfied with the results of a year-long unit in which she took part. The unit, which blended social studies and science, was organized around a "1492" theme. Roth felt that the unit did not do enough to help students grow as scientific thinkers. "Despite careful, collaborative planning, I was unable to create activities that fit the theme and connected with the social studies activities while simultaneously engaging students in active, meaningful scientific inquiry," Roth has written. "We called this unit integrated science/social studies, but it really felt like social studies."

Her experience was not unusual, Roth believes. Thematic units often fail to focus on powerful ideas or organizing concepts from the disciplines, she says. In selecting concepts for such units, teachers often choose what fits best with the theme, rather than emphasizing the ideas that are most important and useful within the discipline. As a result, content is "compromised or diluted." Teachers shouldn't just assume that curriculum integration is inherently a good thing, Roth says. They should explore what *kinds* of integration yield benefits for student learning.

Experience with interdisciplinary teaching led Suzanne Krogh of Western Washington University to a similar conclusion. When developing her book, *The Integrated Early Childhood Curriculum*, Krogh took a sabbatical to teach 2nd grade, so she could "try everything out" in the classroom. She was badly shaken when a visitor asked her class what they were learning in social studies, and the children just looked at her blankly. "They didn't know what 'social studies' meant," Krogh realized. In trying hard to integrate content, she had failed to give her students any conception of the subject areas and their meaning—something she believes students should know and understand.

Since that time, Krogh has tempered her thinking about interdisciplinary efforts in general. She had assumed that the second edition of her book would take a more radical, far-reaching approach to integrating content than the first, she says. But in surveying the literature, she discovered a lot of concern (even among advocates of curriculum integration) that the integrity of specific subjects could be lost. Because she shared this concern, even at the early childhood level, she decided to retain the first edition's conservatism.

The concern over losing important content is "very reasonable," says Jacobs, who emphasizes that teachers should fuse the disciplines only when doing so allows them to teach important content more effectively. By providing a context for the knowledge and skills students learn, interdisciplinary teaching can improve students' retention, Jacobs notes. But if teachers feel that a particular effort to integrate content is "sabotaging" their work, they simply shouldn't do it.

Teachers might want to reflect on why they feel that way, however. Often, when teachers begin to blend the disciplines, they feel "a nagging fear that they're not doing their job," says Wasley. Trained as single-discipline teachers, they worry that they may be "shirking their curriculum responsibilities."

This fear stems from the old conception of learning as simply the acquisition of content knowledge, Wasley says. If a teacher believes that students should learn a great deal of vocabulary in Biology I, for example, then using an interdisciplinary approach focused on broad concepts might constitute "shirking." But for many teachers today, Wasley notes, the goal is to ensure that students *understand* what they know. A teacher who wants students to understand interdependence within biological systems, for example, might better achieve that goal by using an integrated approach that pays less attention to vocabulary.

In a well-designed integrated unit, less is more, says Jane McGeehan, a former teacher who now works for the consulting firm Susan Kovalik and Associates in Kent, Wash. Although some topics will not be addressed, the most powerful skills and concepts from the disciplines can be woven into a year-long theme that is relevant to young people's lives, she says. This approach gives students opportunities to *apply* knowledge—instead of just "going through the motions" of memorizing and then forgetting information.

Teachers can't be sure students really understand what they've learned unless students apply it in a different context, Jacobs believes. For example, a math teacher could find out what students *truly* know about statistics, she says, by asking them to apply statistics to demographic patterns in immigration.

AVOIDING THE PITFALLS

In revising the curriculum to focus on themes or problems, how can teachers prevent essential learnings from winding up on the cutting room floor?

Team planning is "vital" to ensure subject integrity, says Orme. When two or more subject-area experts plan curriculum together, "each person is going to protect her discipline," she says. When Orme, an English teacher, planned and taught a two-hour Humanities course with a social studies teacher, she was able to teach the same number of novels and poems as she had in English, but "what we got across was richer," because the literature was placed in a historical context. Now, as a teacher solely responsible for teaching Humanities, she gives "a real English slant" to social studies, she concedes, because English is her area of expertise.

The benefits gained when teachers represent—and defend—their disciplines during planning have been demonstrated in the Bellingham, Wash., schools. According to Peggy Taylor of the district's central office, a committee of Bellingham educators worked three months to develop an interdisciplinary curriculum framework, which is now being used in 75 classrooms.

Initially, the framework focused on math, science, social studies, and reading, Taylor says. It took only "a brief swipe" at music and physical education, listing songs and activities such as square dancing. This "cursory endorsement" did not satisfy some music and physical education teachers, who wanted to see "depth, and a spiral of skills" in their disciplines. At their own request, specialists in music and physical education, and a media technician, have been added to the interdisciplinary committee.

Teachers' defending their disciplines can be a two-edged sword, however, says Grady. Although teachers should protect the content that is integral to their subject areas, they shouldn't try to make their own disciplines dominant. Teachers also need to appreciate that sometimes another subject might take the lead, Grady says. "Next time it might be yours."

Another way to avoid losing important content in interdisciplinary units is by paying explicit attention to standards and outcomes, experts say.

Because teachers in Bellingham were concerned about coverage of important content in interdisciplinary units, Taylor says, the district has emphasized the need for unit outcomes that are well articulated from the beginning. The "driving force" in planning, she says, is to ensure that "critical content" is clearly identified. Otherwise, "you can have cutesy activities, but what do they add up to?"

The process for curriculum planning that McREL promotes pays close attention to standards and benchmarks, says Grady. Typically, teachers select a theme or topic focus, then identify the standards—from their district or state, or from national subject-area groups—that must be embedded in instruction.

Teachers feel comfortable with the McREL approach because it yields curriculum strongly founded in standards, Grady says. Teachers *don't* feel "my subject is losing out," she says. And the standards basis makes the new curriculum easier to sell to parents, because educators can show that it's "not just a lot of fun activities that kids like to do."

Like discipline-based courses, interdisciplinary courses benefit from clearly defined performance expectations, says David Ackerman, superintendent of the Catalina Foothills School District in Tucson, Ariz. Teachers should be able to state, "By taking this course, students will be able to . . ." The performance expectations should make clear the "value-added dimension" of the interdisciplinary approach, Ackerman says, which should "help make the case for it."

Doing interdisciplinary teaching well is very powerful—but very difficult, Roth says. Although she was not happy with the "1492" unit, she had better success with another effort to merge science and social studies. In science, she taught her students about things that dissolve; in social studies, she taught about farming in the United States. Then she pulled the two subjects together by teaching about farmers' use of pesticides and insecticides, including what dissolves in rain water. Because interdisciplinary connections were made *after* students had a base of understanding in both subjects, they were "easier for the kids to grasp," she believes.

In planning integrated curriculum, teachers need to ask, "Is it a natural connection, or a forced and superficial one?" Roth says. "Naturally occurring links are extremely powerful."

◆

REFOCUSING THE CURRICULUM

SCOTT WILLIS

Unlike some other trends in teaching, interdisciplinary education has captured and held the interest of teachers. What accounts for the lasting appeal of interdisciplinary teaching? One reason is that it allows teachers

This article was originally published in the January 1995 issue of ASCD's *Education Update* newsletter.

to organize the curriculum around themes, problems, or essential questions that students find more engaging than discipline-bound instruction.

"It's the natural way that human beings learn," says Suzanne Krogh of Western Washington University, author of *The Integrated Early Childhood Curriculum*. Daily life constantly calls on us to cross disciplines, she notes. When buying a car, for example, a consumer must read about different cars (English), analyze numerical data (math), negotiate with sellers (social skills), and so on. Schools shouldn't always break life experiences into fragmented subject areas, Krogh believes—and many educators today agree with her.

But interdisciplinary teaching represents a major departure from past practice. How can educators ensure that efforts to blend the subject areas are successful?

When planning interdisciplinary curriculum, teachers should be sure to "make it meaningful to the kids," advises Joan Grady, a senior program associate with the Mid-continent Regional Educational Laboratory (McREL) in Aurora, Colo. Teachers should tap into local issues, Grady suggests. If students can see the relevance to their own lives, they will put more effort into their schoolwork.

Grady offers examples of schools where teachers have successfully engaged students in real issues:

• At a high school in North Dakota, teachers of physics, algebra, and English used the school building itself as the focus of a problem-solving project for 11th and 12th grade students. The school had been designed during the early '70s as an "open space"; interior walls had been added later. As a result, some classrooms were numbingly cold while others were too hot.

Teachers asked students to examine the school's heating and ventilating system to discover the cause of the problems, then research and propose a solution. After students had presented their solutions to their classmates, the class chose the best one—which was then proposed to the principal and school board. "Obviously, the kids had a lot of buy-in," Grady says.

• At a rural school in Colorado, teachers asked students to advise the town government as to which of two local industries—ranching or mining—should be encouraged, based on the effects each had on the environment and the economy. One group of students who promoted ranching produced a videotape making the case for raising buffalo instead of cattle.

• At a Texas school in a town having trouble with its drinking water quality, teachers asked students to investigate the cause of the problem and to suggest ways to solve it without hurting the local economy.

Grady emphasizes that teachers need administrative support if efforts such as these are to succeed. "Administrators don't understand that it takes a lot more planning time" to create interdisciplinary curriculum, she says. Too often, such lessons get designed "between 2 and 4 a.m."

Scheduling is also critical to the success of efforts to fuse subject areas, says education consultant Heidi Hayes Jacobs, editor of ASCD's *Interdisciplinary Curriculum: Design and Implementation*. Schools must find ways to schedule opportunities for teachers to work together, and to provide longer blocks of time for students to pursue interdisciplinary projects, she believes. The flexibility or rigidity of the schedule can be the determining factor, Jacobs says: "Schedule is destiny."

Efforts to integrate subject areas are more likely to succeed if teachers learn about group process and develop the skills, such as negotiation, that will help them collaborate, says Pat Wasley, a senior researcher with the Coalition of Essential Schools at Brown University. Particularly at the high school level, teachers can influence others positively and "sail along," or they can alienate others and draw battle zones, Wasley says. Curriculum integration disrupts the department structure of the high school, she notes, and "that's a big deal."

Teachers need to be sensitive to interpersonal issues, Grady agrees. Interdisciplinary teaching may require them to serve on a team with someone they don't know—or don't respect, she points out. And interdisciplinary teams *must* have a leader to provide direction.

Krogh offers a caveat based on her own experience. Teachers who have created integrated units need to realize that this year's children might have different interests from last year's, she says. Krogh herself taught a class of four- and five-year-olds who constantly asked her, "When are we gonna do dinosaurs?" To capitalize on their interest, Krogh spent hours developing lesson plans on brontosaurs and stegosaurs. The children loved the unit, she says.

The next year, however, her students were apathetic to dinosaurs; the subject left them cold. "I was extremely frustrated," Krogh says. "I had all these wonderful materials." Yet, the following year, the class was again very responsive to the topic.

Krogh believes teachers need to honor students' own interests. "Listen to the children: they'll tell you," she advises. And she recommends that teachers not create units that last the entire year.

START SMALL

When teachers decide to blend disciplines, they should "start with something fairly small and manageable," such as a short thematic unit, says Kathleen Roth, an associate professor of teacher education at Michigan State University. "A [whole] curriculum organized around themes can be overwhelming to a teacher," she says.

Roth emphasizes the need for teachers to be reflective about the changes they make. Too often, she has seen teachers "buying into" the idea of interdisciplinary education without asking when and why it makes sense. When creating new lessons, teachers should ask themselves, "Would students be interested in this?" and, more important, "What would they be learning from this?" Developing curriculum that promotes critical thinking and deep understanding is not something many teachers have learned to do, Roth says.

In merging disciplines, teachers should avoid a level of intensity they can't sustain, says Robin Fogarty of IRI/Skylight Publishing, author of *The Mindful School: How to Integrate the Curricula*. Trying always to work in a team of five or more teachers, she cautions, will demand too much time and energy; it will also be difficult to schedule meetings everyone can attend. Therefore, teachers should consider doing "an intense model" only once a semester or so.

"Moving to more integrated, holistic learning won't happen overnight," Fogarty says. Instead, teachers should try "easing into it." A good way to start, she recommends, is to inventory what's already being done at the school—writing across the curriculum, for example—and build on those efforts.

Teachers should avoid making integrated activities too elaborate, agrees Bena Kallick, an education consultant from Westport, Conn. "Be careful not to make a three-ring circus out of it," she says, because if the effort is exhausting, teachers may never do it twice. Kallick also cautions teachers against "force fitting" their instruction around a theme, which she says can lead to superficial teaching.

Public support is another necessary ingredient to the success of interdisciplinary teaching.

"I don't believe the public has embraced interdisciplinary education as something they think is important," says David Ackerman, superintendent of the Catalina Foothills School District in Tucson, Ariz. But that doesn't necessarily mean they're opposed to it, he adds.

One way to garner public support, Ackerman says, is to demonstrate that academic rigor is not being sacrificed on the altar of curriculum integration. The Humanities course at his district's high school, which combines history and English, has clearly defined performance expectations in both subjects, he says.

Allowing students to choose whether they take interdisciplinary classes can also help win community acceptance, Ackerman says, because "reform goes down better when people have choices." Efforts to combine disciplines in his district have succeeded, in part, because "students and families can select a pattern of courses that best matches their needs." Ackerman himself believes that a *portion* of each student's school experience should be interdisciplinary. "To never have a course that tries to break down discipline boundaries is to miss a valuable experience," he says.

Experts are cautiously optimistic that interdisciplinary teaching will become more popular in the future.

Enough teachers are dissatisfied with the status quo in schools, Grady believes, that they are willing to be risk takers; and these teachers are likely to be attracted to interdisciplinary education. "We need to start teaching students how to think, in much broader ranges than before"—including across disciplines, Grady says. "This is the way we need to go."

Kallick believes the degree to which interdisciplinary education will take hold depends on "how willing people are to really restructure." Will schools really let teachers work in teams, give them more planning time, and find new ways of assessing the quality of student work?

Kallick admits to being somewhat fearful about the recent popularity of teaching across disciplines. If interdisciplinary education becomes faddish and is practiced in superficial ways, it could lose credibility with teachers and the public. But "it will never go away," Kallick says. "It just plain makes sense. We live in an integrated world."

MULTICULTURAL EDUCATION

<hr>

MEETING THE CHALLENGES THAT ARISE
IN PRACTICE

SCOTT WILLIS

All students in U.S. schools—whether they are Arapahoes in New Mexico, Mennonites in Pennsylvania, Cuban immigrants in Florida, Korean-Americans in California, Mormons in Utah, or African-Americans in Georgia—should learn about their own culture and the cultures of others. This simple premise underlies the far-reaching—and sometimes controversial—concept of multicultural education.

Why should schools teach more about various cultures? For too long, American schools have presented a narrow, Eurocentric viewpoint, advocates of multicultural education claim. Scant attention has been paid to non-European cultures. History has been seen from one perspective only—that of the victors. The achievements of European-Americans, including their art and literature, have been trumpeted, while those of other cultural groups have been overlooked.

Such a limited view is unacceptable in a pluralistic democracy, experts contend. To correct this bias, multicultural education opens the curriculum to the histories and perspectives of the many diverse groups that form America.

The goals of multicultural education are also diverse. Those most often cited include imparting more accurate and complete information, reducing prejudice and fostering tolerance, improving the academic achievement of minority students, building commitment to the American

<hr>

This article was originally published as "Multicultural Teaching: Meeting the Challenges That Arise in Practice" in the September 1993 issue of ASCD's *Curriculum Update* newsletter.

ideals of pluralism and democracy, and spurring action to make those ideals a reality.

Multicultural education should permeate the curriculum, most advocates recommend. Rather than adding separate units about various cultural groups, educators should transform the curriculum as a whole to affirm diversity and honor multiple perspectives. Social studies, history, and literature classes are the most fertile ground for this change, experts generally agree.

Clearly, multicultural education, as theorists envision it, calls for sweeping changes. How can teachers make this idealistic vision a daily reality in their classrooms? How can they resolve the dilemmas that inevitably arise when dealing with the specifics of diverse cultural groups? This article tries to address these challenging questions.

WHO GETS INCLUDED?

In pursuing multicultural education, one of the first challenges that teachers and curriculum developers must confront is choosing which groups to teach about. Of the hundreds of distinct cultural groups in America, which groups should the curriculum feature, and why?

A multicultural curriculum should address (at least) the five major ethnic groups in America: Native Americans, African Americans, Latinos, Asians, and Europeans, says Carlos Cortés, a history professor at the University of California–Riverside. "You need something from each group to be multicultural."

A group's numbers in the population, however, shouldn't be the only criterion for inclusion, says Gary Nash, a history professor at the University of California–Los Angeles. Although one can allot space in the curriculum by population—so that "Icelandic Americans will get half a line"—that approach is "not very workable or historically responsible," he says. One must also weigh the importance of a group's role in American history.

For example, Native Americans and African Americans both deserve a good deal of attention on historical grounds, Nash says—the former, because they were the indigenous peoples who confronted the newcomers; the latter, because the problem of slavery is "so central to the whole paradox of the American experience."

German Americans, by contrast, became part of the dominant group, like other Western European immigrants. Although they made great contributions, "their story doesn't need telling so much as a distinct German-American story," Nash says. They should be given much less attention in the curriculum than their numbers in the population would dictate.

The question of which groups to study is important but secondary, says James Banks, who directs the Center for Multicultural Education at the University of Washington. The first priority, he believes, is to teach students about *concepts*—such as immigration, intercultural interactions, and racism—using various groups and their experiences as the vehicle to explore them.

Teachers should focus on key ideas, not on single groups, agrees Gloria Ladson-Billings, an assistant professor of education at the University of Wisconsin–Madison. To explore issues of language, for example, teachers might have students study the French Canadians or consider why Americans from Mexico and Puerto Rico tend to retain their native language (many travel back and forth from their homelands). A unit on migration could deal with the Irish, Native Americans, and Chinese, she says.

MULTIPLYING PERSPECTIVES

Educators must also help students see historical events from a variety of perspectives, experts insist. Meeting this challenge requires recasting the traditional curriculum.

The Westward Movement, for example, has been seen by European Americans as "a wonderful expansion of the country," says Dianne Boardley-Suber of Hampton University, a consultant on multicultural issues. The same historical movement may appear very different, however, when viewed from another perspective—that of the displaced Native Americans, for example. The notion of "the West" itself reflects a European perspective, Banks points out: for the Mexicans, it was the North; for the Chinese, the East; for the Sioux it was the center of the universe.

Multiple perspectives should be woven throughout the curriculum, says Ladson-Billings. A unit on World War II, for example, could examine how the war affected the lives of Japanese Americans (who were sent to internment camps), women (who took jobs in the defense industry),

African Americans (who fought in a segregated army), and Mexicans (who worked in this country under the bracero program), among others.

One teacher who tries to present multiple perspectives is Pat Anderson, who teaches U.S. history at Memorial Academy, a junior high school in San Diego, Ca. She begins by discussing Pancho Villa, whom her Mexican-American students consider a hero. "When I was raised," she tells them, "he was a bad guy, a bandit." This cultural contradiction provides "a nice way for me to approach very complex questions," she says.

"I try to show my students as many [perspectives] as I can, as honestly as I can," Anderson says. During a unit on the Civil War, her students role-played slaveholders, Northern factory owners, and abolitionists, and argued their respective points of view. "The kids really got into it," she says. "They're feeling more comfortable seeing different sides."

Opening history to multiple perspectives requires a new conception of what history is, many experts believe. Schools should teach "people's history, rather than just the history of the military and governmental leaders, who were primarily European Americans," says G. Pritchy Smith of the University of North Florida, who has served as vice president of the National Association for Multicultural Education.

Schools need to place more emphasis on social, economic, and cultural history, says Juan Gomez-Quinones, a history professor at the University of California–Los Angeles. "There's a lot more depth and richness in U.S. history" than we've portrayed, he says. For example, the movement for American independence was "more complex and inclusive than the Minute Men and the leadership of George Washington." Schools must take a broader view of who makes history, he asserts.

"There's a vast body of social history" that schools often overlook, agrees Nash, including the stories of groups who, by and large, did not dominate, whose voices struggled to be heard. Schools should intertwine this social history with traditional political history, he advises. "They're not mutually exclusive," he says. "Each works best in conjunction with the other."

BEYOND VICTIMS AND HEROES

Deciding *how* to portray various cultural groups poses another challenge for multicultural educators. This issue is "enormously sensitive," says Nash. "It's hard to [present] history and not offend somebody."

Teachers and curriculum developers need to steer a course between two extremes, Nash advises: "victims history" and "contributionship history." Victims history focuses on how certain groups—women, African Americans, Jews, and Eastern Europeans, for example—have been oppressed and exploited. It portrays these groups primarily as victims and objects. Contributionship history, which focuses on "heroes," is equally dangerous, he says, because it implies that ordinary people don't make history.

According to experts, members of minority groups sometimes want to downplay negative aspects of their history—such as slavery and poverty—out of concern that focusing on such topics is stigmatizing and likely to perpetuate stereotypes. This concern raises a difficult question: Should schools try to counteract prejudice by emphasizing the positive aspects of minority groups and their experiences—or does such an approach sugarcoat history by downplaying oppression and prejudice?

"History is not all positive," says Cortés. Looking only at the positive distorts history. "If you avoid issues like racism, prejudice, and inequality," he says, "you've ripped the guts and truth out of history." But schools should "avoid wallowing in negativity," he adds.

"I've been trying to get away from [an emphasis on] victimization," says Anderson. In teaching African-American history, "you don't have to stay within the slavery issue," she says. She teaches also about black people "who did incredible things"—who were mentors, doctors, and entrepreneurs. For example, she shows her students a film about the publisher of *Ebony* magazine, who succeeded in spite of the racism he encountered. "The kids need to have this kind of model as well," she says.

Teachers *do* need to present positive images of ethnic groups to counteract the negative ones prevalent in society, says Banks. Young children, especially, need to see models of people of color who have accomplished great things. Teachers should help students develop more positive attitudes toward minority groups during the early years, he believes; when students are older, they can also examine more negative aspects.

Laurie and Jeff Chapman, who team teach 5th grade at Boulevard Elementary School in Cleveland Heights, Ohio, take a "critical thinking approach" to teaching history. They discuss both good and bad aspects of historical events and figures—explaining that Thomas Jefferson and George Washington were great leaders but also slaveowners, for example.

Students "want to know the whole story," Jeff Chapman says. "We're not rewriting history; we're making a more balanced presentation. Kids respect that." Presenting "the whole picture" is best, he advises; otherwise teachers lay themselves open to charges of bias.

Avoiding stereotypes is yet another challenge for teachers when discussing cultural groups, experts say.

Using primary resources and authentic voices can help, Banks suggests. Teachers also need to underscore the difference between characteristics of groups and the behavior of individuals, he says. (For example, many Hispanics speak Spanish—but some don't.) While there is "some validity" to describing global characteristics of ethnic groups, teachers should emphasize that class, gender, region, and religion all influence individuals. (Northern blacks can be very different from Southern blacks, for example.) "Identities are multiple; they can be fluid and complex," Banks points out.

Teachers should avoid catchall names, experts say. There really is "no such thing as an Asian-American," Nash notes. Chinese-, Japanese-, Filipino-, and Korean-Americans all have separate identities; their histories have distinct threads. Similarly, Native American tribes have very different societies. Teachers should use tribal names—Cherokee or Hopi, for instance—to recognize that diversity.

As a teacher, "you walk the fine line between generalizing and stereotyping. We all do," says Cortés. "But without generalizations, you've got nothing. There's no way to study a group or a nation or a religion." Teachers need to remind students—repeatedly—that they are generalizing, he says. And they should tell students that generalizations give clues, while stereotypes purport to give absolute answers.

HIGHLY CHARGED ISSUES

Conducting discussions of such highly charged issues as racism and oppression can also pose a challenge for teachers. Such discussions can be divisive, putting white students on the defensive and making minority students feel resentful or humiliated.

"Creating bad feelings among cultural groups represented in the classroom is always a possibility," says Smith. But that is "a necessary risk." If a conflict among students erupts, teachers must help the class work through it. "Teachers have an intuition about how to deal with these issues," he believes.

Teachers can "flow with important points made by students," says Gomez-Quinones. "Young people are much more ready to talk about these issues in ways that are sensitive to one another than adults are ready to imagine." A teacher who fears such discussions will be divisive is "probably underestimating the students' knowledge of the world," he says. Students are already well aware of the problems that divide America.

Yet another knotty problem teachers face is how to treat elements of certain cultures that conflict with American values—for example, the oppression of women and minorities, caste systems, and deeply rooted racial hatreds. How can teachers foster respect for other cultures yet avoid implying that all cultural attitudes and practices are equally acceptable?

Teachers need to be clear that everything they present about various cultures does not have to be tolerated and accepted, says Cortés. If teachers avoid all moral judgment, they imply that "anything goes," he says. But teachers also need to help students understand *why* they are making certain judgments.

"This is something teachers have to bite the bullet on," Cortés says. Otherwise, they back themselves into a corner: they will have to teach that the Nazi Holocaust, for example, was just an expression of Hitler's culture.

While we don't have to sanction all cultural practices, we do need to look at them in the context of the culture, Banks says. *Why* are they done? Without sensitivity to the cultural context, our judgments can be ethnocentric, experts warn.

Part of teaching students about diversity, says Nash, is teaching them that cultural practices Americans find offensive—the "medieval" treatment of women in Saudi Arabia, for example—may be seen quite positively in that culture (as a means of strengthening the family, in this instance).

But there are some boundaries the human race has decided we shouldn't cross, Nash points out. Genocide, for example, has been prohibited in the United Nations Declaration of Human Rights. Teachers can also point out that other countries look to American values as a model. But "we don't say that American culture is better than Japanese culture— I don't know why you'd want to do that."

"Values are relative to situation and culture," says Smith. Students should analyze how different values shape the thinking of people in America, he suggests. Is gender equality, for example, really an American value? Who says it is or isn't? "The analysis of the different values—the debate—constitutes the fun and excitement of the class," he believes.

UNITING OR DIVIDING?

A final challenge facing multicultural educators is to refute critics' claims that multicultural education is divisive because it fosters a subgroup orientation, downplaying and eroding our commonalities.

The belief that multicultural education will undercut unity is a "misconception," says Banks. Multicultural education is trying to *unite* a deeply divided society, he says. The goal is to create an authentic unity— one that reflects all people's experiences—instead of the imposed Anglo-Saxon one.

When carried to extremes, multicultural education *can* foster a subgroup orientation, Nash believes, where society is seen as "various social groups struggling for a share of power." But only a "poorly wrought" approach would focus on how we're different and submerge what we have in common, he says.

Schools must show both our diversity and our unity, which is based on our country's founding principles, Nash says. The stories of people who have crossed racial, gender, class, and religious lines to stand shoulder to shoulder in support of those principles are "some of the most exciting stories" in our history, he asserts.

Multicultural education "is really the only kind of education that is truly democratic and pluralistic," says Smith. "I'm somewhat astounded that people are threatened by it." He adds simply, "It makes good democratic sense."

Choosing Multicultural Literature

Scott Willis

No area of the curriculum lends itself more readily to a multicultural approach than the teaching of literature. Teachers can present diverse perspectives simply by choosing literature written by—and about—people from a variety of cultural groups. Nevertheless, schools still place too much emphasis on the English and European-American works traditionally taught, some believe.

American teachers "continue to [assign] the same titles over and over," charges Joan Cone, an English teacher at El Cerrito High School in Richmond, Calif. While Cone agrees that classroom perennials such as Shakespeare, Dickens, and Salinger are worth reading, she believes teachers should also introduce students to authors such as Amy Tan, Richard Rodriguez, Isaac Bashevis Singer, and Toni Morrison.

"We keep making white European males the model," she says. "What about Latino or Jewish students, if they never see their cultures represented?"

Children need to "see themselves" in books, affirms Pat Crook of the University of Virginia, an expert on children's literature. "It's very important to attend to that first." Teachers can give *all* students that experience more easily today, she says, because "we're allowing people other than the white middle class to be characters in books."

Children's literature has become very multicultural, Crook says. Folk tales, for example, are no longer limited to those of Europe; publishers are offering "lots of wonderful ones from Africa and China that kids love." Good historical fiction is also available, such as Elizabeth Speare's *The Sign of the Beaver,* a book for 5th graders about the clash between Native Americans and whites. Other books convey an inspiring message, such as

This article was originally published in the September 1993 issue of ASCD's *Curriculum Update* newsletter.

Mary Hoffman's *Amazing Grace,* which tells of a black girl who lands the role of Peter Pan in a school play.

THE QUALITY QUESTION

"It's good that we're getting away from a restrictive and fixed set of texts," says Peter Smagorinsky of the University of Oklahoma, who has written about the ethical problems teachers face in selecting literature. But he warns against trying to include every discrete cultural group—a task he deems impossible. And, he adds, if teachers focus on inclusiveness, they may "lose sight" of the quality of the literature.

The question of literary quality is often raised in discussions of multicultural literature. Will the literary quality of the canon be compromised if some "classics" are displaced by works added in the name of diversity? Most advocates stoutly answer, "No."

"Go to a good bookstore these days," says Cone. "There's wonderful literature being written" by authors of many cultures. "I'm able to find enough [diverse] books of good literary quality," Crook reports, adding, "That's a must."

Others sound a note of caution. Including diverse voices can conflict with teaching top-quality literature, says Sandra Stotsky of Harvard University, if educators insist on a strict formula of inclusion. "If you teach a work from every group at every grade level, you'll teach some bad literature," she predicts. She also advises against "dredging up" mediocre works simply to represent a certain group during a certain era. If no first-class works exist, teachers should discuss *why* rather than "falsify history," she believes.

BALANCED PORTRAYALS

To avoid stereotyping, teachers should ensure that portrayals of any group are both varied and balanced, experts agree. Providing a variety of portrayals is important so that single works of literature are not presented—either overtly or by implication—as representative of a group's characteristics or experiences. In choosing books about family life, for example, a teacher shouldn't make Alice Walker's *The Color Purple*, which includes elements of incest and wife beating, the only novel about African Americans. If teachers must choose a single book about a cultural group, they should be careful to avoid a portrayal that is "on the fringe," says James Banks of the University of Washington.

"There's also diversity *within* cultures," Crook points out. If teachers want their students to learn about Native Americans, for example, they must examine various tribes, which can differ widely. "You can't just give kids little Thanksgiving books" that portray "the Indians" in a generic form, she says.

Providing a balance of positive and negative portrayals is equally important if teachers are to avoid stereotyping, such as casting a group solely in a victim or oppressor role, experts say.

In the past, portrayals of the African-American experience have been primarily negative, says Michele Bajek, language arts supervisor for the Arlington, Va., public schools. In fact, blacks were so persistently portrayed as poor that when one class in her district read Steinbeck's *Of Mice and Men,* the students assumed the characters were black. Today, the Arlington schools avoid such one-sided treatment. Besides showing students the negative effects of prejudice, they make "a conscious effort" to provide images of blacks succeeding, Bajek says.

Similarly, teachers should take care with works that single out whites as villains, Stotsky says. If teachers assign *The Bluest Eye* by Toni Morrison, for example, in which "all the white characters are despicable," then they need to discuss that depiction with students and help them think critically about it. Ideally, students should see balance in characters and some positive interracial relationships, especially during the K–8 years, Stotsky says. "You want [students] to develop healthy attitudes," including respect for other groups as well as for their own.

Teachers need to let students see a range of possibilities within a cultural group and make their own judgments, agrees Smagorinsky. Yet he concedes that providing the right balance of portrayals can be difficult. He himself used to teach Richard Wright's *Native Son,* "a pretty horrific view of black experience." In retrospect, he believes he should have balanced that bleak vision by teaching a more upbeat work about African Americans as well.

STUDENTS' RESPONSES

Teachers of multicultural literature also need to be sensitive to the ways different students may react to different works, experts say. For example, teachers should think carefully before assigning a book whose characters express overwhelmingly bigoted views—such as *Huckleberry Finn,* a book many consider the great American novel.

Teaching the Twain classic caused Smagorinsky misgivings. Although Twain's intent is to condemn racist thinking, *Huck Finn* became "emotionally difficult" for him to teach, he says, when he saw how hurt his black students were by its expressions of bigotry, including use of the word "nigger." Some students found the book "devastating"—even though they understood Twain's use of irony, he says.

While many white teachers say black students shouldn't be offended by *Huck Finn,* Smagorinsky finds that attitude facile. He draws an analogy to the Spike Lee film, *Do the Right Thing,* noting that many white people called the filmmaker racist for the way he depicted black-white relations. "Whites cannot create the same emotional distance from the movie" that they expect black students to create when studying *Huck Finn,* he believes.

Despite the sensitive nature of the issues, students themselves have a great ability to make sense of literature that raises thorny cultural questions, Cone has found. "They're sophisticated readers."

After students read a work, she asks them to write down their reactions before discussing them with the rest of the class. Then, during discussions, she herself remains quiet, refusing to act as moral arbiter. "Kids call each other on their misreadings and their cultural biases," she says.

Students' responses to unfamiliar literary devices can also be problematic for teachers. For example, students sometimes mock the elements of magic in Hispanic literature. "Kids'll say, 'This is really dumb,' when a character floats up to heaven," Bajek notes. Teachers need to help students understand the significance of such devices—in this case, the religious overtones and symbolism.

WHO CHOOSES?

Of course, whether or not students read multicultural literature may depend on who has the power to select what books are taught.

According to Stotsky, classroom literature is selected in "extremely varied" ways. Some school boards exert heavy influence; others do not. Many teachers must select from a list of required works. At some schools, however, especially "progressive" high schools, teachers have almost unlimited choice.

Teachers must feel free to discuss the relative merits of literature selections openly, Stotsky says. Too often, teachers hesitate to question non-traditional works out of fear that they will be accused of being sexist, racist, or homophobic. "Many of the issues simply aren't discussable," she says.

Students themselves should be given more power of choice over what they read, Cone believes. "For too long the choice of books has been in the hands of teachers and university people," she says. "We can open up the canon more quickly by allowing more student choice."

Empowering students will also help them become self-motivated readers, she contends. Too many students don't read willingly, she says. "Somehow we've got to invite them in. They can't just be the receptacles of our choices." When given some guidance, "kids truly choose to read good books," she asserts.

Cone has her students ask their parents, peers, and other teachers to recommend books; then they choose from among the suggestions. (She does reserve veto power, however.) To create a community of readers, she asks her students to choose a book about a culture they identify with and then convince three other students to read it with them. She also asks students to choose books about groups they *don't* identify with, "so a black kid will read about Koreans," for example.

How can teachers learn what good multicultural literature is available? Teachers need well-stocked school libraries, Crook says, adding that "rural districts often have scant resources."

To encourage teachers to become familiar with more diverse works, the Arlington public schools used central office funds to create a traveling library, Bajek says. About 30 books covering a variety of cultures, for all grade levels, were rotated among the schools, giving all teachers an opportunity to read them.

Then, using funds saved through keeping (rather than replacing) a grammar book, the district gave each school $5,000 to buy student copies of books from the traveling library. "Now we have a much better representation in our schools' literature of the cultures we have in Arlington and in the United States," Bajek says.

Cone emphasizes the need for teachers to educate themselves. "The average teacher has to read widely," she says, and teachers need to nurture each other. A core of teachers in her school have agreed to try new books and share suggestions. "We're always looking for new writers."

Teachers without such a network, she advises, should go to a good bookstore (not one of the ubiquitous chains) and ask a salesperson: "What's a good book about a modern dilemma that involves Native Americans (for example)?" Bookstore employees can be a wonderful resource, she says. "Those people love books."

Like other advocates of multicultural literature, Cone emphasizes that the benefits of including diverse voices far outweigh any missteps made in pursuit of that goal. "In integrating new writers into our classes, we're going to make some mistakes," she says. "But it would be much more of a mistake to omit those people" from the curriculum, she believes. "Our American identity becomes enriched by including our diversity."

"This is new ground," she says. "We don't quite know what we're doing. But we're headed in the right direction."

TEACHING STRATEGIES FOR MULTICULTURAL EDUCATION

SCOTT WILLIS

Multicultural education isn't just about *what* students are taught, many experts believe. It also concerns *how* students are taught.

This article was originally published as "Multicultural Teaching Strategies" in the September 1993 issue of ASCD's *Curriculum Update* newsletter.

Teachers need to practice "an equity pedagogy," says James Banks of the University of Washington. To help diverse students achieve, teachers should use "a variety of teaching styles that are consistent with the wide range of learning styles within various cultural and ethnic groups," Banks has written. For example, teachers should be "demanding but highly personalized when working with . . . Native American and Inuit students, and [use] cooperative learning techniques in math and science instruction to enhance the academic achievement of students of color."

Do students from different cultures really learn differently? Not all experts agree, but many are persuaded that valid generalizations can be made.

"Socialization within a particular culture shapes a student's idea of what is important to learn, and of how to go about learning it," says G. Pritchy Smith of the University of North Florida. For example, "some cultures condition children to approach the structure of knowledge holistically rather than in small, separate parts." Students from these cultures are placed at a disadvantage because schools tend to emphasize breaking knowledge into parts (analysis) over seeing the relationship among parts (synthesis).

Cultural learning styles also affect what type of classroom interactions students prefer. For example, Hispanic students tend to be field-sensitive learners, Smith says. The social context of the classroom is important to these students; they learn best when they have a personal relationship with the teacher and can interact with peers. Most American schools, however, are geared to field-independent learners: students who work well on their own and tend not to involve their emotions in learning academic content.

VISUAL, ORAL, TACTILE

Different ethnic groups *do*, by and large, prefer certain teaching strategies, agrees Dianne Boardley-Suber of Hampton University. African-American students, for example, respond better to collaborative, hands-on approaches, she says. "This is something we've known instinctively for years." (But she warns against overgeneralizing: "You can't say *all* African-American students learn best a certain way.") To accommodate students' cultural differences, teachers should use a variety of visual, oral, and tactile approaches, she advises.

Laurie and Jeff Chapman, 5th grade teachers at Boulevard Elementary School in Cleveland Heights, Ohio, are converts to the view that culture affects learning style. When first exposed to learning styles theory through staff development training at Kent State University, they were dubious. "I resisted it at first," says Jeff Chapman. "It bordered on sounding racist."

But in time they became convinced. They "threw out" a textbook that fostered a linear, skill-based approach, which harmed some students, Laurie Chapman says. (In Asian and Native American cultures, she notes, learning is not linear but "circular.") Now when teaching, they both place more emphasis on oral discourse and active learning—changes that have been "really beneficial to many of our white kids as well," Jeff Chapman says.

CULTURALLY RELEVANT TEACHING

Content issues are "only the tip of the iceberg" of multicultural education, says Gloria Ladson-Billings of the University of Wisconsin-Madison. Unless teachers modify their teaching strategies, changes to the curriculum won't ensure success for all students, she believes. "The students [who were] failing U.S. history are now failing black history," she notes wryly.

While she "stays away" from learning styles, Ladson-Billings promotes the concept of "culturally relevant teaching," which has three main concerns:

• *How teachers see themselves and their students.* Do they see their African-American students, for example, as "the sons and daughters of slaves or as potential doctors and lawyers"?

• *How teachers structure social relations in the classroom.* Teachers must be willing to share their power and allow students' input into decisions, she believes. (Some urban teachers' over-riding concern is "to get these kids under control," she says.)

• *How teachers conceive knowledge.* Teachers should hold that "what is true" is always open to challenge, not fixed or static. "Knowledge is not dropped out of heaven into textbooks," she says. Students should be empowered "to bring knowledge to the classroom, to say 'That's not true' when something doesn't jibe with their own experiences."

To adapt instruction to students' cultural backgrounds, teachers should relate new content to students' own experiences, emphasizes Carl Grant of the University of Wisconsin–Madison. For example, teachers should "start teaching science from the students' point of view," by showing them how science affects their lives. Science is typically taught in a way that "mystifies the concepts," Grant alleges. He cites the instance of a teacher he observed who taught a lesson on the step-down transformer using a diagram. The teacher never thought to point out the window at a transformer that was within plain sight.

ONE MORE LABEL?

While he admits that "the body of hard research that undergirds the concept of cultural learning styles is [only] in the developmental stage," Smith believes the theoretical base is well enough established to warrant discussing the concept in teacher education courses.

But he notes one important caveat. "Some educators fear that cultural learning styles will become one more label of inferiority for non-whites, one more cause for segregating students," he says. Multicultural educators must guard against this unintended outcome, he believes, as they work to equalize opportunities for success for all students.

MULTIPLE INTELLIGENCES

◆

THE WELL-ROUNDED CLASSROOM

SCOTT WILLIS

Sandy, an elementary student, is struggling with the concept of multiplication. Because she is talented in art, her teacher asks her to create visual representations of the times tables. Sandy dives into the task with relish, drawing configurations of objects to depict "two times two," "two times three," and so on. When she is finished, she understands multiplication, because the concept has been expressed through visual images.

In tapping Sandy's visual-spatial intelligence, her teacher is applying the theory of multiple intelligences, which Harvard psychologist Howard Gardner set forth 11 years ago in his book *Frames of Mind*. Gardner argued that our traditional conception of intelligence—as primarily linguistic and logical abilities—is too narrow, and that all human beings actually have seven distinct intelligences.

Some educators who find Gardner's theory intuitively appealing are working to address all seven intelligences in their classrooms. Doing so helps students become more well-rounded, makes school more engaging and motivating, and enables more students to succeed, these educators say.

By cultivating a broad range of intelligences, teachers can uncover hidden strengths among students who don't shine at verbal or mathematical tasks. Similarly, students who are gifted in a paper-and-pencil environment may be weak in other areas, such as bodily-kinesthetic, spatial, or interpersonal skills. Teachers should nurture all students' strengths and challenge them in areas where they are less developed, says Thomas

---

This article was originally published in the October 1994 issue of ASCD's *Update* newsletter.

Armstrong, an education consultant and author of ASCD's *Multiple Intelligences in the Classroom.*

There is no recipe for applying the theory of multiple intelligences. Gardner himself considers his theory "a Rorschach blot," because educators can draw diametrically opposed conclusions from it. Some might choose to identify students' strengths and focus on nurturing them; others might identify weaknesses and work to shore them up; still others might give equal time to all seven intelligences. Although Gardner does not endorse any particular approach, he urges educators to take the differences among their students "very seriously." Get a lot of detailed, personal knowledge about how children's minds work—then use it to guide instruction, he advises. "Don't treat everybody the same."

A self-described "purist," Bruce Campbell, a teacher and staff developer in the Marysville (Wash.) schools, weaves all seven intelligences into everything he teaches in his nongraded elementary classroom. In teaching about photosynthesis, for example, Campbell might have his students read about the concept (linguistic), use diagrams (spatial), analyze the sequence of the process (logical-mathematical), dramatize the process or manipulate fact cards (bodily-kinesthetic), create a song about it (musical), work in groups (interpersonal), and do a reflective activity, such as comparing photosynthesis to a change in their own lives (intrapersonal).

To make this approach feasible, Campbell has created seven centers in his classroom, each focused on one intelligence. Students rotate through the centers for half of each day. Campbell emphasizes that he organizes the curriculum around themes. Teaching the traditional curriculum in all seven ways "would take 100 years," he says.

Dee Patrick, a teacher at Russell Elementary School in Lexington, Ky., also uses centers to help her students develop all seven intelligences. Five or six children work at each center for about 35–40 minutes, then rotate to the next. The centers are named after famous figures who exemplify the intelligences, including Martin Luther King Jr. (interpersonal) and Leonardo da Vinci (spatial).

Like Campbell, Patrick uses a thematic approach. In learning about outer space, for example, her students might design a constellation pattern (spatial), simulate walking on the moon (bodily-kinesthetic), and reflect on the Challenger disaster (intrapersonal). Students love working at the centers, Patrick says, and many strengths are revealed when they do.

Addressing multiple intelligences "provides more students with opportunities for success," Campbell says. Among his students, he sees "different kinds of leadership emerging spontaneously" as children identify their own strengths and those of others. Some students are learning much better, he believes—those whose strengths do not lie in the linguistic or logical areas. And students are more accepting of one another.

One boy who had poor basic skills, low self-esteem, and no friends was transformed after other students realized he had "a remarkable propensity" for music, Campbell relates. As the boy began to use his new-found musical ability, his popularity and self-esteem rose. With a new, positive attitude toward school, he made strides in other areas, including reading and writing.

Recognizing multiple intelligences gives every student "the feeling of success," says Rhonda Flanery, another Russell Elementary teacher who uses intelligence centers. Because her class is not tracked into "the dummies, the okays, and the smarties," her students are less competitive and more willing to cooperate and share, she adds.

Teachers should not feel they have to work all seven intelligences into every lesson; such an approach is too rigid, says Linda Campbell of Antioch University, primary author of *Teaching and Learning Through Multiple Intelligences.* Incorporating even four intelligences into a lesson can be "a stretch," she believes. "You need some depth; otherwise teaching becomes cute and fluffy."

Teachers should not assume that all seven intelligences can be used to teach everything, Gardner cautions. In considering potential learning activities, teachers must ask first, "Is it sensible?" and second, "Does it work?"

USING PROJECTS

While some teachers use centers, others apply Gardner's theory through interdisciplinary projects that call on students to use several intelligences.

Seven Ways to Be Smart

According to Howard Gardner's theory of multiple intelligences, all people possess seven distinct sets of capabilities. Gardner emphasizes that these intelligences work in concert, not in isolation. The seven intelligences are:

Spatial: The ability to perceive the visual-spatial world accurately and to perform transformations upon one's perceptions. This intelligence is highly developed in hunters, scouts, guides, interior designers, architects, artists, and inventors.

Bodily-Kinesthetic: Expertise in using one's whole body to express ideas and feelings and facility in using one's hands to produce or transform things. Highly developed in actors, mimes, athletes, dancers, craftspersons, sculptors, mechanics, and surgeons.

Musical: The capacity to perceive, discriminate, transform, and express musical forms. Highly developed in musical performers, aficionados, and critics.

Linguistic: The capacity to use words effectively, either orally or in writing. Highly developed in story-tellers, orators, politicians, poets, playwrights, editors, and journalists.

Logical-Mathematical: The capacity to use numbers effectively and to reason well. Highly developed in mathematicians, tax accountants, statisticians, scientists, computer programmers, and logicians.

Interpersonal: The ability to perceive and make distinctions in the moods, intentions, motivations, and feelings of other people. This intelligence can include sensitivity to facial expressions, voice, and gestures, as well as the ability to respond effectively to such cues—to influence other people, for example.

Intrapersonal: Self-knowledge and the ability to act adaptively on the basis of that knowledge. This intelligence includes having an accurate picture of one's strengths and limitations, awareness of one's moods and motivations, and the capacity for self-discipline.

Adapted from the ASCD book *Multiple Intelligences in the Classroom* by Thomas Armstrong.

At Skyview Junior High School in Bothell, Wash., 7th grade students study an integrated unit called "Genetics: Who Am I?" Science and math are the primary focus, teacher Jeff DeGallier explains, but the three-week unit also incorporates art, music, and other activities, "to hit all the intelligences at least once."

Besides reading about genetics, students observe a simulation of pulling apart strands of DNA, write essays and poems on "nature vs. nurture," and create murals to express their identities. In math, students study probability to explore variation among traits—examining questions such as "What is the chance of having blue eyes?"

Teachers at Lincoln High School in Stockton, Calif., use a project-based approach that integrates science, social science, and language arts, says Pam Martin, a science teacher at the school. Teachers insist that students develop areas of weakness as well as capitalize on their strengths. "We emphasize students' looking at themselves holistically," Martin says.

One Lincoln student researched the antidepressant Prozac. She interviewed professors of pharmacology, created a dance that expressed the drug's effect on mood, and—to stretch herself in a weak area—spoke on the topic before a group. Another student studied caffeine. He extracted it in a chemical experiment, wrote about its role in our culture, and created a musical medley to convey the sensation of drinking one's first cup of coffee in the morning.

When schools honor multiple intelligences, students achieve more overall because they can draw on their strengths, Martin believes. When students receive accolades for their special talents, their sense of self-worth and comfort level are bolstered, sending them into an "upward spiral" of greater enthusiasm for school.

But even if teachers want to address all seven intelligences, it's natural to shy away from one's weaknesses. How can a teacher who is tone deaf help students develop their musical intelligence, or a teacher who is uncoordinated teach bodily-kinesthetic skills?

Teachers cannot escape their bias toward their own strengths, says Linda Campbell. Therefore, they must team with others who have expertise in areas where they themselves are weak. Teachers in a school should acknowledge their strengths and rely on one another, she advises. "We're not all Renaissance people."

Teachers at Skyview Junior High School act as "intelligence experts" for one another, DeGallier says. In planning how to teach a novel, for example, an English teacher might ask a science or math teacher, "How would you incorporate logic?" Teacher teams share a daily planning period, and the synergy among team members is "amazing," DeGallier says. "The ideas fly."

Teachers can also call on outside expertise. One Washington school coordinated parent volunteers to teach weekly enrichment activities, Linda Campbell says. Students could choose from a menu of topics, including gardening, cooking, music, and various forms of art. "It was not a one-shot but a yearlong effort," she says. Because the intelligences are so diverse, Bruce Campbell believes teachers should bring into the classroom a variety of experts—such as visual artists, musicians, and newspaper reporters—and coordinate apprenticeships, if possible.

Although tapping expertise is important, teachers should not always avoid using an undeveloped intelligence, experts say. By occasionally working outside their comfort zone, they can set a valuable example for students.

MULTIPLE ASSESSMENTS?

As teachers work to develop a wider range of student intelligences, assessment must also change, experts say. Relying heavily on paper-and-pencil tests "ropes kids back into a unidimensional concept of intelligence," Armstrong points out.

"It's hypocritical to teach in seven ways and assess in one," he believes. "It sends a mixed message to kids." If teachers use varied forms of assessment instead, they will gather more diagnostic information and allow more students to successfully demonstrate what they know.

Assessing learning through multiple intelligences poses a challenge, however. Should teachers allow a child to paint a picture or create a dance to show understanding of a concept?

Linda Campbell believes it's feasible for students to demonstrate their learning in multiple ways, *if* assessment criteria are clearly articulated in advance. If students choose to write a song to show their understanding of air pollution, for example, the teacher should specify what the song must convey: major sources of pollution, its political implications, and potential solutions, for example. To define criteria to guide student work, teachers can develop rubrics for major curriculum units in collaboration with students, she suggests.

"We have to be willing to allow various methods of assessment," says DeGallier. He agrees that using rubrics can help teachers determine if students grasp a concept such as economic interdependence—whether students write an essay, create a diagram, or perform a skit to show what they've learned. Certain skills are intelligence-specific, however, and should be assessed directly, he says. If the objective is for students to learn to write a five-paragraph essay, then they should be required to write one for assessment purposes.

According to Gardner, "the important thing is whether you, as the teacher, can evaluate whether the kid does or doesn't understand" on the basis of the assessment. A promising approach could be to "co-interpret" the assessment with the student, he says. But teachers mustn't sacrifice their critical faculty just to allow flexibility.

LABELS AND LIMITS

Ways to apply Gardner's theory may vary, but educators are unanimous that multiple intelligences should not be used as labels that limit students' opportunities or their sense of their own potential. "When someone says, 'There's Sally—she's linguistic,' I just cringe," Gardner says, "because of the implication that that's the last word on the subject."

Linda Campbell is "very concerned about teachers labeling students and students labeling themselves." Teachers may fail to appreciate that intelligences can be enhanced and changed, based on need, motivation, and opportunity. "Intelligence is dynamic and modifiable," she emphasizes. "Each intelligence has its own developmental timetable; some develop later than others," she adds.

If the theory of multiple intelligences is "misinterpreted," it could become the basis for another form of tracking, says Cindy Catalano, a teacher at Madrona School in Edmonds, Wash. Teachers must recognize that students' strengths change over time, she says, noting that she herself did not begin to develop her kinesthetic intelligence until college. Teachers should underscore that people have more than one strength and give students experiences in all the intelligence areas.

While teachers should celebrate the areas where students are gifted, they should not "cut them any slack" in other areas, says DeGallier. For instance, students who are very kinesthetic but not verbal can't be allowed to use the excuse "I'm a kinesthetic person" to justify poor performance in English class. Teachers should not "shut down or demean" these students, DeGallier says, but encourage them to think, "If verbal-linguistic intelligence is lowest on my totem pole, then I have to work that much harder in that area."

Gardner says he is "delighted" that teachers are trying to translate his theory into classroom practice—an undertaking he considers "very hard." Often, he believes, applications of his theory are "more well-motivated than demonstrably effective." But if his theory prompts educators to reflect on teaching and learning, he's glad.

The appeal Gardner's theory has for educators is well expressed by Joan Sorenson, principal of Expo for Excellence Middle School in St. Paul, Minn. "If education deals only with the linguistic and logical-mathematic intelligences—if it sees the others as unimportant, as extras—then we miss out on a lot of what motivates and drives human beings," Sorenson says. Rather than ignoring certain intelligences, teachers should be calling them *all* into play to improve learning.

PREPARING STUDENTS FOR THE WORKPLACE

SCHOOL-TO-WORK

MARY ANNE HESS

A kindergarten teacher in Wayne County, Mich., spent two weeks last summer getting some hands-on experience working alongside the meter installer for the local water department. "He didn't see how I could tie this kind of work into the classroom," laughs Catherine Watson. Quite to the contrary, Watson's internship experience inspired seven lesson plans focusing on math, science, safety, and teamwork. Other ideas, she says, are still making their way to the surface.

Rick Dawes, president of Enoch Manufacturing outside Portland, Ore., opens his doors to both student and teacher interns each summer and says his employees relish the interaction. "People are proud to show others what they're doing," he says. Dawes is expanding his interaction with the schools this year. He plans to hire two seniors to work part-time with a guarantee of full-time jobs plus college tuition reimbursement after graduation.

With lots of passion and despite a multitude of challenges, teachers like Watson and employers like Dawes are banding together with students, parents, and entire communities to connect the work of the classroom to the demands of an everchanging workplace.

Legislation passed by Congress and signed by President Clinton in 1994 calls this movement School-to-Work (STW) and makes it the only

This article was originally published in the Fall 1997 issue of ASCD's *Curriculum Update* newsletter.

federal initiative under the jurisdiction of two departments—Education and Labor. Despite the official title, many states and communities have come up with their own monikers, such as School-to-Career and Career Connections. Much of the sensitivity to the name, officials say, stems from efforts to emphasize that STW isn't just another vocational ed or job-training program directed at students not destined for college. Rather, STW programs convey to students that learning is a lifelong pursuit that prepares them to adapt to the changing needs of the workplace.

Whatever it's called, STW is rooted in the realization that many of our youth are ill-prepared to enter the work force and just don't have the skills—from basic reading, writing, and math to advanced sciences—to keep our economy competitive with other industrialized nations, experts say.

FINDING A PLACE FOR WORK IN SCHOOL

In countries such as Japan and Germany, the workplace plays a "crucial" role in educating young people, writes Thomas Bailey of Columbia University's Institute on Education and the Economy in the book *Learning to Work*. When U.S. education reformers looked to these countries for examples of successful programs, the structured apprenticeships available to students made the transition between school and work or career in the United States seem "haphazard and disorganized," he notes.

For the most part, Bailey explains, U.S. schools do a decent job of helping students prepare for and connect to colleges. However, he adds, students "know little about work, have no clear idea about what they must do to enter a particular career or occupation, and do not know what might be expected of them at work."

This situation is especially troubling, experts note, because only about 60 percent of high school graduates go on to college and half who start don't earn a degree. However, STW advocates are quick to point out, even those who go on to earn Ph.D.'s need to get jobs someday. All students, they contend, benefit from a curriculum that, throughout their education, emphasizes problem solving, teamwork, and hands-on learning in a real-world context. "Students whose learning has a connection with reality tend to be more successful," says Halyna Bialczyk, executive director of the Wayne County (Mich.) School-to-Work Partnership in suburban Detroit. "Any person who's focused does better."

In the past, says Bialczyk, schools tended to offer either an all-academic or an all-vocational program for students. What all children really need, she asserts, is "a balance of both. Some of us tend to forget that we all work. School-to-Work is not an add-on. Rather, it's a strategy that supports instruction, supports learning, and blends career development into the learning process."

Reading teacher James Maxfield can certainly relate to STW's emphasis on erasing the line between academic and vocational learning. He was a carpenter for 15 years before going back to school to earn his teacher's certification.

This past summer the schools in Austin (Tex.) got a "two for one" deal, he says, when they hired him for a pilot STW program called "Summer Success"—aimed at getting students who had failed 8th grade ready for high school. For six and a half weeks, the 16 boys and girls under his tutelage spent half the day in school and half out in their own community working on four projects—painting a house for an elderly woman, repairing a picket fence, helping in a child-care center, and making food for the homeless. The students were paid $4.75 per hour for both their time in class and at labor. If they weren't "on task," he says, their pay was docked.

"For a lot of the kids it was the first job they ever had," says Maxfield. "They really liked that. They developed a sense of responsibility and got a real feeling of accomplishment when we finished the house."

Maxfield tied math activities to the work, having the students figure out the square footage of the house and order the paint, and so on. He also asked students to keep journals, write resumes, and identify career options.

"It's hard to tell what will happen to these kids," says Maxfield. "We will track them. I know some will continue not to do well. But my gut feeling is that it's a good thing."

SOME SCHOOL-TO-WORK SKEPTICS

Although there seems to be a groundswell of support for STW, the initiative does have its detractors—those who despise any notion of "outcomes-based education," those who label it a "communist conspiracy," or those who fear it will lock students into career paths before they're old enough to make an informed decision.

Jondel "JD" Hoye says she's not surprised by some of this reaction. Hoye, national executive director of the federal School-to-Work Opportunities Act, acknowledges that there is "an incredible degree of mistrust" with the federal government's involvement in education. "But we're simply not doing what some people think we are," she says. "We have a consensus in this country on raising math and science standards. The problem is: How do you get a majority of our children performing at that level?" Many educators, Hoye asserts, believe a curriculum that links learning to the world beyond the classroom can do that.

She urges parents to question teachers if any program tries to force their children to make choices too early. "It's important for kids to be able to learn what [kinds of work] they want to do and what they don't want to do. School-to-Work isn't meant to be a lock-in program. We're emphasizing broad, industry-based studies—a kind of surfing the industries. Basically, students should be meeting high academic standards."

As STW's top advocate, Hoye is firm in her stance that an engaging, real-world context for learning can help students meet rigorous standards. But even she injects a note of caution: "We need to be careful that we don't get so excited about the *context* that we lose sight of keeping high *content* standards in the curriculum."

Veteran teacher Milinda Schwab would agree. Schwab has had little involvement with STW, but she expresses concerns of many educators. "We need to distinguish between education and training," says the high school English teacher. "We shouldn't push kids to specialize too early. The most important job skill you can have is to be an independent learner—to be able to think critically. Students should have time to explore ideas for their own sake."

Schwab, who teaches Advanced Placement, honors, and other classes, says she'd resist if asked to include a specific skill like memo writing in her curriculum. "What you're doing in a memo is stating your case and backing it up." In high school these skills are more appropriately learned through analyzing literature, she says. The same holds true for spending class time learning how to decipher technical material. "If you can read T.S. Eliot, you can read a computer manual," she laughs.

Dana Peterson, school-to-career specialist at LEED (Linking Education and Economic Development) in Sacramento, Calif., understands these arguments and says her group's yearly integrated training institute encourages teachers to retain the creative element in the curriculum while still incorporating industry skill standards.

That usually means pursuing "action-based projects," she says. For example, students still study *Romeo and Juliet* but throughout the year also work on short- or long-term activities such as creating a carnival booth. Those interested in health careers may take their Shakespeare studies a step further and research the diseases and medical care of that era.

PERSUADING POTENTIAL EMPLOYERS

Like the dubious teachers, some employers wonder about the value of school-to-work endeavors. Although hundreds of thousands of businesses nationwide participate in school-to-work partnerships, many employers (and their employees) are still reluctant to forge any kind of relationship with today's teenagers.

Janice McCall, co-chair of Career Connections in Montgomery County, Md., plans to tackle this hesitancy head-on by using STW grant money to hire a consultant to train potential mentors to feel comfortable working with youth.

"We didn't expect these barriers," McCall says. "I think it's partly a result of the media poorly portraying kids. Employers don't appreciate what's being taught in schools, and they don't know how capable kids are." McCall is also looking for funding and willing business partners to set up a STW program to help children with emotional disturbances.

In addition to selling STW to employers, McCall says she has a job to do with parents, who too often ask young people: Are you going to work or are you going to college? "We need to change the mindset of parents," she says. "We need to give kids the permission to do both—to have a career focus plus college preparation." Plans are in the works to develop a strategy to market the school-to-work philosophy to parents, at first targeting families in a consortium of five high schools. The model will then be used county-wide.

The STW Partnership in Wayne County, Mich., just outside Detroit, has learned all about the importance of marketing and communication, says former newspaperman Craig Farren. Farren has spent much of his time the past year getting the word out about STW. Calling Michigan "a hotbed for education reform," Farren says "everyone was doing lots of things [involving STW] but no one was telling anyone else." With 33 school districts in the county, his initial thrust was internal communications. "We needed to break down the walls between districts. We needed to say: 'If you've got a good program, create a model and share it for the good of all the kids.'"

So now there is an internal bulletin and a contact committee, composed of a key person in each district who can funnel information back and forth on successful practices. "We know our internal network is good because districts are starting to repeat programs that work," Farren says. Creating a press packet and a newsletter for the general public were also critical elements of the communications strategy, he explains.

Because Wayne County is at the tail end of its federal STW funding, it is essential, Farren adds, to let parents, labor, and business know the importance of their support to the program's longevity. A supercoalition of Wayne and three other counties hired a regional marketing firm to develop a STW awareness campaign, which airs on a Detroit TV station (the station donated production help and the services of an on-air personality).

For years businesses have cried out for a higher caliber of employees, Farren says. "We tell them to put their money where their mouth is. If you want to help make a well-trained workforce, send your professionals to work in the classrooms. Or we ask, 'What funding can you provide to get that class to your business?'"

He praises Wayne County business and labor leaders, who make up 51 percent of the partnership board, for their active support of STW. "They browbeat their peers into submission, saying, 'I'm doing it; why aren't you?'" he explains with a laugh. Businesses are starting to understand. Developing a STW movement isn't the same as coming up with a fixed solution to a problem, he adds. "Instead, it's an infinite process that has to be maintained."

Teacher Training

Maintaining the process means currying the support of the business, political, and educational establishment, but it's also important, Hoye points out, that STW advocates "deal with the high mobility in the leadership" that allows these programs to exist—governors, legislators, school superintendents. "They have some of the quickest job turnovers," she observes, and no one wants to keep starting over. "We're serving students now, but we want those who come after to have the same great opportunities." To accomplish this, Hoye says she's counting on more training for those invested in school districts for the long haul—the teachers.

Sandra Pritz, STW project manager for the College of Education at Ohio State University, couldn't agree more. OSU is developing a framework to give student teachers exposure to STW concepts, which, Pritz thinks, "just aren't well understood."

Last summer, as part of a systems-building grant, 10 teachers from inner-city Columbus schools participated in two-day externships to learn how the SCANS competencies are used in the workplace. Teachers followed up by developing their own plans for bringing this reality into the classroom, says Pritz. During the school year, students from inner-city schools will participate in career awareness activities, job shadowing, or internships, depending on their age.

"It's very important that school-to-work be seen as something for all learners," Pritz emphasizes. "A hundred years ago what was learned in academic programs was seen as separate from the needs of a developing manufacturing economy. That idea has outlived the situation in which it made sense.

"That's why teacher training is so important," she points out. "English and history teachers, for example, need to see how what they teach applies to the SCANS competencies. We need to close the chasm between academic and vocational education. There's not one task in the workplace that can be accomplished without using academic skills."

And, Pritz adds, it's not just the students who benefit from the STW philosophy. "What we're trying to do is actually an antidote to teacher burn-out. If learning becomes more important from the learner's viewpoint, students will be more interested, more engaged. It will make a lot of the stuff (like behavior issues) that leads to burn-out fade away."

After 25 years in the classroom, Bertina Williams was getting ready to join some of her burned-out colleagues. The Montgomery County (Md.) high school teacher was on the verge of retirement, but changed her mind after getting the chance two years ago to coordinate an Academy of Finance (AOF) program at her school. Predating the federal STW Act by 12 years, AOFs are operated in more than 114 high schools in 26 states by the nonprofit National Academy Foundation. Their philosophy of a career-focused education, backed by strong academic skills, blends right into STW.

"I just love it," says the seasoned business teacher, who receives a week of training once a year from the foundation. The four-year curriculum is "structured," she says, and includes accounting, computer programming and applications, economics, and the world of finance, banking, and credit.

What makes this opportunity so rejuvenating to her career, Williams says, is that she gets the chance to recruit 8th graders who really want this focus into the program. "I can get to know them and work with them throughout the four years."

With a 2.5 GPA required for entrance, the AOF offers something special "for the mid-range, the average-to-above-average student," says Williams. "I've fought for them all along. They've always been left out." Many of these children already have an excellent work ethic, she adds, because they have part-time jobs. Enrollment in AOF offers them a chance at paid internships, mentoring, field trips, and service learning—all geared to the financial field. As seniors, students enroll in the local community college for one course and can continue there after graduation.

STUDENT SUPPORT FOR STW

Perhaps the most persuasive arguments for STW are made by students who have thrived in such programs.

Take, for example, Jessica Green. Jessica has her eyes on a seat on the U.S. Supreme Court, and her paid internship last summer at the largest law firm in Louisville, Ky., served only to cement her choice of careers.

"I'm loving it," said Jessica while her stint in the legal world was in full swing. "I'm going to court, talking with the attorneys about their experiences . . . and just soaking up the ambiance." Following in her father's

Resources

There's no need to reinvent the wheel when trying to come up with ideas for implementing school-to-work principles into the curriculum. Here are some of the many STW organizations and resources. The web sites listed link to a wealth of information.

ORGANIZATIONS

The National STW Learning and
  Information Center
400 Virginia Ave. SW
Room 210
Washington, D.C. 20024
1-800-251-7236
http://www.stw.ed.gov

Jobs for the Future
One Bowdoin Square
Boston, MA 02114
617-742-5995
Fax: 617-742-5767

The National Academy Foundation
235 Park Ave. South
7th Floor
New York, NY 10003
212-420-8400
http://www.naf-education.org

National Employer Leadership
  Council
1001 Connecticut Ave. NW
Suite 310
Washington, D.C. 20036
1-800-360-NELC
http://www.nelc.org

Institute on Education and the
  Economy
Teachers College, Columbia
  University
Box 174, 439 Thorndike Hall
525 W. 120th St.
New York, N.Y. 10027
212-678-3091
http://www.tc.columbia.edu/~iee/

PUBLICATIONS

Learning to Work:
Employer Involvement in School-to-
  Work Transition Programs
Edited by Thomas R. Bailey
Published, 1995: The Brookings
  Institution, Washington, D.C.

The Double Helix of Education and
  the Economy
By Sue Berryman and Thomas Bailey
Published 1992: Institute on
  Education and the Economy

Life Beyond the Classroom:
Transition Strategies for Young
  People with Disabilities
By Paul Wehman, Ph.D.
Paul H. Brookes Publishing Co.
Baltimore, 1996

footsteps, the 16-year-old junior says she's known ever since she was "young" that she wanted to be a lawyer. She jumped at the chance to enroll in the legal/government services magnet at Central High School. "I knew I could get an edge up on what I wanted to do with my life."

Since starting at Central, Jessica has served as leading prosecutor on the school's mock trial team, which placed second in the region. She's traveled with classmates to Spain to study law in a different culture and has planned a school trip to a law-related conference in Washington, D.C., this fall. "I don't know any other school in the world that could measure up to Central," she says. "I'm just trying to take advantage of every door life opens up for me."

Jessica says her academic courses, such as English and social studies, offer connections to her legal studies—especially through their public speaking and research requirements. The Magna Charta, for example, was a topic of study in both her legal and social studies classes. The poised teenager discounts the notion that she and her classmates are too young to make career choices. "You should know your interests by the time you're in high school," she says. "And, if you decide you don't like your choice, it's not carved in concrete."

Another teen sure of where she's headed is Carolyn Wacker, a senior in Central's veterinary science magnet. With the help of her teacher, a registered veterinary technician, Carolyn has worked in an animal hospital, running tests and assisting in surgeries. "I've done lots of things high school students wouldn't be able to do," she says. But, she was given the responsibility because the hospital's veterinarian had been to Central "and had seen what we do." The magnet even includes a student-run business where owners can bring pets for grooming and for check-ups for parasites.

"My sister's a vet tech and a lot of what she learned in college I already know," says Carolyn, who put her knowledge to the test recently in a nationwide skills competition sponsored by the Health Occupation Students of America. She placed among the top 10 in vet science in the country (after placing first in Kentucky) and hopes that feat boosts her chance for a spot at Purdue University, which recently became one of Central's partners.

These work-based and school-based experiences, Carolyn says, have helped her focus on a college choice with confidence. "Going through the magnet lets you say, 'Yes, I can do this for the rest of my life' or 'No, I can't.' Then you won't have to spend all that money going to college to find out you don't like your major."

Carolyn's mother, Diana, who's had three daughters at Central, agrees. "A college education is so expensive, you really need to choose the field you're going into before you start." High school's not too early to make that choice, she adds. "By that time kids know what their strengths are. This [program] gives them a chance to expand on their strengths."

◆

MAKING SCHOOL-TO-WORK WORK

MARY ANNE HESS

When a school decides to implement a School-to-Work focus, it requires having "lots of conversations, taking down walls, and making communities responsible for preparing their children for the future," says JD Hoye, national executive director of the federal School-to-Work Opportunities Act. She adds that educators, parents, and community members "need to talk about what we want our children to know and to know how to do" and then discuss how to change the school structure to enable students to reach those goals.

"It's really quite simple," explains Jim Wernsing, a colleague of Hoye's at the National STW Office in Washington, D.C. "As educators it's our obligation to give our children the skills and ability to succeed. It's a much bigger world out there, yet most high schools haven't changed their structure for 100 years."

ATTRACTING CAREER-FOCUSED STUDENTS

One century-old school that *has* changed its structure is Central High School Magnet Career Academy, located in the business sector of downtown Louisville, Ky. Calling itself "today's school for tomorrow's

This article was originally published in the Fall 1997 issue of ASCD's *Curriculum Update* newsletter.

leaders," Central recently graduated its first class of students who had spent their entire four years under the new magnet organization.

Previously a traditional comprehensive high school, Central now features 10 specialized career-oriented curriculums in business, law and government, and medicine and other health professions. As part of a state-wide reform effort, passed in 1990, 14 other high schools in the Jefferson County system also have career-related curriculums, ranging from performing arts to fire and emergency services, but Central is the only one where all 900 students follow a career path. With the advice of counselors, 8th graders from all over the county apply to various high schools after taking an assessment test that points out their strengths and weaknesses, explains Brenda Schmidt, Central's magnet coordinator.

Central accepts students with a wide range of interests, achievement, and ability levels, including some diagnosed with learning disabilities, says Schmidt, a former business teacher. Some youngsters know what they want to do, while others aren't so focused. So, all 9th graders spend three weeks in each of the 10 career clusters and, after extensive counseling, eventually choose one concentration for the next three years.

With a growing number of employer-partners (30 at last count), the school can offer sophomore students job shadowing—everything from sitting on the bench with a judge during a court trial to watching surgery. Local attorneys, nurses, and a variety of other businesspersons serve as mentors, particularly during students' junior year.

During the summer between junior and senior year (and sometimes even earlier), students who meet certain academic and behavior criteria get the chance for paid internships, says Schmidt. More internships and co-op work experience are available for seniors—with a goal set for all seniors to get this opportunity. Sometimes, she says, students need to juggle internships with after-school jobs—with the school recommending that any combination of the two shouldn't exceed 15–20 hours a week.

A close relationship between the school and local community colleges and universities adds to the pool of mentors as well as to the school's academic rigor. College instructors teach physics, psychology, engineering, and some math courses at Central—all offered for college credit to students with at least a 3.0 average.

Since launching its whole-school magnet, Central has seen its percentage of students bound for college jump from 79 to 93 percent. "It's fantastic," says Schmidt, particularly for an inner-city school where 57 percent of the students receive free and reduced meals. But, she adds, it's not surprising. "School-to-Careers really fosters a community and a culture here. No one asks 'if you're going to college.' The question is 'What college are you going to?'"

Some of the money for college tuition comes from the profits of a Kentucky Fried Chicken (KFC) mobile unit, owned and operated by business management students who sell food twice a week at lunch and after school (and get lots of mentoring from KFC officials). The store generated $20,000 in scholarships this year, says Schmidt. "It's really amazing."

Over the past few years Schmidt says she's heard the argument that schools or programs such as Central's channel students into a career direction too early. She thinks the advantages outweigh any perceived drawbacks. "Students simply learn better by seeing a connection to the real world," she explains, citing the example of a girl in the pharmacy magnet who was having trouble with metrics until she started using the system in a job setting.

The magnet also means improved behavior and attendance and an overall jump in student enthusiasm, says Schmidt. "Urban schools just aren't supposed to be this good," she laughs. "We don't have hard-core data, but we just don't have a lot of problems. The magnets give students a focus."

And some students do change their focus even after spending their years on one career path. A recent valedictorian, who spent lots of time job shadowing and interning during her three years in the legal magnet, said there was 'no way' she wanted to work the long hours of an attorney, explains Schmidt. "She's now majoring in elementary education and says she may use her magnet experience to run for school board some day. She had enough opportunity for career exploration to make an intelligent decision."

Some teachers in the academic subjects expressed initial apprehension about the changeover to a magnet, but efforts continue at co-curricular teaching, teaming, and linking areas—such as humanities with business, and Latin teachers with the medical magnet, says Schmidt.

Through summer internships, teachers also get exposure to the same fields their students are exploring. Schmidt hopes that a switch to block scheduling during this school year will allow more room for electives such as music, satisfying requests of staff and students.

Although federal STW dollars are on the wane, the magnet coordinator says the School-to-Careers philosophy has so much support—among government, business, students, and parents in Jefferson County—that there's no going back. "We just see too many benefits."

A FOCUS ON TEACHER TRAINING

Also upbeat about a similar movement in his school district is Michael Kaiel, coordinator of the K–12 school-to-careers program at the North Clackamas (Ore.) School District outside Portland.

As one of the first communities to receive federal STW funds, North Clackamas is now at the tail end of its three-year grant, which provided $55,000 annually for staff development. But Kaiel is forging ahead with his plans, counting on the regular school budget, other grants, and the continuing support of the business community. "This has been a high priority of the superintendent," he says. "We've made sure School-to-Careers is not an add-on. It's simply the philosophy we have about teaching and learning." The district's efforts also have state backing, as Oregon had already established a framework for building STW with the passage of its Educational Act for the 21st Century in 1991.

At about the same time that Kaiel came on board to head the program, North Clackamas, along with Jefferson County, Ky., and three other school districts, was selected as a "Benchmark Community" by Jobs for the Future (JFF), a national, nonprofit organization. Founded in 1983, JFF conducts research, provides technical assistance, and makes policy proposals on the interrelated issues of work and learning. In addition to the technical assistance and the prestige of being associated with an outside organization with "credibility," Kaiel says the opportunity "to share our successes and our failures" with other communities in the JFF initiative has proved invaluable. "Without all this we wouldn't have been able to move as far ahead."

The arena where Kaiel's school district has pushed ahead most is teacher training. "From the beginning we identified this as essential," he says. At first, the emphasis was on getting teachers out to observe for a short time in local businesses—to identify how the Secretary of Labor's SCANS competencies are used in the workplace. Kaiel envisions expanding the program to two-to-three days so teachers can get a better idea of how to mesh the context of the workplace into the content of a curriculum that meets state standards. "Teachers are driven by state standards," he explains, and they couldn't be expected to accept any content that would sidetrack them from those goals.

North Clackamas has also put together cadres of K–12 teachers who will spend the next year or more practicing project-based teaching under the direction of a master teacher on a contract from JFF. The teachers will also be looking at what tools they might use to assess whether this kind of teaching has an impact on student performance. A grant from the Goals 2000: Educate America Act will also help the district develop model curriculums for contextual teaching and learning.

Kaiel says that about 65 percent of high school graduates in his district head for college or other postsecondary training. That's only one percent or so higher than before school-to-careers came into effect, but he's not surprised. "We haven't yet put in our career pathways in our high schools," he says. That kind of curriculum reform is now in progress, and he expects the percentage of college-bound to increase once each student has a pathway. As proof he points to the fact that 70 percent of the district's students who enroll in advanced technical courses at a regional skills center end up continuing their schooling. "Once students have a focus they're more likely to go on to higher education," he says.

Reflecting on her organization's work with North Clackamas, Jefferson County, and other communities, Mary Ellen Bavaro, JFF's director of communications, says she sees a new phase coming—the development of a better connection between the STW movement and the push to raise standards. Prior to the 1994 federal STW act, she explains, most educational efforts to connect work and learning had concentrated on "at-risk" students. The legislation moves the focus "to improving education for all kids," she notes. "I feel confident about its sustainability. School-to-work has tons of support. Students and parents are demanding it. It's a train that's out of the station and it won't stop."

◆

GETTING A HEAD START ON A CAREER

JOHN O'NEIL

Ten years ago, students in David de Leeuw's anatomy and physiology course studied an abstract academic curriculum, loaded with material to memorize but short on real-life applications. When they learned about the heart, for example, they memorized its chambers and the order in which blood passes through them. Meanwhile, students in a health occupations course taught by one of de Leeuw's colleagues learned to take a person's blood pressure, without really studying the anatomy involved. The two curriculums, generally studied by different groups of students, were separate and distinct. Neither provided learning experiences that allowed students to combine both the theory *and* the practical applications of the discipline in a real-life setting.

That's all changed under the revamped curriculum used at the Oakland Health and Bioscience Academy in Oakland, Calif., where de Leeuw now teaches. The curriculum in anatomy and physiology teaches students the applications of academic knowledge, using a focus on diseases to place the study of the human body in a real-world context. Through experiences such as internships and long-term projects, the students, who are interested in possible careers in the health field, learn firsthand how medical professionals draw upon academic knowledge in their daily work. In the revised anatomy and physiology course, "our kids not only learn how to take blood pressure," says de Leeuw. "They learn to think, 'What does it mean?' and 'What would you tell people'" to explain the results?

This article was originally published in the October 1994 issue of ASCD's *Update* newsletter.

The Academy, which opened in 1985, has paid dividends for students like Leuckessia Spencer. A self-described "worst-case scenario," Spencer had to endure a chaotic home life, shuttled from one foster home to another. Before entering the Oakland program, she eked out a "D" average and had no real plans for college or a career. "I was more concerned about how I was going to survive day-to-day," she says. But the school's distinctive curriculum and supportive atmosphere helped her to earn a straight "A" average by her senior year. She began college this fall and is thinking of a career as a health care advocate or medical journalist.

Driven by new economic realities, educators in Oakland and elsewhere are trying to revamp school curriculums to better prepare students for eventual careers. Good-paying jobs, once available even to unskilled laborers, today require workers who are able to solve complex problems, work well in teams, and learn new information and skills as conditions change. While preparation for work traditionally has been considered the province of the vocational education system, many experts now believe that curriculums for *all* students should address the knowledge and skills they'll need for today's jobs.

That goal raises a host of difficult questions, however. To what extent should the curriculum reflect the world of work? Should the curriculum for the future sheet metal worker and the future doctor be similar? And how can the curriculum be designed so that students are not forced to choose a career path prematurely?

ACADEMICS, JOB PREP SEPARATE

Perhaps the biggest obstacle to designing a curriculum better suited to the new workplace is the historical separation of academic skills and knowledge and the learning of a trade or job skills. Since the early part of this century, schools have maintained an "academic" track suitable to prepare students to enter a four-year college or university. Pupils in this track seldom experience a curriculum that pushes them to explore careers or ties their academic studies to information about their intended career field. Students in the "vocational" track learn job skills, but the academic component of their programs frequently is weak. By default, other students end up in the "general" track, where they choose from a mishmash of courses, often getting neither a solid grounding in academics nor salable job skills.

Although the system of tracks may have served its purpose during a different economic era, it no longer benefits today's students or today's workplace, experts say. Students today don't fit into neat categories like "college-bound" or "vocationally trained." Sixty percent of students who take vocational courses go on to some form of higher education, according to Brett Lovejoy, acting executive director of the American Vocational Association. And students going to four-year colleges are also well served by a curriculum that helps them learn about careers and that features links between their academic coursework and careers that may interest them.

If America is serious about preparing students to enter careers, then programs to improve their transition from school to work must include *all* students, experts say. Programs should be designed so that all young people will remain eligible for college, even though some may not go, says Larry Rosenstock, principal of the Rindge School of Technical Arts in Cambridge, Mass. "At its core, what this has to be about is detracking schools."

But what routes will permit most, if not all, students to succeed in the new economy? Increasingly, experts say that *multiple* pathways to careers need to be established—but they warn that pathways must not become euphemisms for high-status and low-status tracks. All students should have a challenging curriculum, infused with applications from real workplaces, that keeps open the options of going on to a four-year college, a technical or community college, a training program, or a job.

Creating "career pathways" or "career clusters" is one way to arrange the curriculum to preserve these options. These pathways should exist in a largely untracked system, with high academic standards for all students, Lovejoy says. For example, students in a health careers pathway would learn about the health field through electives and material integrated into academic courses. They would also learn about the different roles played by health professionals such as radiology technicians or doctors—and the kind of preparation needed to enter these professions. Such an approach, Lovejoy and others say, gives students a solid academic footing and helps them to see more clearly the path from school to a career.

Central Valley High School in Veradale, Wash., requires each student to select a career path as part of its Student Career Opportunity

Paths in Education (SCOPE) program. The career paths are grouped into job families such as "engineering, science, and medical services," "creative and applied arts," or "business marketing and management."

School officials meet with employers to get a better sense of what skills jobs require, and to begin to develop curriculums to prepare students to enter those careers, says Dan Ruddell, community resources coordinator at the school. "We'll go into a personnel office and get the job descriptions" to see what each job entails, he says. The school's counseling program provides clear direction to students about what courses students should take to enter the various careers in each of the job families.

In each job family, entry-level, semi-skilled, and skilled and professional careers are described to students. In the engineering family, for example, avionics technician is an entry-level career, aerospace engineering technician is a semi-skilled career, and aerospace engineer is a professional career. In addition to fulfilling basic graduation requirements, students take the elective and advanced academic courses and undergo the work-site experiences necessary to stay on the track toward their intended career.

Although students often postpone thinking about careers—and how their curriculum may help or hinder their path to a good job—SCOPE helps students see how what they study in school is necessary in the workplace, Ruddell says. Ian Hughes, a senior at the school, agrees. SCOPE "has helped a lot of students get a head start on planning," he says.

To keep students' options open, Central Valley tries to give all students a thorough grounding in academics that will serve them no matter which path they take. Central Valley no longer refers to students as "college-bound" and "non-college-bound" ("We call them all lifelong learners," says Ruddell), and the school groups students heterogeneously in many of the courses. "In the real world, people with all different capabilities and interests work side by side," notes Ruddell.

BROAD PREPARATION

The use of career pathways or clusters is, in part, a move away from a focus on training students for specific occupations. In the past, some experts say, vocational students have been shortchanged because they didn't end up working in a job for which they trained, or because the skills they learned in vocational programs didn't match the skills needed in the rapidly changing work force. "Technical skills don't transfer," says Rosenstock. "Clearly, we should not have programs that are occupationally specific."

A recent federal assessment of vocational education supports the notion that preparation for work ought to be more broad-based. The final report to the U.S. Congress of the National Assessment of Vocational Education (NAVE) said that traditional vocational education programs are "too narrowly defined and too narrowly based." Instead of focusing on teaching students the particular processes and procedures used in a specific job, the NAVE suggested a system of "industry-based majors" that would prepare students, as much as possible, for some form of postsecondary education. According to the NAVE report, "occupationally specific procedures would be used primarily to teach underlying principles and concepts. Thus students might examine automobile engines to learn how electricity and combustion are put to work, but not specifically how to repair automobiles."

The call to submerge occupationally specific skills worries some experts, however. Vocational educators "for the most part, are increasingly teaching broad skills" useful in many occupations, says Lovejoy. But some students want to learn skills to take a job immediately upon graduation, he says. "There is a danger in the pendulum swinging too far" toward broad skills, he says. "I have some trouble seeing how you train an auto mechanic without going through specific training in automobile engines." A student might reasonably ask: "Is my skill in this cluster called 'transportation'? And have I really learned to diagnose engine trouble?" Lovejoy says. Educators should ensure that school-to-work programs are as flexible as possible so that students retain the choice of receiving direct training for jobs, he says.

CAREERS, NOT JUST JOBS

The Oakland Academy, which enrolls about 240 students, tries to offer viable options for all of them, although their ultimate career goals differ. "We want students to be both job-ready and college-ready," says Patricia Clark, the Academy's director. Because many students in the program gain work experience in health facilities, some may end up taking jobs as hospital ward clerks or lab assistants upon graduation, says de Leeuw. The school also offers a training program for students who are at least 18 years old that leads to certification as an emergency medical technician, he says.

But the reality is that "there aren't that many good jobs that don't require *some* postsecondary training," says de Leeuw. So the Academy offers a "2+2" program that links students' last two years at the Academy with two years of study at a community or technical college. Other students attend four-year colleges, and many students combine their postsecondary education with a part-time job, capitalizing on the work experiences gained through the Academy. "We want kids to be able to go out and get jobs, but we want them to go for careers, not just jobs," says de Leeuw.

In a marketplace that is extremely competitive, it's more important than ever for students to develop solid academic skills and knowledge of—and experience in—a career field that interests them. Because the Bay Area is such a desirable place to live, it's not unusual for people with master's degrees to apply for jobs as secretaries at local hospitals, says Clark. But Academy graduates will have extensive experience working in hospitals, as well as communication and computer skills, she points out. "We've got to show that our kids are just as well prepared."

PREPARING STUDENTS FOR WORK

JOHN O'NEIL

For more than a half-century, preparing students for work meant sorting out the "sharp" ones from those deemed less able. Students seen as college material took a core curriculum of challenging academic courses in preparation for a professional career. The rest got less academic

This article was originally published in the November 1994 issue of ASCD's *Update* newsletter.

content and, perhaps, enough vocational training to take a low-skill entry-level job.

This practice is slowly changing, however, with the introduction of efforts called "applied learning" or "applied academics," or, simply, "integration." These are all names for a curriculum that better integrates the academic material in courses such as English, math, and science with the knowledge and competencies used in actual workplaces. Experts on school-to-work transition say that regardless of the path students take through school, they are more motivated to learn the content when they see how academic skills are used in real workplaces.

As a student, "I always asked: 'Why am I learning this?'" says Brett Lovejoy, acting executive director of the American Vocational Association (AVA). "It wasn't until I took carpentry and had to cut the rafters for a house that I knew what the Pythagorean theorem was for." Schools "need to drastically change curriculum to make it more practical and applicable," Lovejoy says.

The idea of linking academic and vocational content has emerged as a key component of the new thinking about how to better prepare students for the world of work. The Perkins Act, the federal government's major program for vocational education, requires schools to integrate academic and vocational content to receive funding under the Act. And some schools are using applications from the workplace to illustrate academic concepts even in classes not populated by students in the vocational "track."

A Focus on Health

At the Oakland Health and Bioscience Academy in Oakland, Calif., a program for students interested in possible careers in the health field, applications of academic concepts are a central feature of the curriculum. In David de Leeuw's anatomy and physiology course, for example, students learn about the human body and how it works through a study of diseases.

In one unit, students study health problems related to particular occupations. Students first interview workers about typical health problems in their occupation. For example, a student interviewing a worker in a frozen foods factory might find that employees, who move items in and out of room-sized freezers, often get respiratory infections. The student then researches the topic and writes a report, using material from the research and the interviews, suggesting what relationship might exist between sudden temperature changes and respiratory infections. Such an activity "helps students see the relevance of their academic classes," says de Leeuw.

Information about occupations and the workplace can be woven into different subject areas. Workplace safety, for example, may seem like a dry topic marginally related to traditional academics. But a curriculum developed as part of the Pennsylvania Youth Apprenticeship Program shows it can be a fertile theme.

In social studies, students read about and discuss the 1911 Triangle Waist Company fire, which killed 146 people trapped in a crowded, unsafe factory. The fire spurred major changes in worker safety laws and had a substantial impact on New York City politics for years to come. In science, students learn the scientific principles behind what firefighters call "lapping in," which happens when fire in one floor of a building shoots out the windows and enters through the windows of the floor above. And in math, students calculate volume in order to see the inadequacy of the regulation that required 250 cubic feet of air space per factory employee. Before the fire, there were no restrictions on where the air space should be. So many factories with high ceilings placed workers elbow to elbow—a condition that kept many employees from escaping the Triangle fire.

A curriculum that links academic and vocationally oriented content is not only more motivating to students, it is better able to accommodate students of different academic standing, de Leeuw believes.

"People sometimes shy away because they feel that the curriculum is too difficult for students," says de Leeuw. "It *is* more challenging, but kids aren't complaining that it's too hard." Further, the material is appropriate for students on different career pathways. Students who take the course and go on to four-year colleges "feel they're ahead" of their peers from other schools, he says. And students who are academically behind are more

Aviation Program Piques Student Interest

Most children have some idea what they want to be when they grow up. "A doctor." "A sports star." "A firefighter." Their dreams rarely reflect an understanding of what such jobs—and the industries within which they fit—are really like, however. For the most part, these early aspirations are put aside or forgotten, and serious thinking about a career doesn't begin until high school, if then.

Some programs are beginning to educate students about the workplace at a much earlier age, however. When information about industries and occupations is infused in the curriculum, even young students can benefit from a better understanding of careers and how academic skills are used in real jobs.

Aviation 2010, developed by the Regional Airport Authority serving Louisville and Jefferson County, Ky., is a K–12 program with a strong curriculum component directed at young children.

"School-to-work [transition] starts in kindergarten," says Rande Swann, public relations director for the Regional Airport Authority and a former specialist with the Jefferson County public schools. The program has numerous goals, Swann says, among them motivating students to learn the academic skills needed for future aviation jobs and introducing students—especially women and minorities—to career opportunities.

The Aviation 2010 curriculum includes numerous activities that use information on aviation and the airport to buttress instruction in basic academic skills. In one activity, students look at the number of passengers and tons of air cargo carried at a local airfield. The activity requires students to use information in graphs and charts and to hypothesize reasons for increases and declines. In other activities, students build paper airplanes and whirly-birds to learn more about concepts such as lift, drag, thrust, and gravity that are crucial to aviation.

Tangible examples from the world of work can help students become more motivated about—and better understand—academic content, says Susan Rostov, co-developer of the curriculum. "Today, you're competing with TV and video," she says. "You've got to make it relevant."

Swann agrees. Students "want to know: 'Why do I have to learn about positive and negative numbers?' If you can say: 'This is how you're going to learn it, and here's how to apply it,' kids become more interested." In fact, Swann found that even after students "learned" positive and negative numbers in school, they still struggled with the idea of time zones. How can a

westward traveler take a flight that begins at 10:30 a.m. and ends at
10:17 a.m.? So one of the activities in the curriculum puts flight schedules
in students' hands and has them plan an itinerary for a band on a nationwide tour.

Business involvement in developing curriculum is sometimes criticized as
self-serving, but Swann says Aviation 2010 enjoys solid support in the community. The curriculum was not "laid on" teachers, and the airport authority
has been clear about its goals, such as helping to attract students into aviation careers and to educate students about the importance of the airport to
the local community. "We've been real up-front about what we've been
doing from the beginning," she says. The airport authority is in the midst of
a $400-million expansion that will bring new jobs, she says. If efforts to
teach students academic skills and the aviation industry don't begin early,
"we won't have the workforce we need" to take advantage of the new
opportunities, she says.

motivated because the academics are placed in a real-life context. Students
in his course have to learn 160 different terms the first semester, de Leeuw
points out, but they keep up. "It's just not true that the kids with 'lower'
academic skills can't do higher-order thinking and find it satisfying."

A LONG ROAD

Finding links between vocational and academic content "is not hard
to do," says Dave Pacolay, a master teacher with the Pittsburgh public
schools who has worked on the Pennsylvania apprenticeship plan. But it
requires working with partners in business to find out what skills and
knowledge are most in demand and then bringing teachers together to
develop the curriculum. "Our key constraint is time."

In 1987, the Southern Regional Education Board launched its "High
Schools That Work" program, which now encompasses 300 sites in 19
states. A major thrust of the program is linking academic content and
applications drawn from the world of work, says Gene Bottoms, who
directs the program. As a precursor to greater integration, schools in the
program eliminate low-level academic courses, he says. "There's no need
to integrate low-level academics and low-level vocational studies."

Schools in the SREB project use a variety of ways to integrate. Some embed academic content in existing vocational courses; others offer new applied learning courses, often using commercially prepared materials. Team teaching, which brings together teachers from the academic and vocational departments, and project learning, where students do projects that require them to integrate academic and occupational content, are also popular strategies. Although integration takes considerable effort and at least five to seven years to institutionalize, the results are positive, Bottoms says. Some schools have increased student enrollments in higher level courses in math and science, for example. One school, he says, went from offering physics every other year to offering five sections per year.

Efforts to integrate academic and vocational content are on the upswing, but they are still relatively rare. The National Assessment of Vocational Education (NAVE), a recent report to the U.S. Congress, noted recently that "Integrated education as the norm in American high schools is a long way off."

One barrier is that traditional divisions among academic and vocational teachers persist. "Academic teachers are more likely to coordinate courses among themselves than with vocational teachers, and vice versa," according to the NAVE. Much of the pressure to integrate courses has been directed at vocational education, for example, through the Perkins Act, but educators in the academic subjects have not been pushed in a similar fashion, notes Lovejoy of the AVA. In addition, developing and delivering integrated courses requires both time and money. The state of Washington, Lovejoy says, will spend $26 million just to buy time for teachers to plan integrated coursework together. "It boils down to money."

Those offering more integrated courses say such barriers can be overcome. The benefits, moreover, are worth the struggle. Even students who have been unsuccessful academically often thrive when they begin to see connections between what they learn in the classroom and what they may eventually do on the job. "We have honor students fighting to get into this program," says Patricia Clark, director of the Oakland Academy. "Every student is looking for this kind of contextualized learning."

APPLIED ACADEMICS, TECH-PREP PROGRAMS SERVE THE 'FORGOTTEN HALF'

SCOTT WILLIS

At no other time in history has it been so important for American schools to educate every student. So educators, politicians, and business leaders repeatedly insist. Yet, critics charge, American schools serve only one population of students well: the college-bound.

Fully half of all students do not attend college, however. These students—the so-called "forgotten half"—are allowed to drift through the system without gaining the skills that desirable jobs require.

Vocational education can give these students direction, experts in the field assert. In vocational programs, they can train for the highly-paid, skilled jobs that await them if they are qualified.

Today more than ever before, the economic health of the nation depends on the availability of a skilled workforce—and therefore on vocational education, experts maintain. "Quality vocational education is absolutely essential to the international competitiveness of this nation," says Charles Buzzell, executive director of the American Vocational Association (AVA).

The need to educate the forgotten half of students is compelling. But to help fulfill this mission, vocational education must overcome a number of obstacles: declining enrollments, a persistent image problem, and the American public's belief that only a four-year college degree is good enough for my "my child."

This article was originally published as "Vocational Education: Applied Academics, Tech-Prep Programs Serve the 'Forgotten Half'" in the September 1991 issue of ASCD's *Curriculum Update* newsletter.

Vocational education is responding to the challenge. Two major trends in the field hold promise, experts say: the integration of academic and vocational content, and the development of tech-prep programs that link high school and postsecondary study.

INTEGRATION SOUGHT

Years ago, when hiring technicians for the U.S. Air Force, Leno Pedrotti discovered that many applicants had "shied away" from tough math and physics courses during their schooling. Today's vocational students are no different, says Pedrotti, now senior vice president of the Center for Occupational Research and Development (CORD) in Waco, Tex. "These kids have precious hand skills but are bypassing opportunities for getting head skills."

Vocational educators are trying to change that. To ensure that students train *both* head and hand, educators in the field are working to integrate more academic content into the vocational curriculum. The integration movement is "very rapidly growing now throughout the land," says Gerald Hayward, deputy director of the National Center for Research in Vocational Education at the University of California–Berkeley.

Vocational courses are fertile ground for academic learning, experts say. Recent cognitive research shows that learning by doing is "a very powerful educational device," says Hayward. "We all learned how to use a computer that way," he notes.

"Many people learn from the concrete to the abstract," Buzzell says. "Voc ed provides a wonderful environment to experience the concrete." Volumetric measure may not mean much to a high school freshman, he points out, but "piston displacement in his favorite automobile is very important to him; it's part of his lexicon."

Concerns over the "skills gap" are fueling the integration trend. As the skills workers need on the job grow more complex, educators and policymakers are becoming increasingly concerned about the less-than-rigorous academic content of some vocational programs. Many of today's office jobs, for example, require workers to be familiar with complicated technology, such as computers and teleconferencing equipment. In industry, workers often need to know not only how to use machinery but how to troubleshoot and repair it. Assembly line workers may even need to know robotics. Given these growing demands on workers, vocational students need a thorough grounding in math, science, and communication skills, experts say.

The U.S. Congress evidently agrees. The reauthorized Perkins Act, the federal law on vocational education, requires the integration of academic content into vocational programs.

Several states, including Ohio, Oregon, Pennsylvania, and New York, are promoting a new emphasis on academics in vocational programs. Ohio, for example, is "broadening the scope" of vocational education to integrate more academic content, says Darrell Parks, the state's director of vocational and career education. By 1994, science, math, and language arts will be incorporated into all programs, Parks says.

ENOUGH ALREADY?

Despite the calls for change, some experts, like Buzzell, contend that academic skills have always been part and parcel of vocational education. Students can't complete a good program without mastering the basic skills, he insists. "They're just embedded in the fabric."

He cites training for electricians as an example. "The assumption in the minds of a lot of people is that there are no math, no science, and no communication skills taught to electricians." On the contrary, he says, trainees must learn subjects such as geometry and algebra. "I was taught that you find resistance by dividing volts by amps. That's algebra—you're solving for x."

Academic skills are intrinsic to all the vocational fields, Buzzell argues. "Take any quality voc ed program—food service, home economics, industrial arts, drafting, you name it. When you peel layers away, like an onion, you will find layer after layer" of academic skills. Students "aren't typically told, 'Okay, today we're going to do trigonometric functions'," but they are "absolutely" learning those skills, he says.

Other experts, however, contend that vocational students too often learn only low-level academic skills. They are typically given "minimal and diluted academic content," says Larry Rosenstock, executive director of the Rindge School of Technical Arts in Cambridge, Mass.

What Do Students in Voc Ed Classes Study?

Vocational education comprises eight main areas of study, according to the American Vocational Association:

✦ *Trade and industrial education.* Includes carpentry, auto mechanics, metalworking, graphic arts, and cosmetology.

✦ *Business education.* Includes office occupations, accounting, and business management.

✦ *Agriculture.* Includes agricultural mechanics, horticulture, and agribusiness.

✦ *Home economics.* Includes consumer and homemaking education and occupations in fields such as food services.

✦ *Marketing education.* Includes general merchandising, apparel marketing, and real estate.

✦ *Technical education.* Includes communications, technologies related to engineering, and computer sciences.

✦ *Technology education.* Includes study of the materials and processes used in construction, manufacturing, transportation, communication, and other industries.

✦ *Health occupations.* Students in these programs train to be practical nurses, nurses, medical and dental assistants, and radiology technicians.

"The academic content of [vocational] courses needs to be beefed up," Hayward agrees. He quickly adds, however, that it is unrealistic to expect vocational programs to make the change alone. Instead, a stronger connection between academic and vocational courses is needed.

Newly developed curriculums for teaching "applied academics" are helping to provide that connection. Unlike the traditional textbook approach, in which knowledge is often presented in the abstract, divorced from everyday life, applied academics courses link theory and practice. Lab work is central, providing hands-on experiences that illustrate academic principles.

The Center for Occupational Research and Development (CORD) has developed several applied academics curriculums for high school students, says Pedrotti. These include "Principles of Technology," a two-year course in applied physics; a two-year course in applied mathematics; and a new one-year course in applied biology and chemistry.

The CORD curriculums aim to help students overcome their reluctance to confront academic concepts. Because vocational students typically have "a love of devices" and the ability to use their hands, Pedrotti says, the curriculums allow them to work often with equipment—"their trump suit." But they also introduce students to scientific principles, which are demonstrated in concrete ways. "In the lab, students begin to tolerate the abstractness of equations."

Principles of Technology, the applied physics curriculum, uses lab experiences not as ends in themselves but as a context for discussing the principles of physics, Pedrotti explains. In a traditional automotive shop, for example, a unit on brakes would cover such topics as how to raise the automobile safely, remove the wheel, and so on. In Principles of Technology, the instructor also talks about the scientific concepts involved, such as hydraulic pressure, friction, and thermal energy.

When Principles of Technology was introduced, the developers felt "a lot of trepidation" that the physics content would scare students off. Happily, students have not been intimidated. Today the curriculum is being used by 40,000 students in 49 states, Pedrotti says. But students still don't like to read the print materials, he notes with chagrin.

Principles of Technology has been a success at Pendleton High School in Pendleton, S.C., says Harriet Palmer, who teaches the course there.

Palmer's class attracts a mixture of students, vocational and college-bound, and she believes it serves them all equally well. In their lab work, students use equipment such as voltmeters, motors, winches, thermal couples, and an oscilloscope. The course gives students some freedom, Palmer says, allowing them to do problem solving. As a result, they gain confidence in their abilities. "They're enthused about it," she says.

In fact, enthusiasm runs so high that one student came in after school every day for a week to replicate a demonstration. And students are spreading the word that Principles of Technology is "a fun class," Palmer reports.

A TWO-WAY STREET?

While most experts agree that the movement to include more demanding academic content in vocational courses is gaining momentum, the degree to which this trend will influence *academic* courses remains unclear. Academic instruction also needs to be reshaped, some experts contend, to allow students to learn by doing as well as by reading or listening.

Rosenstock, for example, believes that voc ed should "recognize its strengths and share them with the academic sphere." A number of methodologies common in vocational education—hands-on learning, performance assessment, cooperative learning, team teaching—"need to be brought into the rest of the educational arena," he says.

"We ought to teach the standard curriculum with more of an applications slant," agrees Ken Gray, the professor in charge of vocational and technical education at Pennsylvania State University. Too often, "math and science curriculums are barren of application."

Gray considers it a "disgrace" that academic students typically have no access to the sophisticated equipment in vocational schools. "Those classes are going empty, and students who really should understand these things are looking at books in an academic school," he charges. Logistical and funding problems pose a barrier, he concedes; finding a way for academic students to attend vocational schools part-time is a major difficulty.

One school that has solved that problem is the Bethlehem Area Vocational-Technical School in Bethlehem, Pa. Since the school first opened its doors to students from public and private schools in its area three years ago, the program for academic students has "mushroomed," says Don Foellner, the school's director.

Last year, several honors physics students took applied engineering at Bethlehem, and several honors biology students took health-related technology. These college-bound students were attracted to the vocational courses because "so many kids have no applications base to go along with the theory they're getting," Foellner says. The influx of academic students has benefited the school, he adds, by raising expectations and providing a mix of students. Now, coats and ties mingle with blue jeans and tee shirts.

Starting this year, Bethlehem will open all 30 of its programs to students from neighboring public and private schools. Because outside students will be able to attend Bethlehem for two-period blocks of time—less than the traditional half-day program—they will still be able to take full advantage of the offerings at their regular schools, such as foreign language classes, Foellner explains.

Two years ago, enrollment at Bethlehem had "bottomed out," Foellner recalls. This year, enrollment is up almost 100 students, primarily because of the new program for academic students. The school is recognized as a model for integrating academic and vocational studies, and Lehigh University has shown interest in holding a summer practicum for mechanical engineering students at Bethlehem. "We're ecstatic about what's happening right now," Foellner says. "It's exciting times for us."

WORKING TOGETHER

Collaboration between teachers from the academic and vocational realms is critical to integration efforts, experts say.

Academic and vocational teachers at Tyrone High School in Tyrone, Pa., used to keep to their own; the division between them was symbolized by the heavy doors between the two parts of the school. Now, teachers from both sides are often found in each other's classrooms, says Janette Kelly, the school's vocational director.

The collaboration has borne fruit. Vocational teachers and math teachers, for example, have worked together to develop ways to introduce applied technology into math classes. "We don't have 'shop math' any more," Kelly notes. In addition, an industrial technology teacher and a science teacher are co-teaching a course for 8th graders, which is hands-on but deals with "very high-level science."

"The academic teachers are thrilled" to be sharing instructional ideas with their vocational colleagues, Kelly says, and all teachers are excited to be blending the academic and vocational. But "it's not easy to do," she cautions. "We've had this idea that if you're vocational, you're not intellectually inclined—you work with your hands." Changing that attitude is worth the effort, however, she asserts.

The Great Oaks Joint Vocational School District in Cincinnati, Ohio, has also succeeded in fostering collaboration between academic and vocational teachers, says Rosemary Kolde, associate superintendent.

Collaboration in the district started in earnest several years ago, Kolde says, when vocational and academic teachers met over the summer to write a new academic curriculum—one that meshed with the vocational curriculum and used problems and examples drawn from the workplace. Now, academic teachers get an extra planning period so they can team teach with a lab teacher. Concepts that students learn in a trigonometry class, for example, are also used in a lab class to reinforce them. Students are extremely successful in the new program, Kolde says, because they find learning more relevant. "A lot of students are really turned off by a straight academic class," she observes.

While many vocational experts are enthusiastic about integrating academic and vocational content, they also cite numerous prerequisites. "The key thing is to get the teachers to sit down together and have some time to plan," say Hayward of the National Center for Research in Vocational Education.

Teachers need staff development to help them coordinate and articulate what they teach; otherwise, the result may be a "one-sided, superficial version" of integration, says Jay Cummings, director of vocational applied technology education for the state of Texas. "A math teacher might mention that math helps tool-and-die makers," he says. "Some people call that integration."

Staff development may also be needed to provide teachers with new skills. Some vocational teachers with backgrounds in industry are fearful of teaching academics, says Harley Schlichting, director of the Instructional Materials Lab at the University of Missouri and a former high school voc ed teacher. Similarly, academic teachers "need help with the applications side," says Gene Bottoms, director of the Southern Regional Education Board's State Vocational Education Consortium.

"If folks believe that because we now have the legislation, [integration] will automatically happen, that is a major mistake," Bottoms says. Integration will happen only if principals and teachers have a vision of what the high school could be as a result, he says.

THE TECH-PREP ALTERNATIVE

A second major trend in vocational education also holds promise for the forgotten half of students, experts say: the development of tech-prep programs.

Based on agreements between high schools and postsecondary schools (usually community colleges), tech-prep programs provide articulated sequences of courses leading to a certificate or two-year associate degree. Because they span the last two years of high school and two years of community college study, they are also known as "2 + 2" programs.

In his 1985 book, *The Neglected Majority*, Dale Parnell advocated tech-prep programs as a way of "making winners of ordinary students." His logic has proven persuasive. Today, tech-prep programs are "sweeping the country," says Hayward, because the idea simply "makes good sense."

Tech-prep programs have much to offer, proponents say. First and foremost, they provide an attractive alternative for students who do not plan to attend a four-year college on leaving high school. They allow students to acquire lucrative technical skills and a degree, while investing far less money and time. "For a lot of students, the idea of staying in school four more years is out of the question," Hayward says, but many are willing to study two more years to earn an associate degree.

Community colleges support tech-prep programs because, by maintaining close ties to neighboring high schools, they can ensure that students come to them better prepared, Hayward says. Business and industry also support tech-prep programs, because they need the skilled workers these programs produce.

The U.S. Congress also backs the idea. The new Perkins Act authorizes the federal government to spend up to $125 million to fund tech-prep programs. This funding represents a change in thinking, says Ken Gray of Pennsylvania State University; in the past, Congress has frowned upon the idea of 2 + 2 programs. "The federal government felt the reason they were supporting voc ed was because it was a special program" with extra costs, he explains, not an alternate means of preparing for higher education. Gray applauds the turnaround. "It's not only the right thing; it's critical."

Buzzell of the AVA also supports the tech-prep concept but emphasizes that it is not new. "It's been going on for a long time," he says. "It's been quite successful in some places." Programs will proliferate, he predicts, because the federal government is now providing "the tool-up money" to develop them.

Ways to Integrate Academics and Voc Ed

With his colleagues, Norton Grubb of the National Center for Research in Vocational Education at the University of California–Berkeley has identified eight ways that educators can integrate vocational and academic education:

✦ *Incorporate more academic content in vocational courses.* This can be done informally by the instructor, or formally by adopting curriculum materials or developing model curriculums that have academic skills components.

✦ *Use academic teachers to enhance the teaching of academic content in vocational programs.* Academic teachers can teach lessons or modules in vocational classrooms, work with vocational teachers to develop more academic exercises, or serve as remedial teachers for vocational students.

✦ *Make academic courses more vocationally relevant.* Academic teachers can incorporate vocational applications, such as reading materials that describe work-related activities and job-related problems in math and science. The most common approach, however, is to introduce "applied academics" courses.

✦ *Align the academic and vocational curriculums.* Academic courses can be made more occupationally relevant, vocational courses more academically rigorous, and the two linked so as to reinforce each other. This approach requires teachers to work together closely to create coherent sequences of courses for students choosing the vocational program.

✦ *Follow the Academy model.* Academies usually operate as schools-within-schools, staffed by four collaborating teachers: one each in math, science, English, and a vocational subject. Courses are coordinated, and teachers develop special projects that cut across all four classes. Academies often develop relationships with businesses in their area.

✦ *Set up occupational high schools and magnet schools.* Such schools prepare students for jobs in aviation, fashion industries, business careers, agricultural sciences, and the health professions. The culture of these schools readily supports the integration of academic and vocational instruction.

✦ *Offer occupational majors and "career paths."* A few schools have replaced subject-area departments with departments organized along occupational lines; each department recommends specific course sequences for given careers. Students in career paths take academic and vocational courses related to their paths. They also attend career path activities, including field trips and lectures by visitors.

✦ *Use the senior project as a form of integration.* A senior project might consist of a written report, a physical representation of some kind, and an oral presentation. This approach requires students to demonstrate mastery of a variety of competencies, both academic and vocational.

Adapted from "The Cunning Hand, The Cultured Mind": Models for Integrating Vocational and Academic Education *by W. Norton Grubb, Gary Davis, Jeannie Lum, Jane Plihal, and Carol Morgaine.*

Mt. Hood Community College in Gresham, Ore., has had tech-prep arrangements with its eight feeder high schools since 1987, says Jim Schoelkopf, a curriculum specialist in professional/technical education for Multnomah County. Students at Mt. Hood can earn associate degrees in a wide variety of fields, including accounting, landscaping, automotives, cable television, early childhood education, electronics, drafting, tourism and hospitality, journalism, and office occupations. The college and high school faculties meet at least twice year to examine curriculum and technology issues and to ensure rigor, Schoelkopf says.

The program targets that "vast middle ground of students who are merely jumping through the hoops to fulfill institutional requirements," Schoelkopf says. It attracts these student by "giving them some recognition" (including AP credit) and "pointing them toward a higher-paying job." The program also takes advantage of the fact that the community college environment is less intimidating to many students than a university.

North Carolina first implemented tech-prep in 1986 in a pilot program in Richmond County, says Clifton Belcher, who directs the state's division of vocational education services. Today, programs are in place at about 30 sites. "We anticipate by 1995 to have the program in all of the school systems of sufficient size," he says.

North Carolina has aimed its tech-prep programs at "students who were not pursuing the college track but knew they could do better than the general track," Belcher says. These students have not been scared off by the commitment or the stepped-up academics, he reports. "It has become very popular."

Belcher credits this popularity to the "avenue of visibility" that tech-prep provides these students. He also notes that students are "very excited about the kind of education they're receiving," which is application-oriented and promotes teamwork. Added incentives are the convenience and low tuition rates that community colleges offer.

"We're still in our infancy," Belcher says of the state's tech-prep effort, but he is "pleased and encouraged with results" so far.

Tech-prep has also proved successful in the South Carolina counties of Anderson, Oconee, and Pickens, says Diana Walter, executive director of the Partnership for Academic and Career Education (PACE) in Pendleton, S.C. The initiative in those counties has been named the top tech-prep program in the nation by the U.S. Department of Education.

Some high school students have been skeptical of applied academics courses, Walter says. A typical response is, "Hey, wait a minute—I don't do physics." But in time students adjust—and learn to like the challenge. In some cases, enrollments have doubled and tripled in applied classes, she says.

Such success does not come easily, however. Developing a new tech-prep program requires a lot of work, Belcher stresses. "You must provide a minimum of a year for design."

Staff development is also critical, experts say, to help faculty members at both institutions understand the program's aims and to help them collaborate. In addition, programs require strong support from the school board, superintendent, community college president, high school principal, and counselors.

Publicizing tech-prep programs is important to their success, Belcher adds. Most schools host open houses several times during the year to explain the programs to parents, he says, but brochures and newspaper ads may also be necessary to get the message across.

CAUTIONARY FLAGS

While most vocational experts agree that tech-prep programs are a promising means of educating the "neglected majority," some raise cautionary flags.

"One has to be careful that it's not seen as the silver bullet," says Buzzell. In particular, he fears that too much content might be deferred to the community college years. "Don't so water down the high school element that there is no employment at the end of that experience," he cautions.

Schlichting of the University of Missouri worries that tech-prep programs might force high school voc ed teachers to emphasize preparing students for further study, thereby slighting students who plan to join the workforce after high school. If high school course credits are to transfer under the program, the postsecondary school has control over accepting them, he points out.

Others caution against superficial implementation. "Many colleges say they're doing tech-prep when in fact they're [only] doing an elevated level of articulation," says Jim McKenney of the American Association of Community and Junior Colleges. These schools should be going further by "revamping the curriculum on both sides of the aisle," he says.

A major challenge, Walter says, is addressing the concerns of parents, who often ask, "What if my kid changes his mind?" (Nothing prevents tech-prep students from going on to earn a four-year degree if they choose, she notes.) Also problematic is the added work that tech-prep programs create for high school counselors, who often feel overwhelmed by the new demands.

But the benefits far outweigh the drawbacks, experts agree. One of the most important benefits, Kolde says, is that students in tech-prep programs have "a good career plan in mind." As a result, they have a greater investment in their education and are more determined to achieve. Tech-prep programs provide a clear path for students who would otherwise be wandering aimlessly through the curriculum.

Through the integration of academic content and the development of tech-prep programs, vocational educators are helping to change many students' focus from "what you have to do to get out of high school" to "how to prepare best for what's after high school." That shift in focus is perhaps one of the largest contributions that vocational education is making to the cause of educating all students—including the "forgotten half."

DO VOC ED STUDENTS NEED GENERAL OR SPECIFIC SKILLS?

SCOTT WILLIS

A perennial controversy in vocational education is whether students should be taught job-specific skills or more general, transferable skills. Some experts argue that students need job-specific skills so they will be immediately employable on leaving school. Others contend that training students for a particular job does them a disservice, because the job market is unpredictable and workers change jobs frequently. Therefore, what students really need is generic skills, such as how to think conceptually and critically, how to learn, and how to get along at the workplace.

Charles Buzzell of the American Vocational Association is a staunch advocate of teaching job-specific skills. "Is it important for an attorney, a doctor, or an engineer to have specific job-relevant skills?" he asks. "You bet it is. And [it's equally important] for the carpenter, the auto mechanic, and the laboratory technician." Buzzell considers neglecting job-specific skills a form of educational malpractice. "Do you want to dump 60 percent of our high school population into the labor market with no training?" he asks rhetorically.

Many others in the field, however, think vocational education should be providing "broader occupational competencies," says John Wirt of the Secretary's Commission on Achieving Necessary Skills (SCANS). This view is backed by findings such as those reported in *America's Choice*, the report of the Commission on the Skills of the American Workforce: "The primary concern of more than 80 percent of employers is finding workers with a good work ethic and appropriate social behavior. . . . Although a few managers are worried about literacy and basic math skills, education levels rarely seem a concern."

This article was originally published as "Do Students Need General or Specific Skills?" in the September 1991 issue of ASCD's *Curriculum Update* newsletter.

Harley Schlichting of the University of Missouri claims employers don't really mean what they say. "A student needs a job-specific skill; I don't want to teach my secretary how to type or to use good grammar." Advocates of teaching job-specific skills also note that employers do very little training at the entry level. "By and large, the employing community expects workers to be trained when they arrive," says Buzzell.

KEEPING PACE WITH CHANGE

Yet, others contend, instruction simply can't keep pace with changes in the job-specific skills needed in the marketplace.

Buzzell refutes this argument with an analogy to medicine. "Are we going to stop giving [medical students] the skills and understandings for making a transplant with the mechanical heart we have today based on the fact it's going to change tomorrow? Of course not." Similarly, vocational students gain a great deal by learning job-specific skills, even if those skills may someday become obsolete. Buzzell scoffs at the illogical notion that "if I train Charlie as an electrician, I might damage his capacity for future learning."

"There's a place for both" job-specific and transferable skills in the vocational education curriculum, says Gerald Hayward of the National Center for Research in Vocational Education. Specific skills training is needed for the hundreds of thousands of students who go directly into jobs—from secretarial programs, for instance. But students "also need generic skills so they're not stuck in that job forever."

Those who downplay the need to teach job-specific skills are simply naive about the realities of vocational education, Buzzell believes. "We will always have students exiting the high school to work," he says. "We owe it to those students and their taxpaying parents [to ensure] that they are able to go and earn a living when they exit the system."

Obviously, critical to the debate over teaching job-specific skills is the question of whether students who have acquired such skills find jobs related to their studies.

The National Assessment of Vocational Education (NAVE) reported discouraging findings on this question: "We estimate that, for women who get no education beyond high school, about 46 percent of all occupationally specific vocational courses were used in training-related skilled jobs. The comparable number for men was 33 percent. . . . These rates are low enough to call into question the efficacy of highly job-specific forms of occupational training for many students at the secondary level."

Buzzell warns that the NAVE figures are misleading. "You've got to be sure to factor out the difference between a survey course and a concentrated sequence of courses, and the NAVE study didn't do that," he notes. He also points out that the NAVE data are skewed by the fact that some students may have taken only one or two vocational courses and therefore naturally did not find employment in a training-related job.

Buzzell offers his own rule of thumb regarding placement rates: "Find a quality voc ed program and you can expect 90 percent of the students to find employment in their trade/craft area or in a related trade/craft area," providing students are willing to relocate. But he offers the caveat that "you're not served well when you use placement as a surrogate measure of quality of instruction," because the economic climate has a marked effect on placement rates.

THINKING SKILLS

◆

TEACHING THINKING

SCOTT WILLIS

The teaching of thinking has come a long way since the days when teachers directed their students to "put on their thinking caps." Today, many teachers take a much more active role in helping their students to think clearly and logically—and to monitor and assess their own thinking.

Since the early 1980s, the education community has seen a surge of interest and innovation in teaching thinking. Advances in cognitive science—known collectively as the "cognitive revolution"—have encouraged educators to pay more attention to students' thought processes. And with the roar of the "knowledge explosion" ringing in their ears, educators have come to realize that students will be better equipped for the future if they are good thinkers, rather than good memorizers of a fixed body of knowledge.

Experts in the field generally agree on the thinking processes that students need to master, but differ on the best way to teach them. Three approaches to teaching thinking are the most common:

• *Creation of a classroom environment that fosters thinking, without direct teaching of thinking skills.* Teachers following this approach may use Socratic questioning techniques, for example, to prompt students to clarify and refine their thinking. Instruction may be focused around issues, problems, and debates to spur higher-order thinking. Directly taught thinking skills, however, are conspicuous by their absence.

This article was originally published in the June 1992 issue of ASCD's *Curriculum Update* newsletter.

• *Infusion of thinking skills into regular classroom instruction.* This is the most popular method of teaching thinking, experts say. Teachers following this approach generally teach thinking skills directly, in the context of subject-matter content. The thinking skills most often taught include predicting, hypothesizing, remembering, comparing and contrasting, analyzing, inferring, decision making, problem solving, and deductive reasoning.

• *Separate courses for teaching thinking.* In this approach, thinking processes are taught outside the context of regular classroom content. Separate programs for teaching thinking include Feuerstein's Instrumental Enrichment, Lipman's Philosophy for Children, and Pogrow's Higher Order Thinking Skills (HOTS).

Besides debating the best way to teach students to be sound thinkers, experts in the field are grappling with the questions of how to assess students' thinking, and how to revise the curriculum so that it requires more thinking and less factual recall.

ENVIRONMENTAL IMPACT

Teachers who follow the first approach to teaching thinking—fostering a thinking environment in the classroom—provide process-oriented instruction, explains Roberts Swartz of the University of Massachusetts, who directs the National Center for Teaching Thinking. For example, they are careful to ask questions that require higher-order thinking, not just recall (Not "When did the plague sweep Europe?" but "*Why* did it?").

These teachers work at "creating a sense of inquiry by getting students to generate questions," says John Barell of Montclair State College, author of *Teaching for Thoughtfulness*. Use of wait time—"the pregnant pause"—is a key strategy. "Even more important is how we respond to kids," he emphasizes. "Do we respond to them as people or as right or wrong answers?"

In this approach, thinking skills are not directly taught. "Not everybody believes you should teach skills," says Barry Beyer of George Mason University, author of *Practical Strategies for Teaching Thinking*. "Teaching skills is condemned by some as reductionist—as paying more attention to the parts than the whole."

Those who take this view consider it best to teach *thoughtfulness* by asking engaging, thought-provoking questions; requiring students to give evidence to back up their arguments; asking students to explain their reasoning, and so on. Formulating thinking into discrete skills is artificial, they believe.

While he does not condemn the direct teaching of thinking skills, Fred Newmann of the University of Wisconsin–Madison emphasizes the importance of the "generic qualities" of the classroom. Compared with an explicit skills approach, "the more generic approach is likely to be more fruitful." Long lists of skills decontextualized from subject matter can be "unwieldy" and "too mechanistic," he says. To think productively, students need in-depth knowledge, intellectual skills, and dispositions of thoughtfulness, Newmann believes. If teachers take the skills approach too seriously, they are likely to slight the other two areas, he warns.

One drawback of the "thoughtful classroom" approach, however, is the difficulty of using Socratic techniques, experts say.

For teachers to become good Socratic questioners "takes a lot of training, practice, and patience," says Mary Reames, principal of Jamestown Elementary School in Jamestown, Pa. Reames' school has been working toward Socratic teaching for eight years, and spent an entire year clarifying the difference between recitation (question and answer) and discussion.

"It's a lot harder," she says of Socratic teaching. "You can't give students a worksheet." And teachers like to be the only source of information. But children in elementary school "thrive" on a Socratic approach, she adds.

Teachers sometimes get impatient to get to the point, and slip out of the Socratic mode into traditional telling, says Diana Kamp, who teaches 3rd grade at Katherine Curren Elementary School in Hopkins, Minn. "Teachers say, 'I think I'll just tell it to them, so I don't have to keep asking these questions.'"

INFUSING SKILLS

The second approach to teaching thinking is to infuse thinking skills into regular classroom instruction. Those who advocate this approach say

Making Thinking Manifest

Teaching thinking requires that teachers make an invisible process—thinking—visible. For teachers and students to discuss thinking, for example, thinking processes must be made manifest. For teachers to help students improve their thinking abilities, they must provide them with concrete models of good thinking. And students need to make their own thought processes tangible if they are to receive feedback.

Clearly, verbalizing one's thought processes is critical. "The best mirror of the mind is the mouth," says Stanley Pogrow, developer of the HOTS program. But putting thoughts into words doesn't always come easily. "It takes a little practice for kids to do this," says Barry Beyer of George Mason University. "Your first efforts are crude, but with time your representations become more sophisticated."

Teachers can use a variety of means to prompt students to articulate their thoughts, experts say. They can ask students to "talk aloud" their thoughts or to write stream-of-consciousness journals. Discussions and cooperative learning activities require students to put their thoughts into words clearly.

Of course, a verbal model "doesn't represent all that's happening in your mind," says David Perkins of Harvard's Project Zero. But such speech offers a "porthole" on mental processes. Even though think-aloud methodologies don't capture everything, they yield "plenty of payoffs" for both teachers and researchers, he says.

To provide models of good thinking, teachers can "talk aloud" their own thinking and provide written descriptions of how an expert thinker might approach a particular problem.

According to Howard Gardner of Harvard's Project Zero, students learn well when they have teachers who themselves learn well, who exhibit their learning, and who draw students into their approaches. "That is how masters work with apprentices and how professors work with graduate students," he notes.

Teachers, therefore, must be willing to reveal their own thought processes, experts agree. Anyone teaching thinking must have an open mind—literally, says John Barell of Montclair State College. Teachers must reveal how they themselves deal with problem situations. An English teacher, for example, must be willing to analyze an unfamiliar poem, in order to model the interpretive process for students. "Before I can ask, 'How did you approach this?' I need to be open enough to show my own thought processes," Barell says.

that students need direct instruction in thinking strategies if they are truly to sharpen their thinking.

Just creating a thoughtful classroom environment is not nearly enough, says Beyer. "It's like a craftsman going to work with a blueprint but not tools. Thinking skills are the tools of good thinking." Students cannot judge arguments, for example, if they can't reason deductively and detect assumptions.

Too many teachers believe that thinking just happens—and, if it doesn't happen, something is wrong with the student, Beyer says. In general, if students aren't thinking, teachers merely exhort them to. "Teachers rarely bring themselves to focus on thinking; they just teach their content harder." But if instruction doesn't provide an explicit focus on procedural operations, then "it never gets down to really helping kids *do* it."

Experts largely agree on the more important skills to teach, Beyer says. "There are 8 to 10 popular lists" of cognitive operations, including those of Marzano, Gubbins, and Bloom, and the California and Oregon skills lists. These lists overlap a great deal, he says. The thinking skills most often listed include predicting, hypothesizing, information gathering, decision making, problem solving, remembering, comparing and contrasting, organizing, analyzing, inferring, and evaluating.

Tim Melchior, principal of Memorial Junior High School in Valley Stream, N.Y., is a strong supporter of thinking skills based on the work of Edward de Bono. De Bono's thinking skills program, known as CoRT, is intended for students aged 8 through the high school level, Melchior says. While the program is designed as a separate curriculum, Melchior advocates infusing it, because that approach "aims directly at the transfer effect." Transfer occurs when students apply a skill in context different from the one in which the skill was originally learned.

Some of the 60 CoRT "tools" include PMI (Plus–Minus–Interesting points), a decision-making strategy; CAF (Consider All Factors); FIP (First Important Priorities); and OPV (Other Points of View). The CoRT tools are taught directly and independently of classroom content, Melchior says.

The strategies can be used "in myriad ways." OPV, for example, can be used when examining issues such as the Middle East conflict to prompt students to consider multiple points of view, including those of the United States, Israel, and Arab nations. Melchior's school also uses the tools outside of class—in disciplinary hearings, for example.

Use of the strategies leads to strong growth in students' abstract reasoning and confidence as thinkers, Melchior attests. Students' reactions are generally positive, he reports, although "some kids do not see the immediate applicability."

Jay McTighe of the Maryland School Performance Program is an advocate of teaching thinking skills, as a result of his teaching experiences. Having found that Socratic methods worked well with students in gifted programs, he assumed that the approach would benefit *all* students. But he discovered that many students don't respond naturally to problem- and issues-oriented teaching. Gifted students already have a "proclivity for thinking and reasoning," he says, but with most students, "there's a need for being more explicit."

Inner-city students, in particular, need to be taught thinking strategies that the academically able already use, says Judy Lechner, principal of Samuel B. Huey Elementary School in Philadelphia, Pa. Once they are taught these skills, disadvantaged students gain more control over their learning and take more responsibility for it, she says. At her own school, Lechner has seen improvement in attendance, grades, and the number of children at grade level as a result of efforts to teach thinking skills. "Teaching thinking is one of the equalizers," she asserts.

THE CONTEXT CONNECTION

Some experts, however, are skeptical of the value of learning general thinking skills outside a specific context. "I don't believe that one can teach thinking in general," says Howard Gardner, who co-directs Harvard's Project Zero. "One is always thinking about specific problems in specific domains."

"Separate drill or even open-ended practice on the thinking skills isn't going to do much for you," says Lauren Resnick of the Learning Research and Development Center at the University of Pittsburgh. "You can't build up complex abilities out of little bits, so it probably will do very little good to have me practice comparing and contrasting and then put me into a complex situation" calling for that skill. She offers this illustration: In the midst of a complex discussion on what to do with nuclear waste, the teacher asks students to consider a similar question—the disposal of ordinary garbage. "Would it help the kids to have gotten drilled on compare and contrast? Almost certainly not."

Others argue that teaching general thinking skills *does* help students hone their thinking.

Swartz believes that while students may already have certain thinking skills, instruction in those skills helps clarify and sharpen them. For example, while students may already consider options and consequences when making decisions, the teacher who teaches decision making is "guiding them through a more focused and orderly process."

In teaching a general strategy for classifying, for example, teachers will be very specific about what they want students to do, says Robert Marzano of McREL, who developed ASCD's Tactics for Thinking program. This not only provides a common language for discussing thinking but elicits "a level of rigor that we don't need in everyday life."

HOW EXPLICIT?

How explicit teachers should make thinking skills is also a matter for debate. Should a strategy for decision making, for example, be a general guideline or a step-by-step algorithm? There is "great variation" in the degree of explicitness teachers provide—from a quick pass to elaborate structures, Swartz says.

Most experts agree that a fairly high degree of explicitness is necessary. When thinking processes are left implicit, students who are not already good thinkers probably won't catch on, Swartz says; they won't be able to fine-tune their strategies.

"How do you model thinking? You can't open your head and show the wheels turning," points out Richard Paul, director of the Center for Critical Thinking at Sonoma State University. Teachers, therefore, have to be somewhat explicit. "A degree of explicitness is very important," affirms David Perkins, who co-directs Harvard's Project Zero.

However, the same experts also warn against going too far. If thinking strategies become "overproceduralized," then students become captive to procedure, says Paul; they may stop using their own judgment in applying them. Many teachers are "sucked into the trap of taking the thinking out of thinking," he says. Strategies need to be handy, not cumbersome, or students won't use them, Perkins adds.

"I certainly do believe in the direct teaching of certain thought processes," says Barell, "but I feel discomfort because it can be taken to extremes." Teachers must guard against using an overly skills-explicit approach and neglecting pedagogy, he says. "You can get bogged down in every little step; you can micro-manage everything."

Making thinking skills explicit is "too heavy-handed," says Matthew Lipman of Montclair State College, the developer of Philosophy for Children. "It makes students overly conscious of the skills themselves at the expense of the process." If students are weak at drawing inferences, for example, then teachers should break for an exercise that strengthens them in that area. But, otherwise, too much explicitness forces students to be "like the caterpillar thinking about how it walks."

When teachers or programs spend a great deal of time teaching thinking skills in an algorithmic way, McTighe says, the skills become an end in themselves rather than a means to explore content. Barell agrees that teachers must not lose sight of content goals. "If we just focus on skills without reverence for what the curriculum calls for, we are not doing a service to *The Old Man and the Sea* or the quadratic equation."

McTighe also cautions against grafting thinking skills onto the curriculum. Deciding arbitrarily to teach comparison to 3rd graders is artificial, he asserts. The teaching of such skills should arise from the content being taught and the needs of the students.

NEW SKILLS, OLD CONTENT

Experts agree that skills cannot be taught in the abstract; *some* content is needed as a vehicle to demonstrate a new skill. "Almost everybody believes and argues that teaching thinking should be [done] in content, because thinking is content-specific," says Beyer. While many experts recommend teaching skills in the context of new subject-matter content, some disagree with that approach.

"People who are good at skill teaching teach [a new skill] with information the kids *already* know," to ensure that new content doesn't interfere with students' learning the skill, Beyer says. The teacher then helps

Metacognition: Thinking About Thinking

Metacognition—thinking about one's thinking—is vital to being a good thinker, experts agree. Metacognition is "one of the most powerful tactics" for improving one's thinking, says Barry Beyer of George Mason University.

There are three aspects to metacognition, he explains: planning, monitoring, and evaluating one's thinking. Through metacognition, students reflect on, articulate, and become conscious of their own thinking processes; this helps them to store thinking strategies and call them up when appropriate.

Ordinarily, students don't think about thinking. "They think it just happens; they stand around waiting for it to happen," Beyer jokes. But if students become metacognitively aware, they can make their thinking conscious, explicit, and purposeful.

Teachers need to help their students develop metacognitive awareness. "You *can* cultivate it," insists Robert Swartz of the University of Massachusetts. "It's a kind of habit of mind." Means for stimulating metacognition include double-entry journals (notes and reflections on them), discussions about thinking, and modeling.

To foster metacognition, Susan Whitten, who teaches in the Concord, Mass., public schools, has her students write about their thinking. She prompts them to reflect on their own thinking by asking them frequently, "What were you thinking about when you did . . . " In time, they come to reflect on their thinking naturally, she says.

Robert Marzano of McREL warns that metacognition can also be taken to extremes. A lot of mental energy can be spent making thinking *too* conscious, he says. "Automaticity is the goal."

students apply the skill to "increasingly less familiar content and multiple content."

While he believes skills can be taught effectively with new content, Barell agrees that the content can "get in the way" of learning the skill. For example, trying to teach students to identify assumptions during a Shakespeare unit may be a mistake; the difficulty of the vocabulary may get in the way of learning about assumptions.

The CoRT tools are taught using "neutral" examples from the program, Melchior says. A teacher should not use the topic of smoking to teach a decision-making strategy, for example, because the emotional content could be distracting, he says. Instead, the teacher should choose an issue children can look at "purely academically," such as whether seats should be removed from buses to allow more passengers. "Then connect [the skill] relatively quickly to learning in the classroom."

SEPARATE PROGRAMS

The third approach to teaching thinking—separate programs—is least common, experts say. This is primarily because separate programs require their own class periods. This approach also raises questions about whether students will apply what they learn in separate courses to their other classes, McTighe says.

Two highly respected separate programs for teaching thinking are Higher Order Thinking Skills (HOTS), developed by Stanley Pogrow of the University of Arizona–Tucson, and Philosophy for Children, developed by Matthew Lipman of Montclair State College. HOTS is a pullout program that aims to help at-risk students develop their general thinking abilities. (HOTS replaces Chapter 1 programs and programs for students with learning disabilities.) Students attend HOTS classes for 35 minutes, four days a week, generally for two years. Now in its ninth year, the program is used in nearly 2,000 schools, according to Pogrow.

The HOTS program does not take an explicit skills approach. Instead, it helps children develop their thinking abilities through extensive participation in a social setting, Pogrow says. Teachers use Socratic questioning and "bug" students to clarify their thoughts. The aim is "sophisticated conversation" in the classroom.

HOTS is not tied in any way to the content of the regular classroom, Pogrow says. With disadvantaged children, it's necessary to start with general thinking divorced from content, because these children don't understand understanding. "They have no cultural sense of how to deal with ideas; they don't know what it means to think symbolically." HOTS students typically come from environments that haven't enabled them to develop those abilities. "You don't need to think abstractly or to generalize to survive on the street," he notes.

The HOTS program seeks to develop four general thinking areas: metacognition, inferring from context, recognizing ideas in different contexts, and synthesizing information. After HOTS students receive general thinking instruction, they can go on to thinking in content, Pogrow says.

Transfer is not a problem. Helping students improve their general thinking produces "tremendous" transfer, Pogrow asserts. Research findings on transfer have been negative because studies haven't examined the type of transfer sought in HOTS, he says; the subjects have been mainly adults and college students, leading to a "gross misinterpretation" of the potential for transfer.

There is "no question" that HOTS improves students' achievement in their regular classes and their scores on standardized tests, Pogrow says.

Philosophy for Children is exactly what its name implies—a program to help children consider philosophical questions. The program uses novels in which the characters are children who engage in inquiry. Students emulate the characters, who show them how to question. The program is designed for all levels from kindergarten to secondary school; it is taught in a block by a trained regular classroom teacher.

Philosophy for Children "contrasts with the usual approach to thinking skills" because it teaches thinking holistically, Lipman says. The program avoids separating thinking into its component skills; instead, it is "higher order from the beginning." Discussion is central, he emphasizes. In discussion, children spontaneously use skills such as drawing inferences and hypothesizing. "It's done naturally, without [the teacher] having to draw attention to them."

Lipman deplores the "terrible obstacles" raised in the past to helping children think. Scientists, including Piaget, have believed—based on developmental theories—that children are not interested in ideas or abstractions until age 11 or 12. "That's completely wrong," Lipman charges. "Children are excited by ideas" and often show a burning interest in what's fair and true. "It's not surprising that children have a taste for abstraction."

About 5,000 U.S. school districts use Philosophy for Children in at least one classroom, Lipman says. The program is also being used in Russia. Lipman has visited Moscow twice to demonstrate Philosophy for Children, which, he says, comports with the Russians' hypotheses of how children think. In America, by contrast, "it doesn't fit into the Piagetian fabric."

ASSESSMENT

While experts may differ over the best approach to teaching thinking, they agree that good assessment of student thinking is a critical need—especially in light of the cold reality that what gets tested gets taught.

"We need to assess reasoning, not recall," Paul says. But that is not easily done. After all, it is harder to assess whether students can make good inferences than whether they know the capital of North Dakota. Assessment of thinking is a thorny problem, says Barell. "For a lot of people it's a stumbling block for teaching thinking."

Unfortunately, the reigning form of large-scale assessment—standardized, multiple-choice tests—is better at testing factual knowledge than revealing thought processes. Standardized tests rarely reveal *why* an answer was chosen, experts point out. "We've got to get students to expose their thinking," Swartz stresses. "Multiple-choice and true–false tests are the worst way to do this."

Experts agree that performance assessments are much more effective at capturing students' thinking. Moving to performance assessment is "very, very important," says Swartz. Requiring students to provide extended verbal responses, either in writing or through interviews, yields much more information than standardized tests, he says.

While Perkins notes that there are "a few well-crafted commercially available tests that assess some facets of thinking," he agrees that open-ended, authentic assessments such as essays, portfolios, and conversations reveal much more about students' thinking. However, these assessments are not easily standardized, he points out.

Assessments should include challenging tasks without obvious solutions, says McTighe. In addition, assessment tasks should be situated in a context, unlike tests of isolated skills. Of prime importance is the need to collect information on how students approach a problem.

The lack of congruent assessment need not hamstring efforts to teach thinking, Melchior says. As a school principal, he has found that assessment is "not at all a stumbling block." It's "virtually painless" for a school to begin teaching thinking, he says. "Do it but don't make the argument that you're going to derive achievement gains," because current assessment rewards memorization of content, not thinking. "If you get achievement gains, well and good. But you should argue that there will be no losses" on standardized tests. "Strategically, that's the better way to go."

CHANGING THE CURRICULUM

Beyond changing pedagogy and assessment, educators need to modify the curriculum to better evoke student thinking, experts agree. First and foremost, it must be changed to value depth over breadth.

Many subject matters have far too many topics, leading to superficial coverage, says Perkins. The curriculum should encourage active use of the mind—problem solving, inventing, and making connections—not merely memorization. The curriculum should be based on key issues and concepts, says McTighe. "To really stimulate thinking there's a need for curriculum to be framed in problems, issues, anomalies—not just stuff to be learned."

"We need to insert an instructional program in thinking" into the curriculum, says Beyer. Teachers lack knowledge about teaching thinking and need support from instructional specialists and curriculum developers. McTighe agrees that curriculum materials need to provide more suggestions for improving thinking—explicit teaching strategies and open-ended questions, for example. "Thinking skills and processes have to become curricular goals," Swartz adds, so teachers will feel more comfortable devoting time to them.

"Unless the curriculum embodies good models of thinking (within materials and within the teacher) and students have plenty of opportunity to practice thinking, there is no chance that students will learn to think better," Gardner asserts. "Very few curricula anywhere in the world pass this test. When students think well, it is usually because they have had a succession of good teachers who have given them plenty of opportunity to engage in performances of thinking."

WORTH FIGHTING FOR

To transform pedagogy, curriculum, and assessment to support the teaching of thinking may seem like an uphill battle. But experts are emphatic that the spoils of victory—for teachers as well as students—are worth the fight.

The rewards of teaching students to live up to their intellectual potential are "outstanding," says Barell. Teachers get very excited at the "gems of thoughtful responses" that students produce. Teachers are "rejuvenated" by the change in their role from dispenser of knowledge to sparker of ideas, says McTighe.

Teaching thinking also produces some unforgettable moments, as Corrine Hill, ASCD Past-President and principal of Wasatch Elementary School in Salt Lake City, Utah, discovered. For over five years, Hill's school has made teaching thinking a priority. When the 6th grade boys presented Hill with a petition arguing that the school's dress code was unfair in allowing girls but not boys to wear hats, with a copy of the First Amendment attached, Hill felt a surge of satisfaction. "Here was a clear sign that we are a thinking school."

◆

DO THINKING SKILLS TRANSFER?

SCOTT WILLIS

Central to the issue of how best to teach thinking is the question of transfer: whether students will apply a thinking skill learned in one context when the need to use it arises in a different context. For example, will students who have learned "comparing and contrasting" during a unit on governmental systems be able to compare and contrast two novels? The transfer question has important implications, because the rationale for teaching general thinking skills—"making inferences" or "hypothesizing," for example—is based on the expectation that students will be able to use such skills in a variety of contexts.

This article was originally published as "The Transfer Question" in the June 1992 issue of ASCD's *Curriculum Update* newsletter.

Many experts warn that spontaneous transfer is a rare phenomenon. "If there is one dogged finding in educational psychology over the past century, it's the difficulty of obtaining transfer, particularly interesting transfer over some distance," says Howard Gardner of Harvard's Project Zero.

Students fail to transfer skills between dissimilar contexts because learning is largely context-bound, experts say. "The human being is a context-sensitive organism and what is learned in one context generally remains mired in that context," Gardner says.

"Being good at something is very situationally specific," agrees Lauren Resnick of the Learning Research and Development Center at the University of Pittsburgh. "That's a fundamental concept, the most radical of all in recent cognitive research: that we create knowledge as we go and that it is adapted to the [particular] situations we're in."

Being a good mathematical reasoner isn't the same as being a good historical reasoner, Resnick asserts. "Now, that doesn't mean there's *no* transfer from one to the other. There is some—but a whole lot less than we used to hope for."

Whether teachers can reasonably expect spontaneous transfer depends on what is being learned, says David Perkins of Harvard's Project Zero. If the skill in question is something strongly stimulated by the environment, such as reading, then transfer probably won't be a problem. Children readily apply reading skills learned at school when they encounter written material elsewhere. But when the thinking skill is not obviously demanded by the environment—"classifying," for example— then students have to "remind themselves" to use the applicable strategy. "This makes spontaneous transfer much rarer," Perkins says.

Another reason transfer happens so rarely is because the curriculum tends to be fragmented, creating a mindset in students that subject areas are unrelated, says Jay McTighe of the Maryland School Performance Program. This fragmentation offers a "disincentive" to transfer.

Richard Paul of the Center for Critical Thinking at Sonoma State University believes that traditional teaching produces little transfer because most students' understanding is superficial. "If we want transfer, we need depth—and we are far, far away from depth," he says.

Other experts are more optimistic about the likelihood of transfer.

Teaching thinking involves mostly procedural knowledge, much of which cuts across the disciplines, says Robert Marzano, the developer of Tactics for Thinking. "There are generic types of thinking you can do in any content area." If the teacher provides appropriate cueing, the frequency of student transfer is "not bad at all," he says.

Matthew Lipman, the developer of Philosophy for Children, concedes that each discipline has its own idiosyncrasies that might not readily transfer, but argues that there are common elements among them. "The ability to debate, examine, reflect, question, infer—these are not limited to any one discipline."

Barbara Presseisen of Research for Better Schools cautions against defining transfer too narrowly, as "something you're going to expect to see on a test on Friday." Some instances of transfer are more subtle and operate on the level of insight and metaphor, she says. For example, learning a second language may help one become metacognitively aware of one's own language. Transfer "won't happen the same way for everyone."

If students have a deep understanding of a concept, they will be able to apply it in novel situations, asserts John Barell of Montclair State College. "The alternative is absurd. To say that knowledge is going to stay within history or physics doesn't accord with anybody's experience."

TEACHING FOR TRANSFER

The challenge, experts agree, is to teach so that transfer *will* happen. "Transfer can be obtained, of course," says Gardner, "but it generally occurs only when it is mindfully sought—that is, when students and teachers recognize the common elements across two domains and try explicitly to make the connections."

Barry Beyer of George Mason University agrees. "Transfer doesn't just happen on its own. But it will happen with help." Teachers need deliberately to help students transfer skills, he stresses. Students often won't call up relevant thinking operations they have learned because "they don't seem to be appropriate."

To overcome this obstacle, Perkins recommends that teachers give students practice using a strategy in a variety of contexts, perhaps in different disciplines. Teachers should also have students consider potential opportunities for transfer. "You might ask students to brainstorm possible uses" of a strategy in other settings, he suggests.

Teacher modeling of transfer is very helpful, says Susan Whitten, who teaches in the Concord, Mass., public schools. Teachers should try to demonstrate skills in a variety of settings, not only in academic areas but in real-life, social situations, she advises.

The more you teach for transfer, the more it happens, say Robert Swartz of the University of Massachusetts, director of the National Center for Teaching Thinking. Teachers need to remind and prompt students constantly to apply skills they have learned in other contexts. "You've got to keep reinforcing it," he emphasizes.

However, not all transfer is good transfer, Paul points out. Instances of undesirable transfer often occur, as when students overgeneralize or form prejudices. Negative transfer is also to blame when students accustomed to worksheets begin calculating furiously to solve the problem: "The are 75 sheep and 5 sheepdogs in a field. How old is the shepherd?" As Paul notes, "We want enlightened transfer."

UNTRACKING

CAN SEPARATE BE EQUAL?

JOHN O'NEIL

Noble High School, a small school of 800 students in rural Berwick, Maine, is an unlikely place to start a revolution. But Noble—like a handful of other schools around the nation—is seeking to overturn a principle that has guided how schools organize instruction for decades.

Unlike the vast majority of American schools, Noble is challenging the notion that students must be divided into separate ability groups to receive an appropriate education. Except for its Advanced Placement program, the school of 800 students is completely "untracked," according to Principal Pam Fisher. As part of a program that includes 90-minute classes, team teaching, and a theme-based curriculum, Noble mixes together students of varying talents and interests. Since the school launched the untracking process in 1990, students have made strides socially—demonstrating increased tolerance of differences, for example—while also getting better grades, Fisher says.

The efforts at Noble and a scattering of other schools defy convention. As most schools have tinkered with one proposed change after another, the practice of grouping students by ability—or "tracking" them, as the more rigid and long-term version is known—has remained virtually unchallenged.

What started as an effort to "customize" schooling based on students' different needs, however, is now decried by some as producing education's version of apartheid. In schools where rigid grouping practices prevail,

---

This article was originally published in the June 1993 issue of ASCD's *Curriculum Update* newsletter.

low-track students, disproportionately minority and poor, are served up a ditto-driven curriculum by the least experienced teachers. Their largely white and advantaged peers in high-track classes are more likely to be taught by experienced instructors comfortable with varied and rich materials and techniques. Not surprisingly, low-track students fall further behind their peers as they take one slowed-down course after another.

Tracking may have begun as a way to better serve students, but "the system has become very stratified and very entrenched," says Mary Futrell, who as president of the National Education Association helped lead the fight against tracking. In many schools, students are grouped by ability beginning in elementary school, and it's common for the same students to turn up in the low-ability groups again and again as they move through the system, subsisting on a starvation diet of worksheets and skills drills. "Because of what we offer, we don't help students in the low track catch up," says Futrell. "They fall further and further behind." Moreover, students themselves become convinced they are not achievers, and some stop trying, she says. As a result, "We end up hurting more children than we're helping."

New Questions

Efforts to "untrack" schools have raised new questions, however. Are schools to be made more "equitable" by abandoning programs for the gifted or other special needs pupils? Will teachers be able to deal with heterogeneously grouped classes without "leveling down" the curriculum and sacrificing standards of achievement?

"The important thing is that kids get a curriculum that is geared to their current level of achievement and attainment," says James Kulik, a research scientist at the University of Michigan whose studies are frequently cited by advocates of ability grouping. "Not all kids in the same grade are going to benefit from the same material in the same course. It would be a loss for all kids if we made schools 'one-track' and all kids did the same things at the same time."

Peter Rosenstein, executive director of the National Association for Gifted Children, says that programs for gifted students have been cut or curtailed in some communities as educators attempt to move toward more heterogeneous classes. In mixed-ability classrooms, chances are that "somebody's going to lose out," says Rosenstein. Although he and other advocates of high-ability students say they abhor the conditions in low-track classes, Rosenstein says that schools must recognize that some students learn better with peers matched in ability or interests. "The public doesn't seem to hesitate to cull out the best athletes for the football team or the best musicians," he says. "Why not the best scientists or mathematicians?"

Others see things differently. While schools should continue to address students' individual differences, some believe separate homogeneous classes aren't the only way—or even a desirable way—to do so. "It's not that you forget about student differences" in untracked schools, says Robert Slavin, director of the Elementary School Program at Johns Hopkins University. "Student differences are always going to be important, no matter what your school organization is. The question is: can you deal with them within a mixed context in a flexible way that is geared to the needs of the individual children, rather than to simply separate them?"

DEFINITIONS BLURRED

The debate over if and how schools should group students by ability is complicated by confusion over terminology (see box on next page). Those favoring very limited use of ability grouping tend to blur the distinction between ability grouping and tracking. Although researchers usually are careful to distinguish among the various types of grouping, such distinctions are frequently lost in the public debate over whether schools should strive to "untrack."

Some experts feel that advocates of untracking, seeking more equitable treatment of poor and minority students, are deliberately blurring the lines between different types of ability grouping. John Feldhusen, an expert in gifted education at Purdue University, says some advocates for untracking schools are pushing "a social and political agenda" of equity and ignoring careful distinctions between effective and harmful uses of ability grouping. The result, he and others worry, will be that students whose abilities vary widely from the norm will not receive the special attention they need. "It's grossly naive to think that just dumping every-

Some Common Terms

Tracking is generally considered to be the practice of students selecting or being placed in different programs of study—such as vocational, general, or college preparatory—especially at the high school level. In addition, some use the term to describe the phenomenon of students being placed in high- or low-ability groups for extended periods during elementary and secondary school.

Ability grouping takes many forms. Between-class grouping refers to the assignment of students to separate classrooms based on ability. Within-class grouping refers to the separation of children into smaller groups within the same classroom, as is common in reading instruction at the elementary level.

Untracking or *detracking* refers to the efforts to minimize or eliminate separate classes for students of differing abilities.

one together in one heterogeneous mix will solve the problem," he adds. "We need to find ways to teach to students' different styles and interests."

Disagreements over terminology have muddied the debate over uses of grouping, but on at least one point, experts across the spectrum agree: students placed in low-ability classes year-in and year-out receive a strikingly inferior education compared to their peers in high-ability groups. In contrast to high-track classes, low-track classes focus more on basic skills and less on applications and are marked by disciplinary problems and disruptions, researchers say.

But would students currently placed in low-track classes be better off in mixed-ability classes? Those supporting such a change were bolstered recently by a new analysis of a longitudinal federal study that has now followed students as they moved from 8th to 10th grade. Controlling for prior grades, ethnicity, socioeconomic status, and other factors, researchers compared how students in tracked versus untracked schools in 8th grade did when they reached 10th grade. The result? "Students in the low track performed significantly less well than did low achievers in untracked schools on composite and core subject achievement tests" in reading, math, science, and social studies, according to a paper by researcher Jomills Henry Braddock II of the University of Miami. "Yet there was no corresponding benefit of ability grouping for high or average achievers."

Others cite research suggesting that ability grouping is appropriate in some circumstances, however. The University of Michigan's Kulik, for example, has reviewed numerous studies on the effects of ability grouping. His meta-analysis found that students *have* benefitted from some uses of ability grouping, especially when differentiated curriculum was provided for various groups.

CAN TEACHERS ADAPT?

Further, some experts are skeptical that—as schools presently operate—teachers will not be able to deal with the range of students' differences in interests and prior achievement that more widespread use of mixed-ability classes would bring, especially in the secondary grades.

Many of those expressing skepticism are parents of high-achieving students and advocates for gifted education, who are concerned that the top students will suffer in heterogeneous classes. Some parents believe that "there hasn't been a good track record of teachers being able to teach such a broad spread in the classroom," says Cathy Belter, chair of the education commission of the National PTA. "They're afraid that some of the gains [in programs for high-achieving students] may be washed aside."

A recent study by researchers at the University of Connecticut bears out such concerns. The study of 46 regular 3rd and 4th grade classrooms found that teachers made only minor modifications in the regular curriculum to meet the needs of gifted students. Such findings "paint a disturbing picture of the types of instructional services gifted students receive in regular classrooms," the researchers note, especially because gifted students typically spend all but a few hours a week in regular classrooms, and these special services are now being threatened by the budget axe or concerns over equity.

Moreover, there is evidence that most classroom teachers believe in ability grouping. In a 1988 survey administered by the Carnegie Foundation for the Advancement of Teaching, for example, 63 percent of teachers agreed with the statement that, "Tracking students by ability is a useful way for schools to deal with diversity." Says Futrell: "A lot of teachers have reservations and concerns" about more mixed-ability classes. "They have been trained to teach a certain way, and they are comfortable with that."

Teachers will need support to expand their knowledge of strategies to help students in mixed-ability classes, Futrell and others note. "We need to reconsider the predominance of classroom whole-group instruction," remarks Joseph McDonald, a senior research associate for the Coalition of Essential Schools. Team teaching and cooperative learning, for example, are commonly cited as strategies appropriate for mixed-ability settings.

NO SPECTATORS

At Noble High School in Berwick, Maine, teachers are finding they *can* make mixed-ability classes work.

One requisite for success in mixed-ability classes is that teachers don't allow students to be "spectators in the grandstands" while the teacher performs for them, notes Dick Ford, who teaches 9th and 12th grade social studies. Instead, the teacher must provide opportunities for students to take control of their own learning. Then the teacher should coach them as they work to create a product that can be shared with the class. In this approach, there is "a lot *less* teaching to the middle than in the old system," he asserts. In the past, when teachers were the dispensers of information, they aimed for the middle, missing the "two fringes." In the new system, students can work to their potential and have more direct interaction with the teacher.

Another way teachers meet students' varying needs is by regrouping within the classroom—and not solely by ability—explains Pam Fisher, Noble's principal. Depending on the activity in question, students may be grouped by skill level or for diversity. Groups are short-term and flexible, Fisher emphasizes. Deciding how best to group students "becomes a real skill over time, though at first it can be nervewracking."

Other aspects of the school's reform effort support heterogeneous grouping, Fisher says. The teaming structure "really helps us focus on the needs of [individual] kids," she says. Teachers can get to know their students and make appropriate modifications to suit their needs. The 90-minute classes also allow for more individualized instruction by providing the uninterrupted time teachers need to make small-group and one-on-one interactions work.

Students also have opportunities to do honors work or to get extra help, Fisher says. In each class, students can choose to pursue the "honors option," which requires that they meet the standard the teacher sets for honors work (the criteria are spelled out in a scoring rubric). The honors option "really gets the kids to make a personal commitment to do the work," she says. Extra help is available in the school's Learning Center, which has resources to assist students at all levels.

The social benefits of untracking have been dramatic, Fisher says. "We've made enormous strides" in improving students' attitudes toward working with other people, and in fostering tolerance of differences. And discipline problems are "nonexistent," she adds.

Over time, alienated students change their attitude about what they can accomplish, says Ford. Their more motivated peers give them a model to emulate, he says. And, if the teacher pays attention to building a sense of community, even turned-off students come to feel they can cooperate.

Fisher has also seen academic gains since the school untracked. While standardized test data is not yet available, students' grades reflect "tremendous gains in academic achievement and commitment." The whole environment of the school has changed, she says; students are more "academically focused."

Teaching in an untracked school is more difficult, Fisher admits. "My teachers are exhausted," she reports, but "they love it." They like the challenge, and they like being on teams. And when they see students of limited ability rising to the challenge in mixed-ability classes, "that's really exciting."

CHANGING WHOLE SCHOOLS

Experiences at Noble and other schools attempting to lessen or eliminate their use of ability grouping suggest that untracking is just one of a host of changes they will have to make to help more students succeed. "The fact is that, as you move from a tracked to an untracked situation, you're going to create some practical problems," says Slavin. "You're not going to harm students' achievement, but you are going to create a situation where teachers feel unhappy at dealing with very heterogeneous classes, parents are worrying about whether their high-achieving kids are getting an adequate curriculum, and so on." Therefore, untracking forces educators "to confront the issues of curriculum and instruction that you might not have otherwise felt that you had to confront."

The move toward untracking highlights the need to change whole schools while considering the needs of all students, others say. "Clear-thinking people who are concerned with all kids in the school are looking for alternatives that don't ask for some kids to be sacrificed on the altar of educational experimentation," says Paul George of the University of Florida, author of an ASCD book on untracking. "We have to move slowly, but we have to move."

UNTRACKING IN THE MIDDLE

SCOTT WILLIS

Mixed-ability grouping has found some acceptance in middle schools. Here's how three of them make it work.

Wellesley Middle School in Wellesley, Mass., which serves 640 students in grades 6 through 8, began dismantling its tracking system about seven years ago, says Principal John D'Auria. At that time, the 7th and 8th grades were completely tracked, and the 6th grade was tracked in mathematics and language arts. Today, the school has no tracking at all, except for an accelerated program in mathematics in the 7th and 8th grades.

D'Auria promoted the effort to untrack because he feels strongly that negative feedback from adults has "a tremendous impact" on early adolescents. Therefore, students in the middle grades should not be sorted in ways that stigmatize some of them.

The transition to heterogeneous grouping was "rocky in the beginning," D'Auria admits. The town of Wellesley—an upper-middle-class

This article was originally published in the June 1993 issue of ASCD's *Curriculum Update* newsletter.

suburb of Boston—has many professional people, and "a very vocal group of parents felt their kids would be shortchanged," he says.

Parents were dubious of the school's plan to enroll *all* students in the top-track courses. When an honors course is thrown open to all students, "people automatically assume you're going to water it down," D'Auria notes. To win support, the school faculty held a number of public meetings where they presented the rationale for the change and showed examples of learning activities.

D'Auria understands parents' concerns. Slighting top students is "something you have to safeguard against all the time" in a mixed-ability setting, he emphasizes. Similarly, extra help must be provided for students who fall behind their peers (at Wellesley, this is offered after school in the Learning Center). Teaching to the middle is "a risk," but D'Auria is confident that his teachers haven't slipped into it.

To teach a mixed-ability class, teachers need a broad repertoire of strategies, D'Auria says. Cooperative learning, for example, can be a valauble tool when appropriate. And *every* teacher needs to be a teacher of reading and study skills.

To ensure that all students work to their potential, teachers at the school provide "inherently challenging and interesting" learning activities that students can pursue as far as they are able, explains Linda Badgley-Smith, head of the English and social studies departments. As a result, learning is not "shut down" for the brightest students, as could happen with lessons that stay at the basic-knowledge level.

"Teachers say they've never worked so hard," D'Auria reports. The need to serve a wider range of abilities has complicated lesson planning; teachers now need to find two or three alternative ways to get a lesson across. And with no lower track to drop students back to, teachers have the pressure of knowing "it's you or nothing," he adds.

Realizing that mixed-ability classes would be more demanding, teachers at the school stipulated that class size be limited to 20–21 students, says Badgley-Smith, who teaches 8th grade world geography. Moreover, students are not placed in classes randomly, she explains. Classes are carefully balanced in factors such as motivation, ability, race, and gender; and each class has no more than a few students who will be especially challenged.

Untracking has brought academic benefits, Badgley-Smith says. On a holistically scored essay test in social studies, for example, former low-track students' scores improved by about 60 percent over the previous year's scores, while honors-level students didn't lose ground. And longitudinal test data in science are "for the most part favorable," D'Auria adds.

Teachers have also seen social benefits. There is less of an intellectual pecking order among students, Badgley-Smith says. Students are more likely to acknowledge different kinds of intelligence—to show respect for artistic ability, for example. And sometimes students who aren't considered bright by their peers express such interesting insights that their classmates are greatly impressed. Such moments "bring tears to the teacher's eyes," she says.

Given this success with mixed-ability grouping, why has the school kept two tracks in mathematics? "We didn't know as much about how to go after this subject differently," D'Auria says. Math is still taught in a lockstep, linear progression, which is less amenable to mixed-ability grouping, he says.

Untracking the school has been a slow—but successful—process, D'Auria believes. "A critical mass of the faculty are proud and feel that this is the way to go," he says.

Riverview Middle School in Denton, Md.—a rural school serving 500 students in grades 7 and 8—began untracking in 1989, says Principal Harry Martin. Until then, students had been homogeneously grouped in all academic subject areas.

Martin pushed the change because he didn't believe tracking was serving its ostensible purpose of meeting students' varied needs. The grade distribution, for instance, reflected this failure: "The kids in the low-ability sections had extremely low grades," while grades were much higher in the upper track, he recalls. Moreover, if students moved from one track to another, it was almost always in a downward direction.

But what really galvanized his desire to untrack was a climate survey given to all students. The results, when broken down by ability group, were disturbing: compared to their peers, low-track students were alienated from the school.

After he presented this data to his faculty, teachers at Riverview began experimenting with heterogeneous grouping. (They also received training in cooperative learning; and, in 1990–91, the school moved to interdisciplinary teaming.) Today, students are grouped heterogeneously in every subject except math—and the school is slowly moving toward mixed-ability grouping even there, Martin says.

Teachers accommodate the wider range of ability in their classes by using cooperative learning and by providing both extra help and enrichment opportunities, Martin says. They do *not* teach to the middle. "We teach everything to the high end, and modify down" for those who really need it, says Shawn Parks, a 7th grade English teacher. In English, for example, they now teach only the Honors curriculum.

Parks uses cooperative learning to help reach all of her students. "I personally don't think I would try it without cooperative learning," she says. Susan Piavis, a 7th grade science teacher, agrees on the importance of cooperative learning and peer tutoring. "There's no way one teacher can individualize instruction for 33, 34 kids," she points out.

Also helpful are the resource teachers who accompany mainstreamed special education students into regular classrooms. Because these resource teachers can help *any* student in the class, they are "a major source of special assistance to kids who are in need and are behind," Martin says.

Some students also get extra help in math, reading, or writing during the "enrichment period," Parks says. But Piavis notes that many students need "less special help than you would expect." This is because students who used to be low achievers often rise to the challenge in heterogeneous classes, where teachers' expectations for them are higher, she says.

Bright students are "absolutely" being challenged enough, Parks says. In every unit, there's material that is new for all students, and enrichment and challenge activities are provided for top achievers. Piavis affirms that making sure gifted students are challenged and getting along with their peers is "a constant concern."

Since the school has untracked, standardized test scores are slowly creeping up, Martin says. But the main improvement he's seen has been in students' behavior. In his first year as principal at Riverview, there were more than 250 suspensions; this year, there have been only 21 through the fall. Why the difference? "There's no longer a large group of kids who feel disenfranchised," he says.

How can other principals best follow Martin's lead? "You need the teachers on board," he says; and, to persuade them to untrack, "you need to assemble your own data." After teachers at Riverview had been confronted with data from their own school, they could "see themselves and their school" in the literature about tracking that they read.

Despite the hard work involved in moving to heterogeneous grouping, Martin has no regrets. "I've been thrilled with the outcome," he says.

Rutland Junior High School in Rutland, Vt., serves 400 students in 7th and 8th grade, most of whom qualify for free or reduced-price lunch. At Rutland, untracking is only one component of a group of reforms—including block scheduling, an advisory program, and portfolio assessment—that mutually reinforce one another, says Principal Sanford Bassett.

In 1988, the school began to transform itself from a junior high to a middle school. One of the elements of the five-year transition plan was a move to heterogeneous grouping.

Untracking was "extremely difficult" in the face of community skepticism, Bassett says. But he "did his homework," making presentations to the school board, parents, and the superintendent. After this preparation phase, the school was able to untrack the 7th grade in 1991–92 and the 8th grade this school year. Bassett believes the change allows Rutland to "serve all children across the spectrum, [and] not at the expense of any one ability level."

The old, homogeneous system was "a nightmare," says Christine Beacham, a 7th grade social studies teacher. Tracked schools tell low-track students they're stupid, she believes, so they act accordingly; they expect not to learn. In a mixed-ability setting, however, "the difference is unbelievable." Low-ability students rise to the challenge of higher expectations. They want to look good in front of their peers, so they try harder, she says.

Untracking also helps students learn to cooperate and to appreciate each other's talents, says Steve Welch, an 8th grade physical science teacher. Former low-track students can demonstrate their own talents, he says—sometimes they figure out how to string up a pulley, for example, while their "brighter" peers remain perplexed.

Two innovations that help make untracking work at Rutland are block scheduling and the use of thematic units, Bassett says. Block scheduling allows teachers to "mix and match" students—to move them quickly for remediation or enrichment, as necessary. "You need that kind of flexibility," he says, to individualize instruction without slotting students into tracks.

Thematic units help by allowing teachers to bring in a "cross-section" of reading materials. In teaching about the Roman Empire, for example, a teacher can provide a range of materials suited to a variety of ability levels: very sophisticated for top students, simple and straightforward for students who are not strong readers.

Bassett is "absolutely" seeing benefits from the untracking effort. Because classes are more diverse, "you can't teach from the textbook any more," he says. As a result, teachers are being more creative in their instruction, and planning ways to reach all students.

While it's too early to tell what achievement gains will result, the social benefits of untracking have been marked, Bassett says. The school climate has improved greatly. Referrals for disruptive behavior have plummeted, there are fewer cliques, and student teams feel a greater sense of community.

Overall, Bassett has been very pleased with the results of untracking. He concedes that there are "gaps between the rhetoric and reality" but points out that "you don't revolutionize a system that's been in place since the turn of the century overnight." His advice to other schools that are considering a move to heterogeneous grouping? "Go for it. We are a better school than we were."

WHEN ABILITY GROUPING HELPS . . . AND WHEN IT HURTS

JOHN O'NEIL

Update *Editor John O'Neil recently spoke about ability grouping with James Gallagher, an expert on gifted education at the University of North Carolina, and Kati Haycock of the American Association for Higher Education, who has written and spoken out against tracking. Excerpts from the joint interview follow.*

This article was originally published in the June 1993 issue of ASCD's *Curriculum Update* newsletter.

By all accounts, schools rely heavily on ability grouping. When is ability grouping useful and helpful?

Gallagher: Gifted students . . . are often three, four, or five years beyond their grade level in terms of achievement. It's very difficult for a teacher who may have a range of students from the 2nd grade level to the 9th grade level to provide a challenging education for all of them in the same place at the same time. So we find that ability grouping is necessary to challenge youngsters to their full accomplishment.

Haycock: I don't agree with that. My own preference is that gifted kids, in most cases, receive supplemental instruction or enrichment after or before school or during the summer. . . .

Experiences in schools that are beginning to untrack show that if teachers have a good deal of support in learning a range of instructional strategies—how to keep students at all levels stimulated and challenged— that the benefits of putting kids together far outweigh the problems.

Are teachers really ready to teach a wider range of students in the classroom?

Gallagher: We're publishing a study that looks at 46 schools across all regions of the country. The study pairs a child who is average ability with a child who is gifted through two days of observation to see what the teacher does to differentiate the program to take into account the special development of the gifted child. And the short answer is: not very much. So we can talk in theory about how the teacher can adjust the program, but . . . if you talk to parents and students, you find out that not very much differentiation is going on.

Haycock: Dealing with a range of kids is a complicated task for which many teachers are not well prepared. Certainly, moving toward more heterogeneous grouping without support for teachers in training . . . doesn't do anybody any good—gifted, average, or below-average. I'm not one who sees this as a panacea.

Much of the support for changing schools' grouping practices comes from studies illustrating the poor conditions in low-track classes. What kind of education are these students getting?

Haycock: In general, in low-track classes, kids get an education that can only be described as dull, repetitive, and unchallenging. By and large, despite what teachers believe about what they're doing for kids who are behind, they tend to push kids further behind through the strategies they use: lots of drill-and-practice, lots of dittos. . . .

In the middle grades, what you see in high-track classes is a lot of emphasis on algebraic thought and mathematical thought and reasoning. And the same age kids in low-track classes are still working on multiplication tables, and they have been for years. . . . There's nothing interesting or challenging in the kind of instruction they get. The same is true in English, where the low-track classes work on grammar, and literature becomes the core in high-track classes.

If you follow a low-track child at the middle or high school level around for a day and then spend the next day following a high-track child around, you'll think you're in different schools.

Gallagher: I'm not supporting grouping for youngsters at the low end of the developmental scale. What I do see, however, having spent some years with youngsters who are mentally retarded, is that there's no reason why you can't make an interesting and exciting educational experience. . . . Why shouldn't those [low-track] classes be exciting or interesting?

Would providing innovative curriculum materials and more experienced teachers for students in the low-ability groups be enough to make a tracked school work?

Haycock: There's no question that those measures are preferable to what we have now. But I do think that when you group kids by ability for the bulk of the school day, it is inevitable that those at the top will get better instruction than those at the bottom. . . .

No matter how much you're exhorted as a teacher to expect the most of all kids, if you go in day after day to a group of kids who are behind and who don't put out as much effort . . . and that group doesn't include kids who are working hard, who are doing well, who can stimulate a discussion: you will expect less. It is simply human nature. I don't think, no matter how much training teachers get, that these halfway measures will do it.

Has the effort to untrack schools harmed programs for high-achieving students?

Gallagher: It certainly has: not just gifted programs but Honors programs and Advanced Placement classes have been cut out. This attempt to try to level everybody—and say, if we can't bring the bottom up, maybe we should bring the top down—has reached a stage where I don't think we're going to provide the knowledgeable students that we're going to need for the next century.

Haycock: I don't know a soul who's involved in untracking a school whose purposes are to bring the top down. . . .

Gallagher: We can't ignore the central fact that some kids learn faster than others, even given the same environment. Just like cars going down the highway; if one's going 60 miles an hour and one's going 40 miles an hour, the gap between them will increase. . . . Just 'de-tracking,' without doing anything else, would seem to me a disaster.

The one-size-fits-all program brings a chill to me because I deal with exceptional children who are on both ends of the continuum, and when you have . . . one program that will be just wonderful for everybody, you find that the top doesn't do very well and the bottom doesn't do very well either.

Haycock: I don't think that all kids learn at the same rate, or that one size fits all in education.

All that we're trying to do here is to seek ways to get all kids to much higher levels of knowledge and skills and understanding. We know for a fact that the current ways of separating kids stand in the way of doing that. Those who are trying different approaches are simply trying to find out if there are better ways of doing things.

One thing we've got to remember is that the reason that kids at 7th grade or 9th grade or 11th grade have such enormous gaps . . . is that we've separated students from the very beginning. We've educated those in the low tracks in ways that make the differences much bigger than they would be otherwise. . . . We need to begin in the elementary grades by challenging all kids, by not sorting them at that point, and then the gap you'd have by high school would be much smaller.

Where we differ is that you assume that ability is fixed, and I don't. You assume that schools can identify kids' abilities effectively, and I assume that they can't. . . . What I'm trying to say is that ability is not fixed; that we cannot, especially when kids are young, determine who's bright and who's dull; and that we need to challenge all kids, keeping them together for the bulk of the school day rather than sorting them by these bizarre means we use.

So schools *shouldn't* group students homogeneously?

Haycock: Do I think that homogeneous grouping is *never* appropriate in a school? Absolutely not; it's sometimes appropriate. What I object to is the fact that, for most kids in this country, for most of the day, everything they get is homogeneous. . . .

In the hands of a well-trained teacher who has a specific instructional objective, a homogeneous setting is sometimes appropriate, but never if it is a rigid track system.

Gallagher: I couldn't agree more.

What we need to do is to shuffle youngsters into groups based upon their interests and abilities. I don't know anyone who is *for* rigid tracking or for a hard-line [approach] where the same youngsters are together for everything all day long. But I do know people who want to group students who are very good in math or social studies for specific instructional purposes.

Haycock: I think our differences might be in who has the *burden*. For me, the burden is very much on the school. When it chooses homogeneous instruction, it's got to be very clear about why; it's got to have a very specific purpose. Otherwise, heterogeneous grouping is the way to go.

Gallagher: When one talks about heterogeneous grouping, one has to explain how one is going to challenge youngsters at the top and the bottom. Not only to say theoretically it should be done, but to demonstrate that it can be done. Once that is done, I think a lot of the concerns and arguments you hear now would disappear.

Haycock: We're beginning to head in the right direction with the movement toward being much clearer about what we want all kids to learn, and toward having high standards for all kids. . . . Our task has to be enriching curriculum and instruction for *all* kids. If we don't give teachers a lot of support, neither gifted kids nor low-achieving kids nor any other kids are going to even come close to meeting these standards.

INDEX